WHITE HOUSE STUDIES

CHANGE IN THE WHITE HOUSE?

COMPARING THE PRESIDENCIES OF GEORGE W. BUSH AND BARACK OBAMA

WHITE HOUSE STUDIES

Additional books in this series can be found on Nova's website
under the Series tab.

Additional e-books in this series can be found on Nova's website
under the e-book tab.

WHITE HOUSE STUDIES

CHANGE IN THE WHITE HOUSE?

COMPARING THE PRESIDENCIES OF GEORGE W. BUSH AND BARACK OBAMA

MEENA BOSE
EDITOR

New York

Copyright © 2014 by Nova Science Publishers, Inc.

All rights reserved. No part of this book may be reproduced, stored in a retrieval system or transmitted in any form or by any means: electronic, electrostatic, magnetic, tape, mechanical photocopying, recording or otherwise without the written permission of the Publisher.

For permission to use material from this book please contact us:
Telephone 631-231-7269; Fax 631-231-8175
Web Site: http://www.novapublishers.com

NOTICE TO THE READER

The Publisher has taken reasonable care in the preparation of this book, but makes no expressed or implied warranty of any kind and assumes no responsibility for any errors or omissions. No liability is assumed for incidental or consequential damages in connection with or arising out of information contained in this book. The Publisher shall not be liable for any special, consequential, or exemplary damages resulting, in whole or in part, from the readers' use of, or reliance upon, this material. Any parts of this book based on government reports are so indicated and copyright is claimed for those parts to the extent applicable to compilations of such works.

Independent verification should be sought for any data, advice or recommendations contained in this book. In addition, no responsibility is assumed by the publisher for any injury and/or damage to persons or property arising from any methods, products, instructions, ideas or otherwise contained in this publication.

This publication is designed to provide accurate and authoritative information with regard to the subject matter covered herein. It is sold with the clear understanding that the Publisher is not engaged in rendering legal or any other professional services. If legal or any other expert assistance is required, the services of a competent person should be sought. FROM A DECLARATION OF PARTICIPANTS JOINTLY ADOPTED BY A COMMITTEE OF THE AMERICAN BAR ASSOCIATION AND A COMMITTEE OF PUBLISHERS.

Additional color graphics may be available in the e-book version of this book.

Library of Congress Cataloging-in-Publication Data

ISBN: 978-1-62948-920-9

Published by Nova Science Publishers, Inc. † New York

CONTENTS

Foreword   vii
                 Meena Bose

About the Contributors   ix

Part I: Comparing the Domestic Political Leadership
                    of George W. Bush and Barack Obama   1

Chapter 1   Introduction   3
                    Gary C. Jacobson

Chapter 2   Comparing the Constitutional Presidencies of George W. Bush
                    and Barack Obama: War Powers, Signing Statements, Vetoes   15
                    Robert J. Spitzer

Chapter 3   Dividers, Not Uniters: How Presidents George W. Bush
                    and Barack Obama Failed to Unite a Divided Nation   37
                    Richard Himelfarb

Chapter 4   Overcoming a Polarized Congress: The Economic
                    Politics of Bush and Obama   57
                    John D. Graham and Veronica Vargas Stidvent

Part II: Changes in the White House and the World from
                    George W. Bush to Barack Obama   73

Chapter 5   Understanding the Obama Doctrine   75
                    Stanley A. Renshon

Chapter 6   George W. Bush and Barack Obama:
                    Foreign Policy Decision Making   91
                    John P. Burke

Chapter 7   Evaluating Afghanistan and Iraq in the George W. Bush
                    and Obama Presidencies: Change We Can Believe in?   111
                    Carolyn Eisenberg

Chapter 8	Bush, Obama, Polarization and National Security: Some Concluding Thoughts *Dov S. Zakheim*	**131**
Index		**143**

FOREWORD

Meena Bose
Hofstra University, Hempstead, NY, USA

In April 2012, Hofstra University hosted a symposium comparing the presidencies of George W. Bush and Barack Obama. In the 2008 presidential campaign, Obama promised major departures from the Bush administration's approach to political negotiations and policies. But in the White House, several, though certainly not all, of Obama's actions have suggested more continuity than change with his predecessor. What is the Bush (43) Presidency's legacy in American politics and the world? How has that legacy shaped the policies of President Obama? This assessment of both presidencies provides a timely discussion of their leadership successes and challenges in the White House, with attention to immediate results as well as long-term effects.

These two special issues of *White House Studies* (Volume 12, Issues 2 and 3) present the symposium findings, with updates that incorporate the 2012 elections and the start of Obama's second term. The first volume examines each president's ability to mobilize public support and exercise political leadership, both within his own political party and more broadly. The second volume compares foreign policy in the two administrations, focusing on Iraq, Afghanistan, and the Middle East. Contributors include experts on the American presidency, executive-legislative policy making, and U.S. foreign policy.

The Hofstra symposium is part of a tradition going back more than thirty years of sponsoring conferences about the American presidency, with individual conferences to date on all presidents from Franklin Delano Roosevelt through William Jefferson Clinton. In 2007, Hofstra created the Peter S. Kalikow Center for the Study of the American Presidency to promote teaching, scholarship, and commentary on presidential leadership and politics, and the April 2012 event marked the Kalikow Center's fourth symposium. In March 2015, the Center will host a conference on the George W. Bush presidency, and selected articles from that conference will appear in *White House Studies* and edited volumes from Nova Science Publishers.

The Kalikow Center thanks the editors of *White House Studies* -- Tom Lansford, Jack Covarrubias, and Robert Pauly -- for recognizing the scholarly contributions of these two special issues to presidency studies and American politics. It conveys special thanks to the staff of Nova Science Publishers – especially Alexandra Columbus and Senior Editors Donna Dennis and Louis Maurici -- for their ongoing support of scholarly work on the White House and thorough attention to every step of the publication process.

At Hofstra, the Center thanks the President's and Provost's offices, the Hofstra College of Liberal Arts and Sciences, the Hofstra Cultural Center, the Office of University Relations, and the Political Science Department for their steadfast commitment to presidency studies. The Center expresses its appreciation to Political Science Professors Rosanna Perotti and Paul B. Fritz for chairing the symposium panels. The Center also thanks Kalikow Center Senior Presidential Fellows Howard B. Dean III and Edward J. Rollins, and Lord Stewart Wood of Anfield, Shadow Cabinet Minister & Labour Member of the House of Lords, and former Senior Policy Adviser to British Prime Minister Gordon Brown, 2007-2010, for their highly informative keynote panel at the symposium comparing the two presidencies. Finally, the Center thanks the contributors to these special issues for their careful and insightful research on the American presidency in the twenty-first century.

Meena Bose
Hofstra University

ABOUT THE CONTRIBUTORS

MEENA BOSE is Peter S. Kalikow Chair in Presidential Studies at Hofstra University and Director of Hofstra's Peter S. Kalikow Center for the Study of the American Presidency. She is the author or editor of several books on the American presidency, American foreign policy, and American politics. She taught for six years at the United States Military Academy at West Point.

JOHN P. BURKE is John G. McCullough Professor of Political Science at the University of Vermont. His most recent book is *Honest Broker: The National Security Advisor and Presidential Decision Making*

CAROLYN EISENBERG is Professor of History, specializing in American foreign policy, at Hofstra University. She is the author of *Drawing the Line: The American Decision to Divide Germany, 1944-1949*, which was awarded the Herbert Hoover Library Prize and the Stuart Bernath Book Prize from the Society for Historians of American Foreign Relations. She has written numerous articles and lectured widely on the "war on terrorism," and she chaired the drafting committee on the Iraq occupation for the Coalition for a Realistic Foreign Policy.

JOHN D. GRAHAM is Dean, School of Public and Environmental Affairs, at Indiana University. He is the author of numerous scholarly books and articles, including *Bush on the Home Front: Domestic Policy Triumphs and Failures.*

RICHARD HIMELFARB is Associate Professor of Political Science at Hofstra University. He received his B.A. from the University of Maryland in 1985, and his Ph.D. from the University of Rochester in 1993. He teaches courses in American politics, public policy, the U.S. Congress, the presidency, and most recently, the politics of American health care. Dr. Himelfarb's scholarly interests include matters relating to the elderly and health care. He is the author of *Catastrophic Politics: The Rise and Fall of the Medicare Catastrophic Coverage Act of 1988,* published by the Pennsylvania State University Press.

GARY C. JACOBSON is Distinguished Professor of Political Science at the University of California, San Diego, where he has taught since 1979. He specializes in the study of U.S. elections, parties, interest groups, public opinion, and Congress, and is author or coauthor of seven books and more than 100 research articles on these topics. His most recent book is *A Divider, Not a Uniter: George W. Bush and the American People*.

STANLEY A. RENSHON is Professor of Political Science at the City University of New York and a certified psychoanalyst. He is the author of over a hundred articles and sixteen books, most recently *Barack Obama and the Politics of Redemption* (Routledge, 2012).

ROBERT J. SPITZER is Distinguished Service Professor and Chair of the Political Science Department at SUNY Cortland. He is the author of fourteen books, including *The Presidential Veto*, *President and Congress*, *Saving the Constitution from Lawyers*, and *The Politics of Gun Control* (5th ed.). He is a past president of the Presidents and Executive Politics section of the American Political Science Association.

VERONICA VARGAS STIDVENT is a consultant and a lecturer at the Red McCombs School of Business at the University of Texas-Austin. She previously served as the University's director of the Center for Politics and Governance, and as Assistant Secretary for Policy at the U.S. Department of Labor.

DOV S. ZAKHEIM is Senior Advisor at the Center for Strategic and International Studies and Senior Fellow at CNA, a federally funded think tank. From 2001 to 2004 he was Under Secretary of Defense (Comptroller); from 2002 to 2004 he was also DOD's coordinator of civilian programs in Afghanistan. From 1985 to 1987, he was Deputy Under Secretary of Defense for Planning and Resources. He is the author of two books and a dozen monographs on national security issues.

PART I:
COMPARING THE DOMESTIC POLITICAL LEADERSHIP OF GEORGE W. BUSH AND BARACK OBAMA

In: Change in the White House?
Editor: Meena Bose

ISBN: 978-1-62948-920-9
© 2014 Nova Science Publishers, Inc.

Chapter 1

INTRODUCTION

Gary C. Jacobson

The papers in this collection were originally presented in April, 2012, at a symposium organized by Hofstra University's Peter S. Kalikow Center for the Study of the American Presidency. The symposium's purpose was to compare Barack Obama's presidency with that of his immediate predecessor, George W. Bush, on a variety of dimensions. At the time it was unclear whether the sections on Obama's presidency would be preliminary or valedictory. To the evident surprise of Mitt Romney and many Republican officials and conservative commentators, they turn out to be the former. Obama's presidency remains a work in progress and will no doubt evolve in ways we cannot easily anticipate. Still, there is much to be learned about presidents and the presidency by comparing Obama's initial term to the profoundly consequential Bush presidency.

The presidency stands out as the least institutionalized of national institutions and thus the most subject to abrupt change. People who assume positions in Congress, the courts, or the higher reaches of the federal bureaucracy enter ongoing institutions with established routines, norms, practices and precedents, not to mention other more experienced and often more powerful participants. Their individual opportunities to bring about change in policy or processes depend heavily on the preferences of their colleagues and are usually quite limited. But they are also spared the burden of figuring out how to how to organize and manage their jobs and can share responsibility for the consequences of their decisions.

Presidents enjoy far more freedom of action because they alone sit atop their institution and have considerable leeway in shaping not only the objectives it pursues, but also its organization and procedures. But with this freedom comes undivided responsibility for unavoidable choices, often with limited guidance from past personal or institutional experience. Indeed, incoming presidents, such as Obama and Bush, elected on a promise of "change"—the inevitable theme of any candidate pursuing the office when it is currently held by the rival party [1]—seem especially attracted to departures from the immediate past in institutional as well as policy terms. Having run against the mistakes of the past, they plan to do things differently as well to do different things. In practice both turn out to be more difficult than they anticipate, raising the central questions in comparing presidencies: To what extent are presidents able to impose their ideas about what they should do and how they should do it, and to what extent are they hemmed in by received ideas, institutional expectations, political realities, and the vagaries of public opinion? The essays in this volume address this question from diverse perspectives by examining the changes and continuities observable in the transition from the Bush to the Obama administrations.

John P. Burke's essay compares the organization and procedures for formulating national security policies in the Bush and Obama White Houses. His guiding concern is the degree to which each president's National Security Advisors have acted as "honest brokers," following the model proposed by former NSC advisor Brent Scowcroft in 1987 in response to the Iran-Contra affair. He also examines how the deliberative process has been structured in each administration. He discovers considerable continuity across administrations in the formal organization of the NSC - one ready, off-the-shelf component of the institutional presidency - but also considerable continuity in their inability to follow the Scowcroft model with any consistency. In both administrations, the personal often subverted the institutional. For example, during Condoleeza Rice's term as NSA during the Bush administration, strong personalities with strong policy preferences - Richard Cheney, Donald Rumsfeld, Colin Powell - were not inclined to confine themselves to channels or procedures that might limit their influence. Obama's first NSA, General James Jones, faced a similar problem with heavyweights in the Defense and State, but was also weakened by the stronger personal relationships his formal subordinates enjoyed with the president.

That the personal should subvert the formal in the field of national security is not surprising. The world is unpredictable, and the challenges and stakes are enormous.

Time is at a premium and time horizons are often short. Presidents want talented, experienced, and savvy people in the key roles, but such people bring their own policy views and agendas to the table and often disagree with each other. Presidents trying to make the right decision, right now, are not likely to be sticklers for procedure; they will listen to those they know and trust regardless of institutional formalities. But Burke's essay makes it clear that this does not always serve them well. For example, the NSC's failure to plan for the aftermath of invading Iraq and deposing Saddam Hussein contributed to difficulties that proved very costly to the president and the country. Obama has yet to experience a equivalent debacle, but when the memoirs appear, it will be interesting to see how orderly and thorough the advising process has been for informing his decisions regarding, for example, the various hot spots in the Middle East.

Robert Spitzer's essay compares the two administrations on a different dimension: their concepts of the legitimate scope of presidential power. The Bush administration explicitly adopted the "unitary" theory of executive power, developed by conservative legal scholars during the Reagan administration, which posits that the president has sole authority over the executive branch and can use it to nullify the decisions of any other branch or agency that he thinks impinges on this authority. Bush reiterated this uniquely expansive claim to power in numerous "signing statements" in which he declared his intention to ignore those sections of the legislation he was signing that he believed encroached on his executive powers. Spitzer cites the most notorious of these actions, Bush's response to a section of a 2005 supplemental appropriations bill barring cruel and inhumane treatment of prisoners held by the U.S., that was intended among other things to end the practice of waterboarding: "The executive branch shall construe Title X in Division A of the Act, relating to detainees, in a manner consistent with the constitutional authority of the President to supervise the unitary executive branch and as Commander in Chief and consistent with the constitutional limitations on judicial power."

In other words, he was free to ignore Congress and the courts when making decisions about the treatment of enemy combatants.

Obama explicitly rejected the unitary executive theory and, according to Spitzer, has made a much more modest use of signing statements, consistent with the pattern of recent presidents prior to Bush. But on another front, Spitzer finds that Bush followed the law, while Obama did not. Before ordering the invasion of Iraq in 2003, Bush sought and won congressional authority as required by the War Powers Act of 1973 (although the administration claimed he already possessed that authority). Obama, in contrast, ignored the requirements of the War Powers Act both before and after committing the U.S. air force to attacking Muammar Qaddafi's forces in support of the popular uprising against the Libyan dictator. No president to date has conceded the constitutionality of the WPA, which has never been tested in court, but Bush gave it a nod, whereas Obama did not.

Spitzer's analysis of these cases underlines two fundamental realities. First, presidents always face greater expectations than they have the ability to meet, more responsibilities than they have the authority or resources to fulfill. Because so much of what they need to accomplish their goals is beyond their control, presidents have strong institutional incentives to protect and expand the powers they do have, particularly when the rival party controls one or both houses of Congress. Obama in his second term, facing a determined and hostile Republican House, can be expected to rely extensively on executive orders to accomplish his goals, a practice that will inevitably produce noisy disputes about the boundaries of presidential power. More broadly, the unitary executive concept will always be attractive to presidents and should be expected to reemerge in one guise or another as long as it is deployed with sufficient restraint to avoid a constitutional crisis.

Second, when national security is involved and presidents assume the role of commander in chief, they are more concerned with getting the right results than with following the rules. The Bush administration offered only the most extreme illustration of this point. After 9/11, Bush's foremost objective was to avoid another terrorist attack on American soil, and if this required ignoring or twisting the law and the Constitution, it was a price he was willing to pay. The worst possible outcome would have been another successful attack that Bush had not used every available means to prevent. The politics are unambiguous: better to endure blame for civil liberties violations than for failing to protect the homeland.

Obama faces the same political equation, hence his continuation of many Bush administration practices in the national security domain and his expansion of the use of drone aircraft to kill suspected terrorists. On a much smaller scale, Obama's flouting of the WPA involved a similar political calculation: act swiftly and decisively to forestall a potential humanitarian disaster in Libya and to hasten the demise of Qaddafi, and worry about the WPA, if at all, later. Success (Qaddafi gone, no American lives lost) would, and did, more than offset whatever political damage ignoring the WPA might incur. Bush's experience illustrates the risk in this approach. Had his "Mission Accomplished" moment after the initial success of the Iraq invasion been followed by peace, stability, democracy, and a rapid withdrawal of American troops from that country, the fact that no weapons of mass destruction or evidence of Iraqi complicity in the 9/11 attacks were found would have been forgiven. That was emphatically not the case, and thus it was crucial to Bush's reelection in 2004 that Congress, with the support of many prominent Democrats, not least his challenger John Kerry, had authorized the venture.

Carolyn Eisenberg's essay begins by reminding us of the enormous human and financial costs of the wars in Iraq and Afghanistan. She provides a concise history of the two wars, delineating their evolving rationales, trajectories, and consequences for the Bush presidency. She notes that Iraq War's unpopularity, especially among Democrats, gave Obama a crucial edge in his contest for the nomination with Hillary Clinton, for he had opposed the war from the beginning, while she had voted to authorize it (Obama was not yet in the Senate). His early opposition to the war was central to his general election campaign as well, and he promised to withdraw all U.S. combat troops from Iraq within the first couple of years of his presidency. But equally central was his promise to prosecute the war in Afghanistan more vigorously. Like Kerry before him, Obama argued that the appropriate targets were be Osama bin Laden and al Qaeda, the actual perpetrators of 9/11, not Saddam Hussein regime in Iraq, and Bush's transfer of military resources from Afghanistan to Iraq was a mistake that he would correct. As with Kerry, commitment to the Afghan war was also a way for Obama to show that he was willing to use military force to protect the nation even as he criticized the Iraq venture. But he also promised to replace Bush's unilateralism with a multilateral approach to foreign affairs that respected international law, standards, and organizations.

This promise was impressive enough make Obama the improbable winner of the Nobel Peace Prize a mere ten months into his presidency. But Eisenberg argues that the award anticipated less continuity with Bush's foreign and military policies than we have actually observed. His appointments to State (Hillary Clinton), Defense (Robert Gates held over from the Bush administration), and other agencies involved in foreign affairs, and his retention of senior military commanders, did not suggest dramatic departures, for example. As it turned out, the exit from Iraq took care of itself; the withdrawal planned and initiated under Bush continued under Obama, and any question of leaving a residual force was settled by the Iraqi government's refusal to give American soldiers immunity from prosecution in Iraqi courts, a condition Bush would have insisted upon as well. Obama could thus continue on the path laid down by his predecessor because it produced an outcome entirely consistent with Obama's objective, a prompt and orderly American departure from Iraq.

Obama's decision to escalate U.S. involvement in Afghanistan also fulfilled a campaign promise and represented much more a continuation than a repudiation of his predecessor's policy. It embodied the kind of counter-insurgency strategy that had stabilized Iraq and was led by some of the same soldiers, notably Generals David Petraeus. It is easy to imagine Bush take the same action had he continued in office (albeit with more troops and no timetable for withdrawal). As Eisenberg points out, the success of Obama's Afghan policy is still in doubt, even as the planned drawdown continues. The one unambiguous plus for Obama was the killing of bin Laden, the original and primary target of the entire U.S. effort in that country.

Eisenberg argues that, with his decisions regarding Afghanistan and his expanded use of drone aircraft to kill suspected terrorists, Obama effectively abandoned his promise to bring a different mindset to dealing with the problem of terrorism. A truly different mindset would, in her analysis, question—and reject—the idea that terrorism could be fought effectively and at an acceptable human and financial cost by large-scale military actions of the kind undertaken by Bush and continued by Obama. Neither president posed the basic question: is it worth it? Eisenberg believes the answer is emphatically no. The costs have been too high, the benefits too small, for the destruction of bin Laden's original al Qaeda network in Afghanistan has only spawned new waves of vengeful imitators elsewhere.

Even assuming she is correct, it is difficult to imagine a president surviving politically who did not go all out to punish and avenge the worst attacks on American soil since Pearl Harbor. According to Bob Woodward's account, the administration's main concern while preparing to go after bin Laden in Afghanistan was to avoid the perception that it was reacting too slowly or with insufficient force, and anyone who remembers how the vast majority Americans felt immediately after 9/11 (or looks at opinion surveys taken at the time) will understand why. [2] And as I noted earlier, Bush's top priority—inherited by Obama and probably every president for the foreseeable future—was to prevent and other mass attack on the United States. For Bush, this included going after Saddam Hussein if there was even a remote possibility that he might have been involved in 9/11 or might facilitate anything similar in the future. It also explains why Obama could not contemplate immediately withdrawing all U.S. forces from Iraq and Afghanistan regardless of consequences and why he has greatly increased the use of drones to target al Qaeda offshoots around the globe. As Stanley Renshon notes in his essay, "The threat of catastrophic terrorism is now an ongoing feature of American national life, and no president can afford to ignore this fact." The political downside to another 9/11, or worse, makes it implausible that any president would treat terrorism as a crime rather than something to be combated by all available means, including military force.

Renshon agrees with Eisenberg that there are important continuities between the Bush and Obama foreign policies, not only in dealing with Iraq and Afghanistan, but also in Obama's adoption of most of the institutional architecture for dealing with potential terrorists established under Bush by the Patriot Act, the Intelligence Reform and Terrorism Prevention Act, and various executive orders. Given the magnitude of the threat, he believes, Obama could do no other. The difference between the presidents is in their premises. Bush emphasized American primacy and intention to act to defend threats to the nation—even merely anticipated threats such as that posed by Iraq—unilaterally or with ad-hoc alliances, unconstrained by hesitant and unreliable international institutions. He also designated the expansion of democracy as a primary goal to be pursued, under some necessary circumstances, by military means. Renshon calls this approach "assertive realism." Obama is, in contrast, a classic "liberal internationalist" one who believes that American interests are best served by building and participating in strong international institutions and engaging in cooperative, multilateral actions to secure stable and peaceful relations among nations. But in Renshon's view, based on analysis Obama's writings and rhetoric before and after he became president, Obama's liberal internationalism derives from a broader objective, the redemptive transformation of America's foreign and domestic policies to conform much more closely to American ideals of justice, fairness, and equality. Regarding foreign affairs, this involves admission of past mistakes arising from belligerence, arrogance and indifference to the opinions of other nations, and the promise to make America a more modest, cooperative international citizen in the future. Obama's approach does not abjure a leading role in world affairs but has been famously characterized as "leading from behind." Renshon prefers to characterize it as "minimized, embedded, and unobtrusive" leadership, supporting other nations (France in Mali) or alliances (NATO in Libya) with U.S. military assets while letting them take the lead in advocating and organizing the engagement.

The assumption of a more modest international role for the United States is also a practical step to bring aspirations better in line with available resources—an urgent requirement for a president with Obama's domestic policy ambitions and the reality of huge budget deficits. It provides a rationale for downsizing the military, which Renshon sees as holding substantial risks in light of the known and unknown international threats. Thus although Obama has for the most part followed the path laid out by Bush regarding Iraq, Afghanistan, and in coping with the threat of terrorism, he is leading a downsizing and redirection of American military resources that implies a very different concept of the United States' international role than the one that guided Bush. While rhetorically insisting on American primacy and exceptionalism, his policies represent an effective retreat from these claims. Whether international realities will allow him to reduce the nation's global profile in a way that furthers whatever redemptive hopes he still entertains remains in serious question. Assuming Renshon's is right about Obama's redemptive ambitions, both at home and abroad, the Obama presidency will hold lessons about how far such dreams are achievable given the limits imposed by the president's institutional, political, and international environment. The evidence to date suggests that the pursuit of redemption remains far more aspirational than operational.

Renshon views Obama's redemptive aspirations are even more important domestically than internationally, and a reading of his 2013 State of the Union address and other post-reelection proposals certainly supports this claim. But here, Obama faces the reality of a House of Representatives controlled by Republicans and a Republican Senate minority large enough sustain a filibuster. Both Bush and Obama experienced periods of both unified government and divided government during their presidencies. John D. Graham's analysis of the coalition-building strategies pursed by the two presidents in these varying circumstances again suggests a great deal of continuity. It also reminds us that, despite the extreme ideological polarization of the House and Senate parties and opportunities for minorities to block action, both presidents enjoyed some notable successes on major pieces of domestic legislation. Graham's cases include Bush's tax cuts and bailout of Wall Street and eventually the auto industry via the Troubled Asset Relief program (TARP), and Obama's economic stimulus package, the "cash for clunkers" program, and the Dodd-Frank reforms of financial regulation. It would be easy to add others: Bush's "Leave No Child Behind" and prescription drug subsidies for seniors, Obama's landmark Affordable Health Care Act.

Graham delineates three strategies available to Bush and Obama to enact their agendas: cooperative bipartisanship (building a bipartisan consensus through negotiations with leaders of both sides), strict partisanship (relying exclusively on votes from the president's partisans), and cross-partisanship or "cheap" bipartisanship (uniting one's own party and then peeling off enough defectors from the other party to win the votes needed for passage). The clearest lesson from Graham's case studies and other legislative actions during the two administrations is that the choice of strategies is dictated by factors mostly outside the president's control. A bipartisan strategy depends on sufficient inter-party agreement on what should be done to make negotiations possible and fruitful. TARP met this criterion because both parties' more sober leaders believed that the financial crisis threatened a repeat of the Great Depression and that failure to shore up the financial system would lead to a global economic disaster. Leave No Child Behind is another example; cooperative bipartisanship is the obvious strategy to follow when the president's objectives are shared as much or more by members of the opposing party than in his own. As Graham notes, partisan differences have become so wide that instances of this sort are now rare. Moreover, even when outsiders might detect a range of potential bipartisan agreement, at least on the basis of positions taken in the past (Obama's health care proposals serve as an example), the intensely competitive political environment can get in the way. The president's opponents may prefer to deny him a legislative victory that might boost his popular standing and reelection prospects than to cut a mutually agreeable deal.

The partisan strategy is also obviously dictated by circumstances: it works only when the president enjoys united congressional majorities large enough to pass legislation without votes from the other side. These conditions are exceedingly rare now that the 60-vote Senate has become the norm. Obama enjoyed a unified government with 60 Democrats in the Senate for a brief period early in his first term, but even then he could not rely on getting every Democratic vote for his agenda. Thus the only option normally available is to unite one's own party to the maximum extent possible and then somehow to pick up the handful of votes from the other side needed to win.

This has been the dominant strategy of both Bush and Obama, but with and important asymmetry: Republican presidents have an easier time executing it than Democratic presidents. Bush could go after the substantial contingents of moderate Blue Dog Democrats in both houses, most of whom represented Republican-leaning states and districts. Congressional Republicans are more homogeneous ideologically, and fewer of them represent states or districts that lean Democratic and thus have to worry about opposing the president. Bush simply had more potential defectors to target than Obama, particularly in the House; the remnant of relatively moderate Republican senators from the northeast leaves Obama more possibilities in the Senate.

Twice since Obama's reelection we have observed new variant of the a bipartisan strategy: House Speaker John Boehner, violating the Hastert rule, [3] allowed bills to come to the floor to raise debt ceiling and to provide billions of dollars for the victims of Hurricane Sandy even though both were opposed by a majority of House Republicans. Evidently Republican leaders wanted their party to avoid blame for the consequences of blocking the legislation while permitting backbenchers to maintain their ideological purity by voting against more government taxing, borrowing, and spending—as long as these votes were inconsequential. But Obama can expect to win such bipartisan victories only on issues where the political equation makes Republican leaders reluctant to stonewall. The list of such issues is likely to prove very short.

The final contribution to this collection puts me in the weird position of introducing a paper dedicated to attacking my own work, but it also gives me the opportunity to reply. Professor Himelfarb considers my examination of the partisan polarization in popular responses to presidents George W. Bush and Barack Obama to be "unfair and politically biased" and contends that Obama and Bush provoked such responses for equivalent reasons: pursuit of "policies that are highly partisan and ideological" and equally deceptive arguments and "comparably aggressive tactics in pursuit of its goals." He also contends that I exaggerate the "excesses" of the political right while ignoring the equally common outré expressions from the left. As far as I was able to determine, he does not challenge any of the research findings that support my arguments about the sources of polarization during the Bush administration, nor does he reject the survey results I draw on to take an early look at polarization during the Obama administration, but he does take strong exception to how I interpret them. He believes I've been too hard on Bush, his supporters, and Obama's opponents, and too easy on Obama.

The charge of partisan bias is neither disturbing nor interesting—other than as a symptom of the very phenomenon I have been writing about. A central theme of all of this work is just how strongly partisan and ideological priors now shape Americans' responses to political phenomena, and it would be surprising if scholars were somehow immune. That I and Professor Himelfarb interpret the two administrations differently is to be expected. What matters to me is whether my interpretations are based on sound, evidence-based social scientific research. From that perspective, his claims that that the sources of polarization are the same in both administrations and that distorted views of reality are equally common among ordinary Republicans and Democrats and are not only wrong, but miss what is most interesting about the evolution of public opinion about these presidents and their policies.

Bush and Obama are indeed equal in provoking strongly polarized partisan reactions (Obama has now, by a couple of points, exceeded Bush's record for polarization in a Gallup survey [4]), and various exercises in "motivated reasoning" have shaped popular responses to both of them, but the processes producing these polarized reactions differ in both cause and timing. In both administrations, people on the political right have displayed considerably stronger and more impermeable priors—as well as maintaining more blatantly erroneous beliefs that are consistent with their priors—than people on the left. For example, nearly two years into the Obama administration, among Republican Tea Party afficianados—those with "very positive" view of the movement, comprising more than half of all ordinary Republicans—71 percent still believed in Bush's original and long- abandoned claim that Iraq possessed weapons of mass destruction at the time of the U.S. invasion (26 percent said the WMD had actually been found), and 59 percent said they believed that Obama was either foreign born (48 percent) or a Muslim (47 percent) or both. [5] Comparable demonstrably false beliefs are not nearly so evident on the left (Himelfarb's reference spotty data on "truthers" hardly establishes equivalence). In other circumstances this pattern could be reversed—those of us who lived through the 'Sixties will recall a time when preposterous conspiratorial beliefs were rampant on the left. But in recent years, the most striking and widespread misperceptions of reality come from the right. More importantly, the beliefs of conservative Republicans are far more central to explaining why Bush and Obama have become such polarizing figures than are the reactions of Democrats or liberals and they have been far more consequential in explaining elite partisan behavior.

Polarization occurs when presidents retain the approval of the great majority of their own partisans while alienating the great majority of the other party's. A crucial difference between the two presidents is that Bush alienated Democrats by what he did, whereas Obama alienated Republicans by what he was. This is evident in the timing and trends in aggregate opinion across the two administrations. Bush enjoyed relatively high approval ratings among Democrats for almost two years after 9/11; the decline thereafter coincided with revelations that the Iraq War's premises had been faulty and its costs and consequences turned out to be much worse than advertised. The opposite is true of Obama: his most enthusiastic Republican opponents took a strongly negative, and, in some obvious respects, misinformed view of him before he was even elected. The sentiments that bred the Tea Party movement were already observable at McCain-Palin rallies. Their campaign's attempt to portray Obama as a '60s-style radical with a socialist agenda failed generally but succeeded wonderfully among their own voters. [6] Perceptions of Obama as a radical leftist were to some extent projections based on his race, unusual name, personal history, elite education, political career in Chicago, and self-presentation as well as by his Democratic label—unless you believe that Hillary Clinton, with an agenda indistinguishable from Obama's, would have provoked the same intensely hostile reaction from the populist right. Once in office, Obama actions were taken in

Introduction

such quarters as confirmation of their views, with the economic stimulus package and "Obamacare" as the chief exhibits. That is, they immediately evaluated what he did according to what they thought he was.

Himelfarb argues that Obama alienated Republicans in the same way Bush alienated Democrats, equating Obama's marketing of Obamacare with Bush's marketing of the Iraq War in this regard. I leave it to readers to judge (especially after reading the other relevant chapter in this volume) the aptness of this comparison. But that aside, the timing is all wrong for them to provide a common explanation for polarization. Developments in Iraq preceded and fueled the gradual drop in Democrats' support for Bush, which fell 40 points over three years following the war's initial months. Republicans, especially those of the Tea Party persuasion, already held decisively negative views of Obama more than a year before Obamacare was enacted, and its passage has not been followed by any appreciable change in their views of either the law or Obama. In fact, opinions of Obamacare from all quarter have been static from its initial proposal through its enactment and though today, no doubt because the vast majority of Americans have not yet felt its effects one way or the other.

In examining polarization during the Bush administration, it is no mystery why Bush lost Democratic support. The interesting question is why so many ordinary Republicans continued to approve of Bush and support the war despite the yawning gap between the war's initial rationales and unfolding events in Iraq. The evidence suggests that it was their strong commitment to Bush, forged by his response to the trauma of 9/11 and the high regard he enjoyed among religious conservatives, who considered him "one of us" and saw him as God's chosen instrument to lead a global war on terror, that motivated them to remain steadfast, rejecting, ignoring, or downplaying discordant news from Iraq. [7]

In short, they supported Bush for what he was, not what he did. It is not clear whether Himelfarb takes exception to this analysis, although he does point out, correctly, that Republicans could find coherent reasons for continuing to support the war without relying on false beliefs and implies that their continued support for the war is therefore unproblematic. But I strongly suspect that had the actual course of the war and its consequences been foreseen, the enterprise would have received little elite or popular support from any quarter (Himelfarb may of course believe otherwise), and thus the Democratic disillusionment with the war raises less interesting research questions than the Republicans' continued belief that it had been a good idea.

The nature of Republican disaffection with Obama also raises more interesting research questions than does Democrats' support of him. The silly notion that Obama is a socialist (tenable only by people who don't know what socialism is) notwithstanding, Obama is a mainstream Democrat whose policy positions put him at about the median of the coalition of moderates and liberals that he leads. Himelfarb believes "there is a valid argument to be made that Barack Obama is the most liberal president in a generation," but the evidence he cites to support this claim, now updated by its producer, Keith T. Poole, to cover Obama's entire first term, actually ranks Obama as the most moderate Democratic president of any in the postwar period. [8] Democrats have not been thrilled by all of his decisions or the slow economic recovery, but he his policies and their consequences have not raised pointed questions about why Democrats would continue to approve of his performance.

For the same reason, Republican disapproval is not generally hard to explain. The dominant conservative wing of the party would no doubt be unhappy with the policies of any president capable of winning the Democratic Party's nomination. What makes their opposition extraordinary—and important for explaining the level of polarization provoked by Obama—is the intensity of their hostility to Obama, expressed not only through negative opinions of his character and performance, but also through patently false beliefs about his origins, religion, and political objectives (e.g., outlawing guns).

Himelfarb discusses my description of the demographic characteristics and political beliefs of Tea Party sympathizers at some length. At no juncture does he claim that my account of who they are and what they say they believe is in any respect inaccurate. He does object to my reference to Kinder and Sanders' widely used racial resentment scale, on which Tea Partiers score higher than other Americans, labeling it "pseudo-science," I'll leave it to Kinder (one of the leading political psychologists of his generation) and Sanders to defend their work against this slur. All I wrote was that, although there was nothing intrinsically racist about the Tea Party ideology, "it is clear that the movement is more appealing to people who are unsympathetic to blacks and who prefer a harder line in illegal immigration than it is to other Americans." (2011, 10).

IS THIS REALLY IN DOUBT?

Himelfarb also denounces my use an authoritarianism scale as another exercise in "pseudo-science." In fact, the scale also is widely used in the literature on political psychology and has been found to be strong predictor of political and social attitudes. The measure, based on responses to questions about preferred characteristics in children, does not purport to detect "some type of personal shortcoming," as Professor Himlefarb alleges. It simply arranges people on a scale that predicts their attitudes toward order, authority, ambiguity, and difference. That people high on this scale would take a dim view of a president as different from the common mold as Barack Obama is entirely predictable regardless of what one thinks it measures. And that was my purpose in using the scale: trying to explain the intense reactions to Obama among Tea Party Republicans. Himelfarb's charges here of "pseudo-science" reminded me of nothing so much as the right's attempt to discredit the ideologically uncongenial science documenting human-induced global climate change.

A final reason to dwell on the Tea Party faction is that it actually matters. The far left's attacks on Bush, such as those conducted by "truthers," were a minor sideshow, with little resonance beyond a small and inconsequential fringe; no major Democratic leader adopted their rhetoric or arguments. Tea Party sympathizers, in contrast, form a majority of the Republican coalition, have set the rhetorical tone and agenda for the party since 2009. Anyone who doubts their influence need only recall the positions adopted by Republican presidential aspirants during the 2012 primary season. And anyone who doubts their radicalism need only consider the Republican House faction that voted against raising the debt ceiling despite enormous financial turmoil a default on U.S. debt would have inflicted on the national and global economies. Thus in trying to understand contemporary partisan polarization, I find it more important and illuminating to explore Tea Party modes of thinking than to dwell on why ordinary Democrats would generally support a president adopting a position at about the midpoint of the center-left coalition that is the present–day Democratic Party.

Finally, Himelfarb's critique contains a number of tendentious misreadings of my work that have me making arguments that I never actually made. I cannot correct them all here, but one deserves mention. I do not claim that "Bush never believed his rhetoric" about uniting the nation; I merely argue that unity was a secondary goal, less important than other goals such as cutting taxes or pursuing the Iraq War and thus to be discarded if it hindered them. I explicitly concede that Bush was entirely sincere in believing that his policies were best for the nation and that, in his mind, the tactics his administration adopted to further these policies were therefore fully justified. That the policies and tactics were polarizing was a consequence he was willing to accept. I agree with Himelfarb that the same is true of Obama; finding it impossible to build bipartisan for a plan to extend health care coverage to all Americans, he gave up on consensus and went for a partisan victory. And it also was surely a polarizing one, confirming Republicans' already negative opinions of the president. Contra Himelfarb, I do not assign "the political right sole responsibility for the partisan divide" as anyone who reads my work conscientiously will discover; but I do reject on abundant empirical grounds Himelfarb's assertion that the sources of partisan divisions in the two administrations were essentially equivalent.

In any case, readers of this and the other essays in this volume will come away with many interesting and important intellectual issues to contemplate regarding both presidents, both administrations, and the presidency itself. They will also be positioned to observe Obama's second term from a greatly enriched and informed perspective.

REFERENCES

[1] Samuel Popkin, *The Candidate: What it Takes to Win—and Hold—the White House* (New York: Oxford University Press, 2012), 58-63.

[2] Gary C. Jacobson, *A Divider, Not a Uniter: George W. Bush and the American Public*, 2nd Edition (New York: Longman, 2011), 66.

[3] The rule, articulated by Dennis Hastert while he was speaker, was that no legislation would be brought to the floor of House which did not have majority Republican support.

[4] Gary C. Jacobson. "The Economy and Partisanship in the 2012 Presidential and Congressional Elections," *Political Science Quarterly* 128 (Spring, 2013), forthcoming.

[5] Gary J. Jacobson, "The President, the Tea Party, and Voting Behavior in 2010: Insights from the Cooperative Congressional Election Study," paper presented at the Annual Meeting of the American Political Science Association, Seattle, September 1-4, 2011.

[6] Cite relevant Jacobson (pres studies?).

[7] Jacobson PSQ article or book on motivated reasoning (p. 50).

[8] "An Update on the Presidential Square Wave," at http://voteview.com/blog/, accessed February 10, 2013; Himelfarb neglected in his discussion to note that George W. Bush's location on the scale put him furthest to the of right of any Republican president ever.

In: Change in the White House?
Editor: Meena Bose

ISBN: 978-1-62948-920-9
© 2014 Nova Science Publishers, Inc.

Chapter 2

COMPARING THE CONSTITUTIONAL PRESIDENCIES OF GEORGE W. BUSH AND BARACK OBAMA: WAR POWERS, SIGNING STATEMENTS, VETOES

Robert J. Spitzer

Barack Obama campaigned for the presidency in part on a platform of promising to reverse the constitutional excesses of the second Bush presidency. Yet critics of the former law school professor – from both left and right – have been quick to accuse Obama of abandoning that promise by accepting, embracing, and even advancing expansive executive power claims. This article will examine these criticisms by comparing the two presidents' constitutional power claims and actions in the areas of war powers, signing statements, and the veto power.

At least one beneficial consequence of the presidency of George W. Bush was that it brought to public attention a serious debate about the scope and limits of presidential power, especially as that power was seen to rise from the Constitution. This debate was prompted not only by highly controversial actions taken by Bush for which Bush claimed constitutional authority, but because these actions stemmed from a new and highly expansive theory, the "unitary theory" of executive power, which was relentlessly implemented for most of Bush's two terms in office by and through the office of Vice President Dick Cheney and his chief assistant, David Addington.

For his part, Bush's successor made clear well before the 2008 election that he rejected the key tenets of the unitary theory, and also most of Bush's most aggressive power claims. In a widely quoted 2007 interview, Obama stated that he would only authorize national security-based surveillance by following the Foreign Intelligence Surveillance Act (FISA) procedures (Bush authorized such surveillance without first obtaining the assent of FISA judges). Obama agreed that Congress has the power to limit U.S. troop deployments abroad (Bush disagreed). Obama said that presidents have the power to issue signing statements when signing bills into law, but that Bush had abused this power, not only in sheer frequency of use but especially when he used them to "nullify or undermine congressional instructions as enacted into law."

Obama flatly rejected other Bush-era actions including presidentially ordered interrogation techniques otherwise barred by law, military commissions created by the president rather than Congress, the detention of U.S. citizens as enemy combatants without access to procedural safeguards, presidentially-ordered military attacks on other nations absent prior congressional approval, and, after taking office, rejecting a Bush executive order that would have put presidential papers out of reach for generations after the conclusion of a presidency. [1]

Yet Obama took criticism almost from the start of his presidency for failing to fully adhere to his commitments. Foremost and symbolic of these criticisms involved Obama's campaign pledge to close the American military prison at Guantanamo Bay, Cuba. One of his first executive orders called for closing the base within a year – yet it remains open as of this writing (in large part, it turns out, because Congress enacted legislation that made it nearly impossible for Obama to transfer out the last of the prisoners there [2]). In addition to liberals and civil libertarians who felt that Obama had betrayed his principles, especially in the realm of presidential prerogatives, [3] conservatives were divided. Some, such as former Vice President Cheney, criticized Obama for improperly yielding presidential power, including the option of torturing detainees. [4] Others, such as former Bush advisor John Brennan and conservative analyst Kori Schake applauded Obama for functioning as "Bush's third term." [5] *Wall Street Journal* columnist William McGurn concluded that "the same Bush claims of executive authority in war that provoked such apoplexy in our pundits, professors and politicos have for the most part been embraced by Mr. Obama. . . ." [6] (No great leap of imagination is needed to hypothesize that such fulsome praise for Obama from political opponents is animated at least in part by a desire to legitimize the Bush administration and inoculate it from critics who view Bush as a presidential outlier.)

Others who have examined Obama's record on key decisions have found that record mixed. For example, political scientist James P. Pfiffner noted that Obama did end harsh interrogations, abide by existing laws regarding surveillance and the functioning of military commissions, and reined in the use of signing statements. On the other hand, the administration has continued to aggressively defend the state secrets privilege, try some detainees by military tribunals and hold some detainees indefinitely. [7]

As political scientist Richard M. Pious concluded in comparing the two presidencies, in some instances "Obama chose continuity (albeit with some legal twists), and in others he chose significant change. . ." [8] A comparison of Bush and Obama intelligence disclosure to Congress by Kathleen Clark concluded that Obama had broken with the Bush practice of opposing virtually all disclosure efforts to Congress, in that Obama accepted reporting on matters like intelligence contracting, covert actions audits, and creation of an Inspector General for the intelligence community. On the other hand, Clark found that the Obama administration "has continued the Bush Administration practice of resisting robust intelligence disclosure to Congress," including resisting disclosure of covert actions. [9]

In this article, I will compare the two presidencies by beginning with a brief examination of their respective constitutional frames, followed by a detailed examination of their use of constitutional powers in three areas that range from the mighty, to the mundane, to the miniature: war powers, signing statements, and the veto power.

CONSTITUTIONAL EXECUTIVE POWER FRAMES

Both the Bush and Obama presidencies expressly addressed their visions of the constitutional power of the presidency, and while the Obama presidency is not concluded as of this writing, this analysis invites an assessment of those frames. As mentioned earlier, the Bush presidency embraced the "unitary theory" of executive power; the Obama administration rejected that theory, even if the Obama presidency accepted or embraced some executive powers that Bush exercised or defended under the unitary theory rubric.

The unitary theory of executive power emerged in the 1980s in the Justice Department's Office of Legal Counsel under President Ronald Reagan. Under office heads Theodore Olson and Charles Cooper, and Attorney General Edwin Meese, staff lawyers, including future Supreme Court Justice Samuel Alito, formulated the unitary executive theory. With coordinate support from the newly formed organization of conservative lawyers, the Federalist Society, these young legal thinkers were looking for a way to limit federal power and curb, if not dismantle, the modern regulatory state. [10] The phrase *unitary executive* was derived from references in the Federalist Papers to "unity" in the executive. [11] Departing from the traditional conservative view that sought limited executive power, [12] the unitary view argued for even greater presidential power as a means of attacking and routing power in the rest of the government.

Key to the unitary theory is the contrarian and counter-factual assumption that presidential power has declined, not increased, since the enactment of the Constitution in 1789. [13] To rectify this alleged imbalance and recapture presumably latent or dormant constitutional presidential powers, the unitary theory stakes out two sets of aggressive power claims.

The first is that presidents have sole and complete control over the executive branch. As then–federal judge Alito said in a 2000 speech to the Federalist Society, "The president has not just some executive powers, but *the* executive power – the whole thing." [14] This power claim might seem unexceptionable on its face, but it presumes to extend presidential powers beyond the well-established understanding of the president's role as chief executive.

As applied during the George W. Bush presidency, it sought to empower the president to exercise sole control over the removal of executive branch officials, to direct the actions of such officials, and to nullify the decisions or actions of others believed to impede the president's full control over the executive. In practice, this meant that Bush felt at liberty to ignore provisions of laws with which he disagreed (most prominently by relying on signing statements, discussed later), interpret or set aside treaties unilaterally, determine the fate of enemy combatants, use tactics including torture against enemy combatants despite strictures against such actions in federal and international law, allow warrantless surveillance of domestic telephone calls contrary to existing law, and curtail judicial oversight, among other actions. Further, the unitary view questions the very constitutionality of government agencies (and the rules they issue) created to be independent of the president by law – that is, independent regulatory agencies, commissions, and other similar entities. [15]

The second claim of the unitary theory is that the other branches of government may not interfere with presidential actions arising from these executive powers. It was on this basis that Bush argued that he could ignore laws or provisions of laws that, in his view, impinged on his so-called unitary power as chief executive. In addition, Bush administration lawyers also argued that the courts may not adjudicate in areas the president deems within his executive power. Administration lawyers made these arguments in such court cases including *Hamdi v. Rumsfeld* (2004), [16] *Rasul v. Bush* (2004), [17] nd *Hamdan v. Rumsfeld* (2006). [18] Obama disagreed, with Bush, stating his approval of *Hamdi* and *Hamdan*, [19] and has adhered to that to date. [20]

These two unitary theory power claims, as formulated in the 1980s, reject the bedrock notion that the powers of the three branches are in any sense shared or overlap, advancing the unitary belief that Congress, for example, has no constitutional right to create independent agencies within the executive branch, even though such actions have passed constitutional muster. [21] A related goal, as expressed by then-Justice Department lawyer Alito, was to see that "the President will get in the last word on questions of [statutory and constitutional] interpretation." [22] This executive "last word" would preclude accepting any further interpretation arising either from Congress or the courts, since the unitary theory asserts that the executive has sole, exclusive, and final control over that designated as such by the president.

The Bush unitary view placed executive power on a platform far above any conception of executive power found in any other presidential administration, including the Obama administration. To be sure, some have argued that Obama's actions in office "are clearly unitary." [23] But this verdict depends on a kind of "unitary-lite" definition of unitary executive power, where by one definition "the *correct* form of this theory do[es] not claim the president should be free of all constitutional restraints, but argue[s] that the separation of powers requires the president to be responsible for and able to effectively defend those powers that the Constitution gives him." [24] By this definition, any action taken by Obama or other presidents to defend or assert executive power conforms to the unitary theory. This definition, however, simply does not conform to most unitary proponents' views, or those of key members of the Bush administration. The Bush unitary theory was by definition categorically more aggressive and tendentious than anything contemplated or articulated by the Obama administration, at least as of this writing. [25]

This conclusion, however, is a broad brush that does not clarify very specific – and arguably more relevant – elements of executive power claims and actions by the two administrations. It is to these that we now turn.

WAR POWERS

Two clear-cut, if different instances of war-making arose in the Bush and Obama presidencies: the 2003 war with Iraq, and the 2011 action in Libya.

The Iraq War

In the Fall of 2002, President Bush asked Congress to grant him legal authorization to engage in armed hostilities with Iraq. Several justifications for such a momentous action were offered, including allegations that Iraq, headed by the brutal tyrant Saddam Hussein, was providing ongoing support for terrorists, including those who had attacked the U.S. in 2001; that Iraq was actively pursuing the manufacture and production of "weapons of mass destruction," including, (though arguably conflating) nuclear, biological, and chemical weapons, which in turn posed a threat to the U.S. and its allies; that Hussein brutalized his own people, and posed a threat to other nations in the region. With the trauma of the 9/11 attacks still fresh in the minds of Congress and the public, Bush's emphatic insistence for the need of such action from the now-popular president resulted in congressional enactment of the Iraq War Resolution (PL 107-243; 116 Stat. 1498) in October. The invasion of Iraq began on March 19, 2003, and concluded within a month.

In the Resolution, Congress granted the president wide discretion to act, noting in section 3(A) that "The president is authorized to use the armed forces of the United States as he determines to be necessary and appropriate" against Iraq. The Resolution also expressly invoked the 1973 War Powers Act, prescribing that the president was to report to Congress periodically about the progress of the action, should it occur. While Congress, and the Resolution it enacted, were criticized for giving over to the president too much discretion, [26] it is undeniable that Congress employed its constitutional war power to authorize subsequent military action by the president.

Mitigating this legal action by Congress was the political context of the decision. As abundant investigation and reporting has demonstrated, the reasons offered to justify war with Iraq were sheer invention on the part of the Bush administration. In fact, the administration, again spearheaded by Cheney, had set out on a course to topple Saddam Hussein from the very earliest days of the Bush presidency. The alleged connection between the Iraq government and the 9/11 terrorists did not exist. Evidence supporting allegations that Iraq was actively pursuing the development of nuclear weapons and other weapons of mass destruction proved to be false. That evidence, in fact, had been discredited even before the Bush administration made its case for war in late 2002 and 2003. And while the Saddam Hussein regime was tyrannical, allied nations' actions to "keep Saddam in his box" and prevent him from threatening his neighbors after the 1991 Persian Gulf War had been successful. In short, both Congress and the country were systematically misled about every important justification offered on behalf of the case for war. [27] In no instance in American history was the case for war – any war – built on as lengthy and prodigious a list of lies as the Iraq War.

Yet even taking this political context into account, Congress cannot be absolved of abnegating its constitutional and political responsibilities through its own failure to fact-find, investigate, question, and legislate. Still, Congress provided the necessary legal green light, and Bush acted within that constitutional and legal framework.

The Libyan Incursion

The start of 2011 witnessed a remarkable, indigenous movement for democracy across many nations of Africa and the Middle East. Dubbed the "Arab awakening," it began with an uprising in Tunisia, and spread to Egypt (where it succeeded in overthrowing authoritarian regimes in these two nations), Syria, and other nations. By February, protests had spread to Libya, in opposition to its brutal dictator, Muammar Qaddafi. Unlike the reactions of other leaders facing widespread protests, Qaddafi responded with full-out military force, even as large segments of his forces melted away to join the rebels or otherwise desert. Nevertheless, rebels won control of much of the eastern portion of the country, including Benghazi, a city with a population of over a half-million. Fearing the slaughter of thousands or tens of thousands of civilians as Qaddafi's army converged on the city in mid-March – a slaughter Qaddafi boasted would occur – Obama ordered air strikes in coordination with NATO on March 19 to protect the rebels and the civilian population, and to destroy Qaddafi's air defenses, air force, and degrade his ground forces. Thanks in large measure to these actions, Qaddafi's forces were driven back, and in the succeeding months rebels gradually gained control of the rest of the country. Qaddafi himself was finally killed in October 2011. [28]

While there was general agreement that military action by the U.S. and NATO not only averted a large-scale slaughter, but hastened the end of the Qaddafi regime – outcomes that were widely supported both here and abroad – many in the U.S. on both the left and the right criticized Obama for failing to abide by the tenets of the war powers process and sidestepping Congress's constitutional powers over war. In a series of statements and documents, the Obama administration justified its actions on several grounds, including U.N. Security Council Resolution 1973, approved on March 17, deploring Qaddafi's actions and calling for military intervention; authorization from, and involvement of, NATO; the limited, low-risk nature of America's involvement in Libya (no American soldiers were killed in the operation) which Obama claimed did not rise to the level of war, in part because American involvement was limited in time and scope; and support from a March 1 Senate Resolution, S. Res. 85, which included support for imposition of a "no-fly" zone over Libya. And finally, Obama said he was acting pursuant to his powers as commander-in-chief and chief executive, and that past precedent of presidents who intervened militarily without prior congressional authorization in such instances as Bosnia in 1995 and Yugoslavia in 1999 also lent support. [29]

In terms of constitutional war powers, Obama did follow initial actions of the War Powers Act (WPA) of 1973 (PL 93-148; 87 Stat. 555), in that he consulted with top leaders of Congress on March 18 before beginning military action the next day. In addition, he reported to Congress within 48 hours of the initiation of hostilities regarding the specific details of the mission ("consistent with the War Powers Resolution," according to an administration report to Congress [30]), and continued to provide periodic reports to Congress (as per the WPA) and the country. However, he failed to act in conformance with the law in two critical respects [31] First, he acted without any valid prior authorization from Congress. Second, he failed to adhere to the 60 day deadline imposed by the War Powers Act, which requires presidents to withdraw troops from "hostilities" 60 days after the president submits the initial report to Congress, "or [the report] is required to be submitted" to Congress (Section 5(b)) unless Congress votes to extend this period for an additional 30 days or acts in some other manner to authorize a continued military presence. Congress took no such actions.

Regarding initial congressional authorization, the WPA wording in Section 2 is clear:

> (c) The constitutional powers of the president as commander-in-chief to introduce United States armed forces into hostilities, or into situations where imminent involvement in hostilities is clearly indicated by the circumstances, are exercised only pursuant to (1) a declaration of war, (2) specific statutory authorization, or (3) a national emergency created by attack upon the United States, its territories or possessions, or its armed forces. [32]

On examination, Obama's various justifications for sidestepping these provisions fall away like leaves. [33] The attacks against Qaddafi's military and military installations were an attack by one sovereign nation against another, even though they did not involve a land invasion. While these attacks were relatively brief in duration and arguably did not rise to the definition of "war," [34] they undoubtedly are encompassed by the term "hostilities" found in the WPA. Authorizing enactments from the U.N. and NATO, while significant in that they reflect international diplomatic and military support for the actions taken, cannot and do not act as a substitute for Congress's constitutional power to declare war or provide "specific statutory authorization" for U.S. military actions. [35] The Senate's non-binding resolution, while notable perhaps for its sentiment, is not a legally binding enactment, and is no substitute for the normal, two-house law-making process. While Obama is not the first president to act in such a unilateral manner, the prior actions of other presidents that occurred without proper authorization may provide "historical gloss," [36] but do not vitiate the fact that presidents do not possess any constitutionally-based unilateral power to act militarily abroad (except for the circumstances of a sudden attack on the U.S., in hot pursuit of other hostile forces in actions already authorized, or blunting an imminent attack) simply because such actions are small scale. [37] And as the WPA wording just quoted says, the commander-in-chief power is not a springboard for unilateral presidential war.

Obama's other action – his failure to abide by the 60 day limit on maintaining military involvement abroad – is even more stark, in that it represents the first instance when a president has ignored this provision [38]. To its great discredit, Congress failed to act on its own to call the president into account for this. Still, it blows a new hole in the WPA, and while this law has been widely criticized, nothing good can be said for the disturbing precedent that Obama has now set.

Assessment

Both the Iraq War and the Libyan incursion involved American attacks on regimes that neither attacked the U.S. nor posed any threat to the U.S. (although the Bush administration claimed otherwise at the time). But the similarities end there. In sheer magnitude of scale, the invasion and occupation of Iraq by 160,000 U.S. soldiers (and 180,000 civilian contractors) at its zenith and lasting over eight years, and at the cost to the U.S. of 4400 dead, over 30,000 wounded, and a trillion dollars, dwarfs anything the U.S. did in Libya (its cost was about $1.2 billion [39] and no U.S. casualties). In politics and war, scale matters. As policy, if one accepts the axiom that the worst kind of change in a nation is that which is forced from the outside, then one can certainly argue that Obama's actions in Libya achieved a highly desirable outcome and maximum benefit – the overthrow of a brutal dictator by offshore facilitation of an indigenous movement for democratization, opening the way for a democratic outcome – with minimum cost. [40] Nevertheless, in constitutional terms, Bush had the congressional authorization he needed; Obama did not. Ironically, the grotesque scale of, and web of deception surrounding, the Iraqi war suggest that its precedential value for future presidents may be limited, whereas the precedential consequences of Obama's actions – another instance of an intervention without congressional approval, and the first instance of violation of the 60 day limit – are more likely to encourage future presidents tempted to engage in unilateral limited military actions.

SIGNING STATEMENTS

In its essence, a signing statement is utterly unexceptional. It is a statement issued by the president at the time of a bill signing that offers comment on the new law. Signing statements may simply praise the new legislation being signed by the president. They may also be used for political exhortations or excoriations. They may express reservations about portions of the new law, offer interpretations regarding the meaning or implementation of aspects of the statute, or, in extreme form, pronounce a reinterpretation of the law's language or meaning that may itself run the gamut from ambiguous to crystal clear.

As with much of what modern presidents do, the Constitution provides no authorization for such issuances (although the Constitution does require presidents who veto legislation to return vetoed bills to Congress along with the president's "Objections," which has always been taken to mean a written explanatory message [41]). In principle, a simple statement by the president offering comment on the bill being signed seems an eminently reasonable action on the president's part. The earliest such statement is traced to President James Monroe, who issued a statement in 1819 about a bill he had signed into law a month earlier pertaining to a reduction in the size of the army that stipulated how the president was to select military officers. In his statement, Monroe noted that such decisions belonged to the president, not Congress. Even so, he did not challenge the law's validity or constitutionality. [42]

Presidential signing statements during the balance of the nineteenth century were used rarely, even apologetically; rarer still were statements questioning the legality or constitutionality of the bills being signed. By one count, from Monroe until 1945, presidents raised constitutional objections in signing statements in fewer than twenty instances. From Presidents Truman through Nixon, signing statements increased in use, but those raising constitutional objections composed only about 3 to 6 percent of these. [43] Presidents Ford and Carter developed signing statements as coherent political tools to advance policy and power objectives, including a few signing statements that announced presidential intentions to ignore provisions of law considered to be unconstitutional or to assert executive prerogatives. [44]

But two qualitative changes then occurred. The first was during the Reagan presidency, [45] when the frequency of signing statements based on constitutional, power-related claims by the president increased dramatically. [46] The increase was part of a coordinated administration strategy, spearheaded by Attorney General Edwin Meese's Justice Department, to imbue signing statements with legal weight sufficient to influence legislative intent. To that end, Meese succeeded in persuading Westlaw Publishing to include signing statements in the Legislative History section of the authoritative record of legislative history, *U.S. Code, Congressional and Administrative News*, [47] even though the president is not a legislator, and the signing statement always comes after the legislative process (where legislative intent is expressed) is concluded. This development in the Reagan administration, in turn, was part of the development of the unitary theory of executive power discussed earlier.

Bush Unleashes Signing Statements

The second major change occurred during the second Bush presidency, when the administration, spearheaded by Vice President Cheney and his assistant, David Addington, sought a full-bore implementation of the unitary theory. Part of that effort included extravagant use of signing statements that, in both quantitative and qualitative respects, ratcheted up their significance. The effort was as Herculean as it was unprecedented: for eight years, Addington was sent for review all enrolled bills, culling them for any opportunity to defend, assert, or expand unitary presidential power. [48] As a legislative matter, the number of bills with attached signing statements during the Bush years was actually fewer than his immediate predecessors: 161 during Bush's two terms. [49]

More significant, however, is the number of *provisions* challenged in Bush signing statements, because each provision represents a separate, discrete, and distinct challenge to some provision of the bill otherwise being signed into law. In the Bush presidency, this number took a quantum leap. All previous presidents combined issued a total of about 600 signing statement provisions that raised constitutional challenges. In his eight years in office, Bush issued about 1200 such statement provisions. [50] During the Reagan administration, about 34 percent of his signing statements raised constitutional objections; 47 percent of those of the first Bush presidency raised constitutional objections; in the Clinton era, it was 18 percent; for the second Bush, it was 78 percent. [51] In turn, this effort served a larger presidential power meta-purpose, described as an effort "to create a kind of body of precedent. . .to bolster presidential claims to authority or to limit Congress so that, after a time, what are in fact broad claims to power appear to be more or less routine legal formulae that may begin to be seen like little more than boilerplate language not worthy of careful attention" to undergird "a systematic effort to define presidential authority in terms of the broad conception of the prerogative. . .under the unitary executive theory." [52]

Bush's use of signing statements not only increased the number of Constitution-based challenges, but they were challenges that also often found no support in prior court rulings or other established law. Further, it was in frequency and content one manifestation of the unitary theory of executive power. The "boilerplate language" or linguistic flag employed in numerous Bush signing statements was some version of "to supervise the unitary executive branch." By one account, references to the unitary executive appeared in 145 of Bush's 161 signing statements. [53] This arcane, mantra-like wording, and the intent behind it, garnered virtually no notice until a *Boston Globe* reporter began reporting this practice in 2006. [54] Three cases illustrate some of the more aggressive Bush signing statements.

On December 23, 2004, President Bush issued a signing statement when he signed into law the Intelligence Authorization Act for Fiscal Year 2005 (P.L. 108-487). That law included a provision barring U.S. troops in Colombia from participating in combat against rebels there except for self-defense, and it capped the troop presence at 800. Bush's signing statement included a statement that the Executive branch would "construe the[se] restrictions. . .as advisory in nature. . . ." [55] Bush's signing statement for this bill, if taken at its word, changes a legal mandate to an "advisory" statement – i.e., meaning that the president did not consider himself bound by the plain and authoritative language of the law – the law that became law because he chose to affix his signature to it.

On December 30, 2005, Bush issued a signing statement of H.R. 2863 (P.L. 109-148). This bill to provide emergency supplemental appropriations included an amendment, sponsored by Republican Senator John McCain (AZ) to bar cruel, degrading, and inhumane treatment of prisoners being held by the United States. Bush had opposed the amendment but dropped his opposition when it became clear that the measure had overwhelming congressional support. Yet, his signing statement included this phrase: "The executive branch shall construe Title X in Division A of the Act, relating to detainees, in a manner consistent with the constitutional authority of the President to supervise the unitary executive branch and as Commander in Chief and consistent with the constitutional limitations on the judicial power. . . ." McCain protested the implication that Bush might decline to enforce this provision of the law, but the White House refused to explain Bush's intentions.

In 2006, Congress passed the Postal Accountability and Enhancement Act (PL 109-435), which confirmed a longstanding legal standard that mail could only be opened by the Postal Service without a warrant if it posed an "immediate threat to life or limb or an immediate and substantial danger to property." [56] Yet in his December 25, 2006 signing statement for this bill, President Bush said that he was construing this provision to allow "searches in exigent circumstances, such as to protect human life and safety." [57] As Senator Susan Collins (R-ME) noted on the Senate floor, this signing statement changed the law by expanding the definition of allowable warrantless mail opening *beyond* the protection of life and limb to "exigent circumstances." In other words, Bush's statement claimed to insert this additional, more expansive meaning into the law he had signed, based on nothing more than his desire to do it.

Obama Reins in Signing Statements

Obama promised as president to reverse course on Bush's prolific and aggressive use of signing statements, although Obama made clear that he would not abandon the practice. While he has come under fire for mimicking Bush's pattern, [58] the evidence does not support that charge. In the first three years of his presidency, Obama has issued 19 signing statements incorporating 62 provisions of law raising specified constitutional issues, and 4 more raising unspecified constitutional issues.

Examining the text of Obama's 66 Constitution-based signing statement provisions, some seem to mimic Bush-like frontal challenges to law. For example, his March 11, 2009 statement accompanying the signing of the Omnibus Appropriations Act of 2009 (P.L. 111-8) – the one for which he received the heaviest, and most bipartisan, criticism [59] – directs that parts of the legislation that call for congressional committee approval of spending decisions by federal agencies are to be treated as "advisory" and "not. . .dependent" on committee approval. But these statements are endorsed by several Supreme Court rulings including *INS v. Chadha* (1983), which struck down the legislative veto (of which this is an example). While a constitutional dispute between the branches, Obama's statement is backed expressly by past court rulings; similar Bush assertions lacked such prior case law support.

A more ambiguous example is Obama's statement of May 20, 2009, the Fraud Enforcement and Recovery Act of 2009 (P.L. 111-21), in which Obama questioned the requirement that every executive branch agency is required to submit information to a legislative branch agency, the Financial Crisis Inquiry Commission. Obama's statement says that the executive branch "will construe this. . .not to abrogate any constitutional privilege." What, exactly, does this mean? [60] While the dispute was aired during congressional consideration of the bill, the statement is vague as to what action on the part of the Obama administration this might entail, but what it does not do is state any intention by Obama to ignore or rewrite existing law.

A 2011 signing statement for a defense appropriations bill, H.R. 1473, also engendered criticism for some statements within it. [61] First, Obama criticized Section 1113 of the bill, and then said "Despite my continued strong objection to these provisions, I have signed this Act. . . .Nevertheless, my Administration will work with the Congress to seek repeal of these restrictions, will seek to mitigate their effects, and will oppose any attempt to extend or expand them in the future." Here again, Obama's statement expresses displeasure, not disobedience to the law. He then lodged an objection to a different section of the bill, 2262, that barred funding for four so-called "czar" positions (presidential appointees not subject to Senate confirmation who advise the president on specific policy areas and exert great influence over them). Citing the separation of powers and the Constitution's "take care clause," Obama then said "the executive branch will construe section 2262 not to abrogate these Presidential prerogatives." [62] The first comment avoids the Bush-style refusal to accept the terms of the law, or to proclaim that it will be treated as "advisory"; instead, Obama proposes to work with Congress on the matter – a separation of powers-based entreaty too often missing from Bush-era statements. Obama's objection to Section 2262 offers a vague statement that leaves unclear what action, if any, the president would take, although political reporting suggested that this statement would not result in any challenge to law. According to news reports, the four unfunded czar positions were handled by reorganization of responsibilities in the White House. [63]

Two bills signed in late 2011 brought a relative plethora of signing statements in H.R. 2055, the Consolidated Appropriations Act of 2012, and H.R. 1540, the National Defense Authorization Act of 2012. Obama's December 23 statement on H.R. 2055 itemized 23 signing statement provisions. Many of these repeated earlier objections to similar provisions raised in earlier signings, including continuing disputes over the funding of executive "czars" and bill language giving legislative veto power to congressional committees. Other signing statement provisions say that Obama will interpret statute language "in a manner that avoids constitutional conflicts," "in a manner consistent with my constitutional authority as Commander-in-Chief," "will not treat these provisions as limiting my constitutional authorities in the area of foreign relations," will interpret the law "consistent with my constitutional duty to take care that the laws be faithfully executed," and with his recommendation of measures to Congress "as I shall judge necessary and expedient." [64]

Obama's December 31 signing statement of H.R. 1540 capped tumultuous political wrangling over a bill that Obama had earlier threatened to veto. In a compromise version, Congress agreed to drop a provision that would have barred the prosecution of Al Qaeda suspects in civilian courts. It retained, but narrowed, wording that allowed for indefinite detention of al Qaeda suspects, as well as for a requirement that Al Qaeda suspects had to be kept in military custody (the executive could now make exceptions). In his statement, Obama included 14 signing statement provisions. Seven of these, pertaining to ballistic missile information sharing and negotiations with Russia "could be read to require disclosure" of sensitive information and to require the president to "take certain positions in negotiations. . . ." If so, and if these conditions "conflict with my constitutional authorities," Obama concluded, "I will treat these provisions as non-binding." [65] Although modified by two sets of conditions, this final statement is perhaps the closest to any found in Obama's record of signing statements of one which asserts defiance of statutory language.

While these and other of Obama's 66 signing statement provisions reference constitutional disputes, they are consistent with the kind of disputes presidents raised in signing statements back to the nineteenth century. With the possible exception of Obama's "non-binding" statement in H.R. 1540, in no instance does Obama adopt the wording, frequency, or unitary power-type claims so common during the second Bush presidency. Further, the criteria for signing statement use issued by the White House in early 2009 outlined four conditions of use that can reasonably be read as an exercise in restrained signing statement use. The four criteria include informing Congress of White House concerns when legislation is still pending to attempt to head off possible constitutional confrontations; to accept that legislation comes with a "presumption of constitutionality," meaning that any disputes raised by the president would have to be "well-founded"; that objections would be as specific as possible; and that they would be based on "legitimate" constitutional construction. [66] Indeed, one analysis suggested that Obama's statements largely fell into the category of "mere bluster" and "represent only nonbinding public assertions of the president's view of the Constitution." [67] Even with these criteria and considerations, this does not mean that there is no constitutional dispute, but that the nature of Obama-era disputes, to date, conforms to those of the pre-Bush era, especially to the extent that his challenges have been grounded in case law, and that he also has notified Congress of the constitutional question beforehand – elements lacking in Bush's signing statements. [68]

Assessment

Presidents surely have interpretive latitude, especially when legislative language is vague or ambiguous, and therefore open to interpretation. This is nothing new. As President William H. Taft noted after his presidency, "Let anyone make the laws of the country, if I can construe them." [69] And presidents are entitled to log Constitution-based disputes with the other branches of government. What presidents may not do, Bush's unitary theory notwithstanding, is to rewrite legislation at the point at which a bill is presented for signature through signing statement in what some have called a de facto item veto. [70] As James Pfiffner concluded, "Bush's systematic and expansive use of signing statements constitutes a direct threat to the separation of powers system in the United States." [71] Obama has, to date, skirted, if not walked away from, this ambition, especially after the criticism of his 2009 signing statement of P.L. 111-8. Contrary to the claims of some that Obama has assumed the mantle of a unitary president, [72] his signing statement use to date has been comparable to, or less than that of any predecessors from Reagan on. [73] And Bush II's signing statement use continues to keep him in a class by himself.

THE 'PROTECTIVE RETURN' POCKET VETO [74]

Recent presidents have carved out a new presidential power by asserting a constitutional right allegedly adhering to the presidency in the form of the so-called "protective return" pocket veto, by which presidents claim to pocket veto a bill – a circumstance where, by constitutional definition, bill return to Congress is not possible – yet proceed to do the impossible by then returning the bill to Congress, even as they insist that they are exercising a pocket veto. This arcane yet portentous power grab 1) arose, ironically, from adverse court rulings and a repudiation of the procedure, 2) illustrates the accretion of presidential power by the claiming of constitutional (as opposed to Neustadtian political) powers by presidents, and 3) exemplifies the ability of presidents to autonomously define, consolidate, and expand power over time.

The Constitution provides the president with two kinds of vetoes in Article I, section 7. The regular or return veto is exercised when the president takes two steps: withholds executive signature, and then returns the bill "with his Objections to that House in which it shall have originated. . . ." The bill is then subject to override by Congress. The pocket veto, by contrast, not only observes different and more circumscribed procedures, but has a different and more emphatic effect, because it is absolute – that is, the exercise of a pocket veto kills the legislation in question because there is no bill return, and therefore no possibility of override. Congress's only alternatives to dealing with a pocket veto are to either stay in session for at least ten days after the passage of a bill that may be subject to pocket veto, so that the bill can be returned to Congress, or start from scratch and re-pass the bill when Congress reconvenes. As the Constitution says, "If any Bill shall not be returned by the President within ten Days (Sundays excepted) after it shall have been presented to him, the Same shall be a Law, in like manner as if he had signed it, unless the *Congress by their Adjournment prevent its Return*, in which Case it shall not be a Law (emphasis added)." The pocket veto can only be exercised when two conditions obtain: congressional adjournment, and the impossibility of bill return.

The core of the dispute arose over the presidential desire to use a pocket veto instead of a return veto during intrasession and intersession adjournments of Congress. President Gerald Ford issued five protective return pocket vetoes (although this name was not yet in use) to five vetoed bills. Each was issued during an intrasession adjournment of Congress in October of 1974. Ford said that he was pocket vetoing the bills – a power he insisted he retained – but at the same time he also returned the five bills in the manner of regular vetoes to the Clerk of the House (who had been legally designated by Congress to receive veto and other messages, a common and accepted practice). This was done to try and salvage this expansive use of the pocket veto, but hedge his bets by also returning the bills to make it more likely that the vetoes would withstand a legal challenge. This occurred in the context of adverse federal court rulings challenging Nixon and Ford pocket vetoes that sided with Congress, strongly suggesting that the pocket veto could now only be used at the end of a congress. In 1976, however, the Ford administration repudiated its views and accepted the court view of limited pocket veto use.

The Reagan administration revived more aggressive efforts to use pocket vetoes during adjournments, but did not issue any protective returns. The first Bush administration employed two protective returns; the Clinton administration employed three, and George W. Bush used the procedure once. Bush's suspect veto was challenged in court (the protective return procedure was a small part of the challenge), but the Supreme Court failed to address the merits of the issue. [75] In his first two years in office, Obama issued only two vetoes. Both were protective returns.

The protective return gambit is distinctive as an executive power matter for several reasons. First, it is not the specific product of the unitary executive theory. Second, the second

Bush administration's use of this obscure procedure was unexceptional. Third, and most significantly, it is the product of a much more broad, diffuse, and bureaucratic executive process most closely described by political scientist Richard Pious as "a 'deep structure' of [executive] power claims, which do not change – or change slowly – when partisan control of the White House changes." [76] That is, the protective return power gambit arose from an executive power claim, and even though its tenets were eventually rejected by its adherents during the Ford presidency, the mechanisms of the procedure survived to be resurrected expressly during the first Bush presidency; thereafter, the protective return became integrated as one more of many institutional power claims that come to transcend political party, ideology, and rotating presidents.

Unlike high-profile executive power claims including, say, signing statements, the obscurity of the protective return pocket veto all but guaranteed that it could survive within the bundle of executive prerogatives that pass from one administration to the next thanks to the executive bureaucracy that carries over from administration to administration. [77]

A more high-profile example of this phenomenon was the Obama administration's defense of Bush era lawyer John Yoo (as well as other Bush administration officials) in federal court against charges stemming from his authorship of controversial memos, including legal opinions authorizing torture against detainees. While Obama nullified every such legal opinion on taking office, and Obama administration lawyers were unstinting in their criticism of these Bush policies and personnel, they nevertheless found themselves compelled to defend "the prerogatives of government" because the administration has "enduring institutional interests that carry over from administration to administration and almost always dictate the position the government takes." [78]

Thus, in the case of the second Bush's one protective return pocket veto, and the two exercised by Obama, the actions were viewed as utterly unexceptional bordering on the routine, even though congressional leaders of both parties continued to raise constitutional objections to the procedure. [79] Note, however, how the Bush and Obama administrations justified these actions. As Bush's deputy press secretary Scott Stanzel said at the time of the veto, this "process and procedure. . .has been used a number of times over the past couple decades." [80] Similarly, Obama press spokesman Dan Pfeiffer explained Obama's protective returns this way: "The longstanding view of the Executive Branch is that a pocket veto is appropriate in circumstances such as these. . . ." [81]

Assessment

Unlike the other powers discussed in this paper, the Bush and Obama protective returns were nearly identical in form, and both appeared to arise from the bowels of the "deep structure" of the executive bureaucracy rather than from top political aides seeking to expand executive authority. Here is one of the most important, if underappreciated, aspects of executive power accretion: *secular bureaucratic power incrementalism*. A day may come where a constitutional challenge or political flare-up may drag the protective return pocket veto into the intense lights of the legal or political stage, and where a full airing, and final disposition, of this arcane executive power grab may be vetted and resolved. Absent such a moment, however, the executive's "deep structure" will continue to advance the protective return for every subsequent chief executive.

CONCLUSION

The three cases of war powers, signing statements, and the protective return pocket veto offer different facets of the Bush and Obama presidencies in their approaches to executive power, even as both administrations functioned in an era of expansive, and expanding, executive power. George W. Bush obtained from Congress the necessary constitutional authority to launch what became the Iraq War. Admittedly, he did so by adroitly exploiting the mood of a country still reeling from the 9/11 attacks, and by spinning a ginned-up yarn that elevated executive prevarication to a new high (or, more properly, low). Still, Congress acquiesced, and it must accept blame for a defective decision. Barack Obama was relatively transparent in his decision to intervene in Libya; his cause, arguably, was defensible on policy grounds both in advancing American foreign policy goals and in assisting a genuine indigenous move to democracy that may well not have survived without outside involvement. But Obama never obtained congressional authorization, and ignored the statutory 60 day limit enacted decades ago precisely to rein in open-ended executive military actions. To add to the irony of these two cases, Obama suffered no adverse political or legal fallout from this plain violation of law, primarily because, at bottom, his actions were largely seen as just, and coming at virtually no cost (either in money or American lives).

The case of signing statements illustrates a different lesson, in that Bush's explosive expansion of signing statements as a leading edge of his unitary executive power view, both in qualitative and quantitative terms, eclipsed that of his predecessors. Obama, to date, while not abandoning the practice, has put this unitary genie back in its bottle.

The protective return case reflects a different facet of modern executive power, where two very different presidents, with very different views of their office, powers, and policy, behaved pretty much identically, dancing to the same obscure "deep structure" bureaucratic imperative.

Obama is not a unitary theory Bush clone; neither is he a neo-Calvin Coolidge. He has behaved in constitutional terms as a modern activist president who has rejected the tendentious unitary theory, yet also broken one significant boundary in war powers, pulled back on abusive signing statement use to the pre-Bush II standard, but also mindlessly conformed to an obscure constitutional executive power grab in the form of the protective return. In short, Obama's constitutional presidency has been broadly consistent with his post-Watergate strong-presidency contemporaries, but to date at least, he is no George W. Bush.

ACKNOWLEDGMENTS

The author wishes to thank Christopher Kelley and Meena Bose for their advice and assistance.

REFERENCES

[1]   Charlie Savage, "Barack Obama's Q&A," *Boston Globe,* December 20, 2007, at http://www.boston.com/news/politics/2008/specials/CandidateQA/ObamaQA/

[2] James P. Pfiffner, "Executive Power in the Bush and Obama Administrations," *PRG Report,* 33(Spring 2011), 4.

[3] Richard M. Pious, "Prerogative Power in the Obama Administration," *Presidential Studies Quarterly* 41(June 2011): 263-89; Geoffrey R. Stone, "Our Untransparent President," *New York Times,* June 27, 2011, A19.

[4] Dick Cheney and Liz Cheney, *In My Time: A Personal and Political Memoir* (New York: Threshold Editions, 2011).

[5] Kori Schake, "Call it G.W.O.T. or J.I.H.A.D. Obama is Waging Bush's War," *Foreign Policy* August 7, 2009), at http://shadow.foreignpolicy.com/posts/2009/08/07/call_it_gwot_or_jihad_obama_is_waging_bushs_war See also Eric Posner, "Stop Complaining About Harold Koh's Interpretation of the War Powers Act," *The New Republic,* July 1, 2011, at http://www.tnr.com/article/politics/91166/harold-koh-war-powers-john-yoo-libya

[6] William McGurn, "Obama Brings Back the Constitution," *Wall Street Journal,* January 17, 2012, at http://online.wsj.com/article/SB100014240529702044090004577158903842171724.html See also Kimberly A. Strassel, "Obama's Imperial Presidency," *Wall Street Journal,* July 6, 2012, A11.

[7] Pfiffner, "Executive Power in the Bush and Obama Administrations."

[8] Pious, "Prerogative Power in the Obama Administration," 265. See also Hendrik Hertzberg, "Prisoners," *The New Yorker,* April 18, 2011, 45-46.

[9] Kathleen Clark, "'A New Era of Openness?' Disclosing Intelligence to Congress Under Obama," *Constittuional Commentary* 26(Summer 2010): 327-28.

[10] In the words of the Federalist Society, it is "a group of conservatives and libertarians dedicated to reforming the current order." The Federalist Society was formed in 1982. See http://www.fed-soc.org/AboutUs/ourbackground.htm.

[11] Jeffrey Rosen, "Power of One: Bush's Leviathan State," *The New Republic*, July 24, 2006, 8. The phrase appears most famously in Alexander Hamilton's *Federalist Paper 70*, in which he wrote that the "unity" of the executive was one of the important advantages of the executive office proposed in the new Constitution. But, Hamilton's reference was far more straightforward than that ascribed to it by the unitary theorists: Hamilton was simply comparing the presidency as an office occupied by a single individual with competing proposals of the day for a "plural executive," whereby the office would be composed of two or more people who would function as a kind of executive committee. Alexander Hamilton, James Madison, and John Jay, *The Federalist Papers* (New York: New American Library, 1961), 423–31.

[12] James Burnham, *Congress and the American Tradition* (Chicago: Regnery, 1959); Willmoore Kendall, *The Conservative Affirmation* (Chicago: Regnery, 1963); Alfred DeGrazia, *Republic in Crisis* (New York: Federal Legal Publications, 1965). See also Raymond Tatalovich and Thomas S. Engeman, *The Presidency and Political Science* (Baltimore: Johns Hopkins University Press, 2003), chap. 7; Robert J. Spitzer, "Liberals and the Presidency," in *Contending Approaches to the American Presidency,* Michael A. Genovese, ed. (Washington, D.C.: CQ Press, 2011), 79-97.

[13] Bush's Vice President, Dick Cheney, was that administration's foremost proponent of the corollary notion that presidential power was gutted in the 1970s, and that it had not recovered its proper powers from then up to the present. Jane Mayer, "The Hidden Power," *The New Yorker*, July 3, 2006, 44–55. This notion was challenged from all

political quarters. For example, as Reagan Justice Department official Bruce Fein commented about the Bush administration's and Cheney's views of presidential power, "They're in a time warp. If you look at the facts, presidential powers have never been higher." Dana Milbank, "In Cheney's Shadow, Counsel Pushes the Conservative Cause," *Washington Post*, October 11, 2004, A21.

[14] Jess Bravin, "Bush's Power Play Has Key Ally," *The Wall Street Journal*, January 5, 2006, 12.

[15] Bravin, "Bush's Power Play Has Key Ally"; "How Bush Has Asserted Powers of the Executive," *USA Today*, June 6, 2002, 2A; R. Jeffrey Smith and Dan Eggen, "Justice Expands 'Torture' Definition," *Washington Post*, December 31, 2004, A1; Stuart Taylor, Jr., "The Man Who Would Be King," *Atlantic Monthly*, April 2006, 25–26.

[16] 542 U.S. 507 (2004).

[17] 542 U.S. 466 (2004).

[18] 548 U.S. 557 (2006).

[19] Savage, "Barack Obama's Q&A."

[20] For a detailed critique of the unitary theory, see Robert J. Spitzer, *Saving the Constitution from Lawyers* (New York: Cambridge University Press, 2008), Ch. 4; Lawrence Lessig and Cass R. Sunstein, "The President and the Administration," *Columbia Law Review* 94(January 1994): 1–120; Ryan J. Barilleaux and Christopher S. Kelley, eds., *The Unitary Executive and the Modern Presidency* (College Station, TX: Texas A&M University Press, 2010); and Louis Fisher, "The Unitary Executive and Inherent Executive Power," *University of Pennsylvania Journal of Constitutional Law* 12(2010): 569-91.

[21] See for example *Humphrey's Executor v. U.S.*, 295 U.S. 602 (1935). See also Charlie Savage, *Takeover: The Return of the Imperial Presidency and the Subversion of American Democracy* (New York: Little, Brown, 2007), 47-49.

[22] Samuel A. Alito, Jr., "Using Presidential Signing Statements to Make Fuller Use of the President's Constitutionally Assigned Role in the Process of Enacting Law," U.S. Justice Department, Office of Legal Counsel, February 5, 1986, at http://www.archives.gov/news/samuel-alito/accession-060-89-269/Acc060-89-269-box6-SG-LSWG-AlitotoLSWG-Feb1986.pdf

[23] Melanie M. Marlowe, "President Obama and Executive Independence," in *The Obama Presidency in the Constitutional Order,* Carol McNamara and Melanie M. Marlowe, eds. (Lanham, MD: Rowman & Littlefield, 2011), 62.

[24] Marlowe, "President Obama and Executive Independence," 47. Emphasis added.

[25] David Gray Adler, "The Presidency and the Constitution," in *New Directions in the American Presidency,* Lori Cox Han, ed. (New York: Routledge, 2011), 12-32.

[26] For example, Louis Fisher, *Presidential War Power* (Lawrence, KS: University Press of Kansas, 2004), 210-15.

[27] Prodigious writing on this subject includes, but is by no means limited to: John J. Mearsheimer and Stephen M. Walt, "Keeping Saddam Hussein in a Box," *New York Times*, February 2, 2003, 4-15; Joseph Wilson, *The Politics of Truth* (New York: Public Affairs, 2005); Thomas E. Ricks, *Fiasco* (New York: Penguin, 2006); Michael Isikoff and David Corn, *Hubris: The Inside Story of Spin, Scandal, and the Selling of the Iraq War* (New York: Three Rivers Press, 2007); John Prados, "PR Push for Iraq War Preceded Intelligence Findings," *The National Security Archive,* Briefing Book No.

254, August 22, 2008, at http://www.gwu.edu/~nsarchiv/NSAEBB/NSAEBB254 /index.htm; Shirley Anne Warshaw, *The Co-Presidency of Bush and Cheney* (Stanford, CA: Stanford University Press, 2009); Scott Bonn, *Mass Deception* (Piscataway, NJ: Rutgers University Press, 2010); Paul R. Pillar, *Intelligence and U.S. Foreign Policy: Iraq, 9/11, and Misguided Reform* (New York: Columbia University Press, 2011); Kurt Eichenwald, *500 Days: Secrets and Lies in the Terror Wars* (New York: Simon and Schuster, 2012).

[28] U.S. Department of Justice, Office of Legal Counsel, "Authorization to Use Military Force in Libya," April 1, 2011, at http://www.justice.gov/olc/2011/authority-military-use-in-libya.pdf

[29] Louis Fisher, "*The Law:* Military Operations in Libya: No War? No Hostilities?" *Presidential Studies Quarterly* 42(March 2012); U.S. Department of Justice, "Authorization to Use Military Force in Libya."

[30] "United States Activities in Libya," Report Submitted by Obama to Congress, June 15, 2011, 29, at http://www.nytimes.com/interactive/2011/06/16/us/politics/20110616_POWERS_DOC.html?ref=politics

[31] The question of why Obama did not go to Congress for authorization lingers over his actions. While the time frame for action was limited, the U.N. Security Council debated its Libya resolution for five weeks before its March 17 vote, so Obama had a window of time to go to Congress. Surely the most likely explanation is that he assumed that the Republican-controlled House of Representatives would not grant him authority, given the hyper-political atmosphere during this time period, and fearing a preventable humanitarian disaster, he approved U.S. attacks. Paul Starobin, "A Moral Flip-Flop? Defining War," *New York Times Sunday Review,* August 7, 2011, 5.

[32] Quoted in Robert J. Spitzer, *President and Congress* (New York: McGraw-Hill, 1993), 169.

[33] Louis Fisher, "Military Operations in Libya: No War? No Hostilities?" *Presidential Studies Quarterly* 42(March 2012): 176-89.

[34] Linton Weeks, "If This Is Not 'War' Against Libya, What Is It?" National Public Radio, March 22, 2011, at http://www.npr.org/2011/03/22/134762513/if-this-is-not-war-against-libya-what-is-it

[35] Louis Fisher, "Obama's U.N. Authority?" *National Law Journal,* April 18, 2011, at http://loufisher.org/docs/wp/authority.pdf

[36] Michael J. Glennon, "The Cost of 'Empty Words': A Comment On the Justice Department's Libya Opinion," *Harvard National Security Journal Forum,* April 14, 2011, 3, at http://harvardnsj.com/2011/04/the-cost-of-empty-words-a-comment-on-the-justice-departments-libya-opinion/

[37] Spitzer, *President and Congress,* 149-68; Fisher, *Presidential War Power*, chap. 1; Edward Keynes, *Undeclared Wars* (University Park, PA: Pennsylvania State University Press, 1982), 37; David Gray Adler, "The Constitution and Presidential Warmaking," *Political Science Quarterly* 103(Spring 1988): 1-36.

[38] Jake Tapper, "President Obama's Libyan Intervention Hits 60-Day Legal Limit," *ABC News,* May 20, 20011, at http://abcnews.go.com/Politics/libya-president-obama-congress-faces-questions-war-powers/story?id=13642002

[39] Reid J. Epstein, "Libya Clash Reaches Tipping Point," *Politico,* June 15, 2011, at http://www.politico.com/news/stories/0611/57015.html; Don Rose, "Recouping Libya

War Costs," *Chicago Daily Observer,* October 25, 2011, at http://www.cdobs.com/archive/featured/recouping-libya-war-costs-a-crass-2-billion-proposal/

[40] David Remnick, "Behind the Curtain," *The New Yorker,* September 5, 2011, 19-20.

[41] Robert J. Spitzer, *The Presidential Veto* (Albany, NY: SUNY Press, 1988), chap. 2.

[42] American Bar Association, "Task Force on Presidential Signing Statements and the Separation of Powers Doctrine," July 23, 2006, 7; Christopher N. May, "Presidential Defiance of 'Unconstitutional' Laws: Reviving the Royal Prerogative," *Hastings Constitutional Law Quarterly* 21(Summer 1994): 929. According to May, Monroe apparently abided by the terms of the law. Monroe actually issued a second such statement in 1822.

[43] May, "Presidential Defiance," 932.

[44] Ryan J. Barilleaux and David Zellers, "Executive Unilateralism in the Ford and Carter Presidencies," *The Unitary Executive and the Modern Presidency*, 41-76.

[45] Early questions about the constitutionality and propriety of some of these signing statements were raised in Marc N. Garber and Kurt A. Wimmer, "Presidential Signing statements as Interpretations of Legislative Intent: An Executive Aggrandizement of Power," *Harvard Journal on Legislation* 24(Summer 1987): 363-95; and Spitzer, *The Presidential Veto*, 138-39.

[46] Christopher S. Kelley, "The Law: Contextualizing the Signing Statement," *Presidential Studies Quarterly* 37(December 2007): 739.

[47] Christopher S. Kelley, "A Matter of Direction: The Reagan Administration, the Signing Statement, and the 1986 Westlaw Decision," *William and Mary Bill of Rights Journal* 16(October 2007): 283-306; Steven G. Calabresi and Daniel Lev, "The Legal Significance of Presidential Signing Statements," *The Forum* 4, No. 2(2006), 1.

[48] Warshaw, *The Co-Presidency of Bush and Cheney*, chap. 9; Chitra Ragavan, "Cheney's Guy," *U.S. News and World Report,* May 29, 2006; Savage, *Takeover*, 236-41.

[49] T.J. Halstead, "Presidential Signing Statements: Constitutional and Institutional Implications," CRS Report for Congress, September 17, 2007, 3-6; http://www/coherentbabble.com. This website is an accepted and authoritative source of basic information about signing statements. According to that site, Reagan issued a total of 250 signing statements (not provisions), the first Bush 228, and Clinton 381. Signing statement expert Christopher Kelley produces counts that are slightly different, as he includes spoken statements.

[50] Spitzer, *Saving the Constitution From Lawyers*, 96; Charlie Savage, "Obama Looks to Limit Impact of Tactic Bush Used to Sidestep New Laws," *New York Times,* March 10, 2009, at http://www.nytimes.com/2009/03/10/us/politics/10signing.html?hp?ref=fp2.

[51] Halstead, "Presidential Signing Statements."

[52] Phillip J. Cooper, "George W. Bush, Edgar Allen Poe, and the Use and Abuse of Presidential Signing Statements," *Presidential Studies Quarterly* 35 (September 2005): 518, 531.

[53] http://www.coherentbabble.com.faqs.htm. While the "supervise the unitary executive branch" phrasing emerged prolifically in the second Bush's signing statements, similar language appeared as early as 1987 in a Reagan signing statement attached to a bill to increase the federal debt ceiling (P.L. 100-119) on September 29, in which Reagan challenged a provision pertaining to a reporting requirement by the Office of Management and Budget. Reagan said that this provision, in his view, would not

preclude him or other presidents from supervising the OMB director, saying that any other view "would plainly constitute an unconstitutional infringement of the President's authority as head of a unitary executive branch."

[54] Charlie Savage, "Bush Challenges Hundreds of Laws," *Boston Globe,* April 30, 2006, A1. Savage won the Pulitzer Prize for this reporting. See also Savage, *Takeover.*

[55] George W. Bush, "Statement on Signing the Intelligence Authorization Act for Fiscal Year 2005," December 23, 2004, *Weekly Compilation of Presidential Documents,* December 21, 2004, 3012. This brief, five paragraph signing statement actually includes five separate signing statement provisions that assert alterations of language in the bill Bush signed into law.

[56] "Senate Resolution 22—Reaffirming the Constitutional and Statutory Protections Accorded Sealed Domestic Mail, and for Other Purposes," *Congressional Record—Senate*, January 10, 2007, S394.

[57] Quoted in "Senate Resolution 22."

[58] Neil Kinkopf, "Still More on Signing Statements," *Executive Watch,* March 19, 2009, at http://executivewatch.net/2009/03/19/still-more-on-signing-statements/ ; Mitchel A. Sollenberger and Mark J. Rozell, "Obama's Promises Not Kept," *Politico,* April 29, 2011, at http://www.politico.com/news/stories/0411/53909.html

[59] Christopher S. Kelley, Melanie C. Marlowe, and Ryan Barilleaux, "President Barack Obama, Unilateralist," in *The Obama Presidency: Change and Continuity*, Andrew J. Dowdle, Dirk C. Van Raemdonck, and Robert Maranto, eds. (New York: Routledge, 2011), 87-88.

[60] In his analysis of Obama's used of signing statements, Todd Garvey says that in his June 24, 2009 signing statement accompanying the Supplemental Appropriations Act of 2009 (PL 111-32), Obama "stated he would disregard several provisions that he said interfered with his foreign affairs power. . . ." "The Obama Administration's Evolving Approach to the Signing Statement," *Presidential Studies Quarterly,* 41(June 2011): 397. Yet this is not what Obama said. Expressing his displeasure with provisions of the law that direct the executive to "take certain positions" regarding negotiations with various international entities, the relevant portion of Obama's statement said: "I will not treat these provisions as limiting my ability to engage in foreign diplomacy or negotiations." "Statement on Signing the supplemental Appropriations Act, 2009, June 24, 2009, at http://www.coherentbabble.com/Statements/SShr2346-111th-B.pdf. Leaving aside the merits of the dispute, while it is undeniably an expression of displeasure by Obama, and could be viewed as an indication that Obama might contradict the strictures of the law he signed, he by no means says that he will do so. Garvey's analysis in his article suggests, in fact, that such statements by Obama are expressions of displeasure, not Shermanesque statements (like many of Bush's) the he does not consider himself bound by the language of the law.

[61] James Risen, "Obama Takes On Congress Over Policy Czar Positions," *New York Times,* April 16, 2011, at http://www.nytimes.com/2011/04/17/us/politics/17spend.html; Sollenberger and Rozell, "Obama's Promises Not Kept."

[62] "Statement by the President on H.R. 1473," April 15, 2011, at http://www.whitehouse.gov/the-press-office/2011/04/15/statement-president-hr-1473

[63] Mitchel A. Sollenberger and Mark J. Rozell argue that this signing statement "effectively nullified" Section 2262. "Prerogative Power and Executive Branch Czars:

President Obama's Signing Statement," *Presidential Studies Quarterly,* 41(December 2011): 819. This assertion fails on two grounds: first, while Obama's signing statement pertaining to 2262 could be interpreted as opening the door to presidential nullification, that is simply not what the statement says; it could just as easily reference presidential efforts to support the four czar positions in ways that would not contradict the law he signed. Second, Obama did, in fact, find support for the four czars without somehow ignoring or attempting to nullify 2262. See Risen, "Obama Takes On Congress."

[64] Office of the Press Secretary, "Statement by the President on H.R. 2055," December 23, 2011, at http://www.whitehouse.gov/the-press-office/2011/12/23/statement-president-hr-2055. My thanks to Louis Fisher and Christopher Kelley for their interpretive perspectives on this bill. An article by Jeffrey Crouch, Mark J. Rozell and Mitchel A. Sollenberger assert that Obama's signing statement "effectively nullified provisions" of H.R. 2055. "Obama Mirrors Bush in Signing Statements," *Roll Call,* January 19, 2012. Yet none of the wording in Obama's H.R. 2055 statement can be said to "nullify" any provisions of the law, and Obama used no such definitive language. Andrew Rudalevige dubbed Obama's signing statement wording "presumably-intentionally-vaguely-worded." "Another Holiday Tradition," *The Monkey Cage,* December 24, 2011, at http://themonkeycage.org/blog/2011/12/24/another-holiday-tradition/

[65] Office of the Press Secretary, "Statement by the President on H.R. 1540," December 31, 2011, at www.whitehouse.gov/the-press-office/2011/12/31/statement-president-hr-1540. I read the relevant sections of H.R. 1540, but could not discern the extent to which the language was either definitive or ambiguous in relation to Obama's objections.

[66] "Memorandum for the Heads of Executive Departments and Agencies: Presidential Signing Statements," Office of the Press Secretary, March 9, 2009, at http://obamahistoryproject.typepad.com/presidential_memoranda/2009/03/memorandum-for-the-heads-of-executive-departments-and-agencies-presidential-signing-statements-3909.html.

[67] Garvey, "The Obama Administration's Evolving Approach to the Signing Statement," 401.

[68] Kinkopf, "Still More on Signing Statements."

[69] William Howard Taft, *The President and His Powers* (New York: Columbia University Press, 1916), 78.

[70] May, "Presidential Defiance of 'Unconstitutional' Laws," 979; Louis Fisher, "Signing Statements: What to Do?" *The Forum* 4(2006): Article 7, 1.

[71] James P. Pfiffner, *Power Play: The Bush Presidency and the Constitution* (Washington, D.C.: Brookings Institution Press, 2008), 196.

[72] Christopher S. Kelley, "To Be (Unitarian) or Not to Be (Unitarian): Presidential Power in the George W. Bush Administration," *White House Studies* 10, 2(2010): 11-19.

[73] Here are per year signing statement averages, followed by per year average use of signing provisions in parentheses: Reagan: 31 (19); Bush I: 57 (61); Clinton: 47 (19); Bush II: 20 (150); Obama (first three years): 6 (22). Source: www.coherentbabble.com; T.J. Halstead, "Presidential Signing Statements: Constitutional and Institutional Implications," CRS Report for Congress, September 17, 2007.

[74] This account is largely drawn from Robert J. Spitzer, "The 'Protective Return' Pocket Veto: Presidential Aggrandizement of Constitutional Power," *Presidential Studies Quarterly* 31(December 2001): 720-32; and Robert J. Spitzer, "Growing Executive Power: The Strange Case of the 'Protective Return' Pocket Veto," *Presidential Studies Quarterly* 42(September 2012).

[75] *Iraq v. Beaty,* 556 U.S. 848 (2009).

[76] Pious, "Prerogative Power in the Obama Administration," 286.

[77] See Hugh Heclo, "The Changing Presidential Office," in *Understanding the Presidency,* James P. Pfiffner and Roger H. Davidson, eds. (New York: Pearson Longman, 2009), 251-62.

[78] Josh Gerstein, "Obama Lawyers Set to Defend Yoo," *Politico,* January 28, 2009, at http://www.politico.com/news/stories/0109/18063.html

[79] For contemporaneous criticisms of these vetoes, see Robert J. Spitzer, "The 'Pocket Veto' Peril," *Los Angeles Times,* January 8, 2008, at http://articles.latimes.com/2008/jan/08/opinion/oe-spitzer8; Robert J. Spitzer, "Pres. Obama: Don't Make This Veto Mistake, *The Huffington Post,* January 4, 2010, at http://www.huffingtonpost.com/robert-j-spitzer/pres-obama-dont-make-this_b_408119.html; Robert J. Spitzer, "President Obama: Veto, Yes; Pocket Veto, No!" *The Huffington Post,* October 8, 2012, at http://www.huffingtonpost.com/robert-j-spitzer/pres-obama-veto-yes-pocke_b_754660.html; Jackie Calmes, "Much Ado Over. Notarization?" *New York Times,* October 17, 2010, 23.

[80] "Press Gaggle by Scott Stanzel," December 31, 2007, at www.whitehouse.gov/news/releases/2007/12/20071231-3.html

[81] Calmes, "Much Ado Over. Notarization?"; email from White House Communications Director Dan Pfeiffer, October 16, 2010.

In: Change in the White House?
Editor: Meena Bose

ISBN: 978-1-62948-920-9
© 2014 Nova Science Publishers, Inc.

Chapter 3

DIVIDERS, NOT UNITERS: HOW PRESIDENTS GEORGE W. BUSH AND BARACK OBAMA FAILED TO UNITE A DIVIDED NATION

Richard Himelfarb

ABSTRACT

The paper examines the work of eminent political scientist Gary C. Jacobson, specifically his acclaimed book *A Divider, Not a Uniter: George W. Bush and the American People* and his subsequent scholarship regarding public opinion during the Obama presidency. Both Bush and Obama governed a nation marked by wide partisan division among the electorate. Jacobson argues that Bush's policies, particularly the deceptive arguments employed to justify the war in Iraq, increased partisan divisions to a level unprecedented in American politics. Despite alienating the vast majority of Democrats along with political independents Bush remained popular among Republicans, particularly the party's base comprised mainly of evangelical Christians. Motivated by religious kinship with Bush, this group embraced the administration's dubious justifications for the Iraq war even when clearly contradicted by fact.

Although he promised a post-partisan presidency, Barack Obama has made little progress in healing the partisan divide. More than two years into his presidency partisan divisions have reemerged approaching those of the Bush years. While Jacobson's scholarship acknowledges this, he argues that Obama, unlike Bush, bears little responsibility for failing to unite the country. Instead, Jacobson blames the arguable successor to the religious right, The Tea Party, a movement comprised of people who, he argues, are extreme, racist, and unreasonable.

This paper argues that Jacobson's analysis is unfair and politically biased. Specifically, it makes the case for three propositions: 1. Like Bush, Obama has pursued policies that are highly partisan and ideological and consequently politically divisive 2. Obama's arguments justifying his policies have been no more or less truthful or demagogic than Bush's. 3. The political right has no monopoly on incendiary rhetoric or the ability to deny facts. During both the Bush and Obama presidencies, the left has proven itself capable of the same.

According to Gary Jacobson: "...George W. Bush's presidency provoked the widest partisan divisions ever recorded in more than 50 years that surveys have regularly gauged the public's assessment of presidential performance." [1] Despite Barack Obama's promises of a post-partisan presidency the political polarization of the Bush years has "reemerged with a vengeance." [2] Jacobson notes: "Although this partisan divide has yet to reach the record levels inspired by Bush, it has become wider than under any president other than Bush." [3] The key questions, of course, are why the polarization has occurred and specifically what role the two presidents have played in exacerbating and maintaining the divide. The recent scholarship of Jacobson, an eminent political scientist at the University of California at San Diego, addresses them, first in his acclaimed book *A Divider, Not A Uniter: George W. Bush and the American People* and then in a number of subsequent articles focusing on American public opinion during the Obama presidency. [4]

Despite the fact that both presidents governed during periods of unprecedented partisan division and rancor Jacobson is significantly more critical of Bush than Obama. Indeed, in his narrative Bush and the political right bear almost all of the blame while Obama and the left are depicted as little more than innocent bystanders. Jacobson argues that Bush's policies, particularly the arguments employed to justify the war in Iraq (which he argues were extraordinarily deceptive), increased partisan divisions to unprecedented levels. Despite alienating the vast majority of Democrats along with an increasing proportion of independents, Bush remained popular among Republicans, particularly the party's base comprised mainly of evangelical Christians. Motivated by religious kinship with Bush, this group embraced the administration's dubious arguments for the Iraq war even when clearly contradicted by fact.

By contrast, Jacobson attributes Obama's failure to achieve a post-partisan presidency not to liberal governance but rather the ceaseless right-wing efforts to undermine him. The most significant opposition arises from the arguable successor to the religious right, the Tea Party, a movement comprised of people who, Jacobson maintains, are extreme, racist and unreasonable.

This paper argues that Jacobson's analysis is unfair and politically biased. Specifically, it makes the case for three propositions. First, it argues that Obama, like Bush, has pursued policies that are highly partisan and ideological and consequently politically divisive. Second, Obama's arguments justifying his policies have been no more or less deceptive than Bush's and his administration has employed comparably aggressive tactics in pursuit of it goals. Third, the political right is not the sole cause of America's partisan divide. Not only is Jacobson's description of the political right replete with exaggerations but the political left is guilty of many similar excesses, a fact Jacobson overlooks or ignores.

Gary C. Jacobson is one of the discipline's preeminent scholars. He has taught political science at the University of California, San Diego since 1979 where his scholarship has focused on American national politics and congressional elections. He is the author (with Samuel Kernell and Thad Krouser) of *The Logic of American Politics (5th edition)*, one of the most popular undergraduate texts used in introductory classes. His *The Politics of Congressional Elections*, now in its eighth edition is a staple of numerous undergraduate and graduate courses. Two of Jacobson's previous works, *Money in Congressional Elections* and *Strategy and Choice in Congressional Elections* (with Samuel Kernell) are political science classics frequently cited in scholarship. Additionally, he is the author of numerous articles that appear in the profession's most prestigious journals. For much of his career Jacobson's work was free of any political bias, overt or implicit. Indeed, it would likely be impossible to detect any of his personal political leanings from this sizable body of work.

This began to change during the first Bush administration as a perceptible liberal bias began to permeate his scholarship. With the publication of *A Divider, Not a Uniter* in 2006 and continuing with his analyses of the Obama years, one detects a clear narrative of recent American politics where virtually every malady befalling them is attributable to a conservative minority that is both malevolent and immune to facts.

BUSH THE DIVIDER

The title of Jacobson's book is a play on George W. Bush's pledge in 2000 to be "a uniter, not a divider" who could "change the tone of Washington to one of civility and respect." [5] Instead, writes Jacobson, by the 2004 election, "he had become the most divisive and polarizing president in the more than 70 years that public opinion polls had regularly measured citizens' assessments of presidents and he remained so through the end of his presidency." [6] Averaged over Bush's two terms, almost 86 percent of Republicans but only 25 percent of Democrats would approve of his performance. The resulting 61 percent gap is the highest recorded for any president on record. [7]

This finding appears a bit less stunning, however, in the larger context of increasing partisanship in American politics. While the public approval gap for Presidents Eisenhower through Carter averaged 34 points, it rose to 54 points under Reagan, receded a bit under George H.W. Bush but then increased to 56 points under Clinton. Thus, George W. Bush's distinction of being the most divisive president in American history is a title he wins only by edging out two of three immediate predecessors and arguably reflects the long term trend of increasing partisan division in American politics. [8]

Jacobson, however, is not content with such a facile analysis; in the case of George W. Bush something much more sinister and disturbing is at work. He argues that for all his promises to unite the nation, Bush never believed his rhetoric "which was tactical rather than an end in itself, to be discarded if unhelpful for winning legislative and electoral victories." [9] Following the disputed 2000 election Bush entered office a divisive president lacking a popular mandate. However, with Republicans holding only the narrowest of majorities in Congress, he proceeded to govern in a most partisan and ideological manner. According to Jacobson Bush's policy proposals were designed in secrecy and pitched as "a multi-faceted sales exercise where the aim was not to explain the product but to sell it." In the process, "contrary messages and messengers were denounced" while "probing questions from reporters were ducked or ignored."[10] According to Jacobson, "this mindset and consequent emphasis on marketing bred a cavalier approach to truth: dishonesty not by lying, but by a deceptive selection of truthful but misleading statements." [11] As an example, he cites the Bush tax cuts which promised "'the highest percentage cuts to the lowest income Americans.'" Jacobson argues that the statement, though true, was deceptive "...because the lowest income groups already paid so little; reducing a tax liability from $200 to $100 represents a large percentage cut but small substantive benefit for the taxpayer." [12]

All the same, Jacobson believes the events of 9/11 offered Bush an opportunity to depart from this heavy handed approach to governing and unite the nation. Within two weeks, Bush's public approval ratings had soared from the low 50s to over 90 percent (including 80 percent of Democrats). While they would decline over the next year and a half, Bush remained a popular president, enjoying overall support above 60 percent. This appears largely due to Bush's strong response to the 9/11 attacks including his decision to wage war in Afghanistan. Notably, however, by early 2003, the partisan divide would reemerge. By January, 2003, even as Bush continued to win the approval of about 90 percent of Republicans his support among Democrats would drop below 40 percent.

Although Democratic support for Bush was already declining among Democrats (and also independents) during 2002, his decision to attack Iraq accelerated the partisan divide to record levels. To make the case for war, the Bush administration would put forth what Jacobson implies were a pair of dubious justifications. First, it would argue that Saddam possessed Weapons of Mass Destruction (WMD) and was actively pursuing nuclear weapons. [13] Second, "the administration also wanted to tie Saddam to the terrorist attacks of September 11 or at least to al Qaeda more generally." [14] According to Jacobson, while the evidence for each of these propositions ranged between nonexistent and shady, Bush and his advisers repeatedly argued or implied they were true and supported by intelligence.

Following the rapid toppling of Saddam Hussein's regime in April, 2003 and Bush's subsequent pronouncement of "Mission Accomplished" aboard the aircraft carrier Abraham Lincoln, things took a decided turn for the worse. Widespread looting, civil unrest, and the beginnings of an insurgency created an increasingly chaotic, volatile situation. American soldiers attempting to quell the unrest experienced increasing casualties. Arguably most disturbing, however, was the failure to locate Weapons of Mass Destruction that had provided the chief rationale for the invasion. In the absence of such weapons, many believed that Saddam Hussein posed little threat to American national security and the full-scale invasion appeared unnecessary.

In the months following the invasion of Iraq, public support fell for both Bush and the war. However, the decline was not uniform. While support fell precipitously among Democrats and, to a lesser extent, independents, Republicans steadfastly backed both. By the end of Bush's second term more than two-thirds of Republicans remained supportive of both Bush and the war while Democratic support fell to roughly 15 percent for the war and to below 10 percent for the president. [15] Jacobson notes that the wide partisan gap in support for the Iraq war was anomalous; partisan differences in support for previous conflicts including Korea, Vietnam, the Gulf War and Kosovo were significantly smaller. [16]

EXPLAINING THE BUSH DIVIDE:
ANGRY DEMOCRATS VS. DELUSIONAL REPUBLICANS

Why did the Iraq war divide Americans of the two parties so deeply? First, many Republicans accepted the Bush administration's two central arguments for invading Iraq, its purported possession of WMDs and Saddam Hussein's involvement in 9/11. Initially, many Democrats also accepted these rationales. However, when no evidence emerged to support either, they concluded that they were simply untrue and turned decidedly against Bush and the war.

By comparison, as late as 2008, 70 percent of Republicans continued to support the war. [17] Further, two-thirds of Republicans who believed that "invading Iraq was the right thing to do" continued to cling to one or both of these unproven rationales. [18] Notably, however, even among Republicans who came to agree that Iraq had not possessed WMD and that Saddam Hussein was not involved in 9/11, a majority (57 percent) continued to support the war in Iraq. [19] Jacobson explains this by arguing that these Republicans likely came to accept one of the Bush administration's ex post rationales for invading Iraq (trotted out when the others became indefensible) such as the emphasis on Saddam Hussein's brutality against his own people. [20] "In sum," says Jacobson, "revelations that its main premises were faulty did little to undermine Republicans' support for the Iraq war because they were less likely than other Americans to get the message, less likely to withdraw support if they did and more willing to adopt alternative rationales emphasized after the fact by the Bush administration." [21] In other words, while Democrats and many Independents turned against the war after its original justifications were unproven, Republicans appeared intent on supporting it regardless of the facts.

What accounts for this apparent irrationality? According to Jacobson, a key part of the explanation involves white conservative Christians, approximately 38 percent of Republicans in some surveys. [22] In the aftermath of 9/11, says Jacobson, many in this group came to view President Bush "as God's chosen instrument in the battle between good and evil." [23] Believing they had a duty to support Bush without reservation, they steadfastly backed the Iraq war and continued to believe that Saddam had possessed WMDs even when none were discovered. This group, as did many Republicans, relied heavily on Fox News whose reporting confirmed their preconceptions and avoided information that might called them into question. [24] In 2005, 90 percent of white evangelical Christians would support Bush and as late as 2008 (when his overall approval rating had tumbled below 30 percent) support among this group remained strong at 70 percent. [25] In Jacobson's view, Bush's support was always strongest "among those whose notions of reality derived from a priori beliefs that were simply not open to empirical refutation." [26]

Interestingly, Jacobson acknowledges that many Democrats who would come to oppose the Iraq war came to face a somewhat different problem: how to rationalize their initial support for military action and early belief in the original rationales for the war. In later years (2006-2008), many Democrats would possess "faulty memories" about Iraq, with more than half insisting they had initially opposed military action and never embraced either of Bush's assumptions. [27] While Jacobson admits that many Democrats (and Independents) evidently reconstructed their memories to match current beliefs, he doesn't appear to believe this to be as problematic as evangelical Republicans' unquestioning support for Bush and the war. Indeed, given what he views as the Bush administration's extraordinary efforts to manipulate the truth for political gain, Jacobson implies that the changed positions of Democrats were understandable and justified.

In the concluding chapter of *A Divider, Not a Uniter*, Jacobson summarizes his perspective on the Bush administration by citing Scott McClellan, Bush's press secretary from 2003 to 2006. Clearly embittered, he wrote a memoir that was extraordinarily critical of the administration he had served. (Indeed, in 2008 McClellan would endorse Barack Obama.) In it, he accuses the Bush administration of engaging in a "permanent campaign" which is described as a "game of endless politicking based on manipulated shades of truth, twisting of truth and spin." According to McClellan, "the Bush White House...embraced and institutionalized this permanent campaign even more deeply than its predecessors." [28] In Jacobson's assessment, Bush's campaign to rally the country around the war in Iraq was only "the most egregious example" of such efforts [29] While Democrats and, to a significant extent, independents would become alienated by Bush's "strategy of deception" (McClellan's words) [30] Bush and his policies remained popular among the vast majority of Republicans, particularly conservative Christians, who remained immune to objective truth.

OBAMA THE DIVIDER

"George Bush will go down as a consummate divider, not a uniter, of the American people," reads the final sentence of Jacobson's book. [31] Given the author's belief that the divisiveness of Bush's presidency was much his own doing, one might expect that his successor would also be judged on his record in uniting in the country. However, Jacobson acknowledges that within months of taking office partisan divisions over Barack Obama widened to levels approaching those under Bush with over 80 percent of Democrats but only 10 percent of Republicans in support. [32] In fact, by some measures Obama would prove even more divisive than his predecessor. For example, in early 2012 the Gallup organization would note that the partisan gap in Obama's third year, 68 percent, was higher than any other president including George W. Bush (59 percent). [33]

That Obama would prove so divisive is startling in light of the fact that he had risen to national prominence and run for president promising to end partisan discord. Obama's first speech on the national stage, the 2004 Keynote Address at the Democratic National Convention included a "stirring call to national unity" that "suggested the rise of a new, unpolarized politics, a vision that was post- or perhaps- supra-partisan." [34] In an oft repeated line of the address, Obama proclaimed that "there is not a liberal America and a conservative America- there's the United States of America." Four years later, seeking the Democratic nomination for the presidency, Obama would argue that his chief opponent, Hillary Clinton, was too divisive a figure to unite the nation. According to a famous Obama policy memo, Clinton, "embodies trench warfare vs. Republicans and is consumed with beating them rather than unifying the country." [35] The promise of bringing Americans together was a central, perhaps the central, tenet of Obama's 2008 campaign. According to the *New Yorker's* Ryan Lizza, "If there was a single unifying argument that defined Obamaism from his earliest days in politics to his presidential campaign, it was his idea of post-partisanship." [36]

EXPLAINING THE OBAMA DIVIDE: TEA PARTY EXTREMISM

So what accounts for the wide partisan divide under Obama? More significantly, according to Jacobson, what accounts for the controversy surrounding his presidency? The answer, he says, is largely unrelated to the substance of Obama's policies. Indeed, Jacobson is puzzled as to why Obama's legislative victories in passing the stimulus and health care reform "did so little to stem rising dissatisfaction" with his performance. [37] "In historical context (consider the New Deal and Great Society) or cross-national comparison (consider other affluent democracies) Obama's policies hardly seem radical," he argues. [38] Jacobson notes the Congressional Budget Office assessment that the 2009 stimulus legislation may have saved as many as 3.3 million jobs. [39] The Affordable Care Act of 2010 bore numerous similarities to the plan enacted under GOP presidential candidate Mitt Romney when he was governor of Massachusetts and to the alternative Republicans had proposed to the Clinton plan in 1993. [40] Even more perplexing to Jacobson is the rejection of these programs "despite considerable courtship" by Obama. [41].

Part of the problem, although only a small part, acknowledges Jacobson, involves an ineffective communications strategy. Thus, "the Obama administration not only failed to persuade Americans that the stimulus had helped, but also failed to get across the point that it had given 94 percent of working Americans a tax cut and that taxes had gone down- by about $240 billion- rather than up, during Obama's tenure." [42] In the case of health reform, Jacobson does not address the Obama administration's efforts to promote the legislation but he does note that independents, those most susceptible to a public relations campaign, became increasingly opposed to health reform between 2008 and 2010. [43]

If not a poor communications strategy, what accounts for the hostility Obama's policies engendered? Jacobson's research focuses on one answer: the Tea Party. Since 2010, he has written four articles about American politics during the Obama presidency and this single force has been a central theme of each.

According to Jacobson, the most striking element of public opinion during the Obama era is not just the continuing presence of a wide partisan divide but the intensity of the opposition to the president. Much of this emanates from the Tea Party "an assortment of populist conservatives and libertarians" not a few of whom, according to Jacobson, display in classic form Hofstadter's "'paranoid style of American politics.'" [44] Comprising 12 to 18 percent of the population and an additional group of sympathizers (about 1/3 of the public), members of this group are white, older, married, less educated, higher income, Southern and more religious. [45] The more "unhinged" among them believe "Obama is not merely an objectionable liberal but a tyrant..." [46] While Jacobson is careful to say that not all of those identifying or sympathizing with the movement are extreme, he notes that "...they are nearly unanimous in their hostility towards Obama and belief [sic] that his policies are moving the nation towards socialism." [47] A sizable proportion of Tea Party members incorrectly believe that Obama is a Muslim and foreign born and thus ineligible to be president. The Tea Party's bitterly anti-Obama views are encouraged by Fox News and a host of conservative talk show demagogues, the most prominent of whom is Glenn Beck. [48] Their origin lies in the 2008 campaign of John McCain and Sarah Palin which sought to portray Obama "as a '60s style radical plotting to turn the United States into a socialist country." [49] Although Obama won the election many prospective Tea Party members became convinced that he was "an extreme dishonest leftist." According to Jacobson, "the deep recession and high unemployment have fueled a combination of anger and anxiety and have left Americans looking for someone to blame and as exemplified by the "Tea Party" movement susceptible to conspiracy theories involving various culprits." [50]

Importantly though, the Tea Party's radicalism springs from the extreme beliefs of its individual members. Jacobson notes that while identifiers of both major parties have moved away from the political center over the past 30 years Republicans have gone further towards the ideological extreme. Tea Party members essentially constitute the far right of this Republican coalition. [51] Underlying their beliefs, he says, is a deep seeded predisposition to authoritarianism. Measured by responses to a set of questions about which of a pair of attributes is preferable in children, Tea Party members choose respect for elders to independence, obedience over self-reliance and being well behaved to being considerate. Such persons consequently tend to desire order, dislike ambiguity and are "uncomfortable with difference and thus averse to a wide range of groups outside their own." [52] Since persons with such views tend to hold the authority of texts such as the Bible and the Constitution literally, the devoutly religious (i.e., Evangelical Christians) are among those inevitably tagged with the "authoritarian" label.

Equally ominous, according to Jacobson, is that those embracing the Tea Party's principles exhibit high degrees of "racial resentment" although the casual reader might be forgiven for assuming this is simply another term for racism. While acknowledging that "it is difficult to pin down precisely" he argues that there is a "racial component" in negative views of Obama. To discern this he employs a measure developed by two political scientists. [53] Respondents are asked to respond positively or negatively to statements such as: "Irish, Italians, Jews and many others overcame prejudice and worked their way up. Blacks should do the same without special favors." or "Over the past few years blacks have gotten less than they deserve." Apparently, answering affirmatively to the first and negatively to the second leads one to score high in "racial resentment." Jacobson finds that such racial resentment was particularly high among McCain voters and "positively related to assessments of Obama as dishonest and as an extreme liberal." [54]

According to Jacobson, "The combination of Obama's own background and traits and the nature of the economic crisis and the government's actions (to) manage it, could hardly have been better designed to heighten right-wing populist antipathy and anger." [55] The combination of Obama's middle name (Hussein), his upbringing in Moslem Indonesia, Ivy League education, career as a community organizer, connection to radical Rev. Jeremiah Wright were a perfect recipe for the "racist, xenophobic, anti-intellectual, and anti-elitist as well as the anti-liberal strands lurking within the right-wing populism." [56] In 2009 and 2010, these elements emerged to oppose Obama's efforts to pass health care reform, angrily confronting Democratic incumbents at town hall meetings. Following its passage they would mobilize for the 2010 elections and provided much of the energy and enthusiasm that led to Republicans gaining 63 House seats and retaking majority control of the chamber. Their anger at Obama and his policies would create a significant enthusiasm gap between the two parties and endanger Obama's hopes of reelection as well as Democratic control of the Senate.

While Obama would remain significantly more popular than had Bush during his second term, (with public approval ratings never sinking below the low to mid 40s), his presidency would prove to be almost every bit as divisive as his predecessors. However, in Jacobson's perspective the two presidencies could hardly have been more different. In his perspective, Bush the cynic was the consummate divider while Obama harbored no such inclination. While Bush would pursue his policies through a combination of lies and distortions Obama's main shortcomings involve his inability to communicate effectively and perhaps a naïve belief that reaching out to Republicans would usher in an era of bipartisanship.

For all the differences between Obama and Bush, Jacobson believes that one common element links their presidencies, the consistent presence of ultra conservative Republicans who are immune to facts. During the Bush presidency, this element consists of evangelical Christians who steadfastly support him because they believe he was chosen by God. They believe the administration's central rationales for the Iraq war even after they are demonstrated to be false. During the Obama presidency, they are succeeded by the Tea Party (which also contains a fair share of evangelical Christians but includes a broader sector of extreme conservatives). Driven by authoritarian beliefs and racism they blindly hate Obama and enthusiastically embrace beliefs about him and his policies that are simply false. In both eras, American politics are continually perverted by a divisive, fervent minority of conservative kooks who are dangerously unmoored from objective reality.

Analysis

Coming from a highly respected political scientist with a substantial record of scholarship, these critiques merit serious examination. Is Jacobson correct that the presidency of George W. Bush was marked by an unprecedented degree of duplicity and cynicism? More importantly, are radical conservatives solely, or even largely, to blame for the increasingly acrimonious and divisive political climate in the United States? My analysis argues that Jacobson is incorrect on both counts and that the scholarship just described suffers from both an absence of fairness and a significant degree of political bias. The result is a tendency to find fault with virtually any person, policy or group associated with conservatism while ignoring similar shortcomings or foibles among the left.

Ideology and Partisanship

First, Jacobson exaggerates Bush's ideological and partisan leanings while overstating Obama's moderation. [57] Arguably perhaps the most objective measure of ideology is derived from a system called DW-Nominate. Developed by a group of political scientists it creates a score for each president "based on cases where the outcome he desired from a vote in Congress was clearly articulated." [58] Using this measure, the *New York Times* Nate Silver finds George W. Bush to be more conservative than his father but similar to Ronald Reagan. [59] That is, his degree of conservatism is comparable to that of an extraordinarily popular president widely regarded as possessing mainstream conservative convictions. By comparison, Obama rates as slightly more liberal than presidents Johnson, Truman, and Franklin Roosevelt. [60] While this measure admittedly ranks Obama as slightly more conservative than other Democratic presidents (Kennedy, Carter, and Clinton) one might be forgiven for perceiving him as a relatively liberal president.

Of perhaps greater importance are the specific policies that Bush and Obama pursued. While the tax cuts passed under Bush are undeniably conservative a number of his other significant accomplishments are not: the No Child Left Behind Act, which significantly increased the federal role in education, and the Medicare Modernization Act, a massive unfunded entitlement providing prescription drug coverage for seniors. Combine this with Bush's support for moderate immigration reform and the TARP bailout in late 2008 as well as his acquiescence to rising domestic discretionary spending and you have a record that falls well short of doctrinaire conservatism. While Jacobson is correct that the Iraq war would almost certainly overshadow all of this, it is no surprise to find significant antipathy among movement conservatives towards the Bush presidency. [61]

By comparison, Obama's signature legislative achievements, the stimulus and health care reform, may be accurately characterized as major *liberal* achievements. True, parts of Obama's base were clearly dissatisfied and disappointed- many argued that the stimulus was too small while health reform was criticized for failing to include a public option. But it is indisputable that the scale of government intervention and spending in each was extraordinary by any measure.

The $787 billion American Reinvestment and Recovery Act was described variously as "a presidency in a box," [62] a behemoth," [63] and "unprecedented." [64] According to the *National Journal's* Ron Brownstein, Obama "achieved more of his aims in this single legislation than many achieved in an entire term." He continued: "I mean there is more new net public investment here on things Democrats consider essential for- like education, scientific research, alternative energy- than Bill Clinton was able to achieve in two terms." [65] Allan Lichtman, a history professor at American University agreed. "No one's going to have 100 days like Franklin Roosevelt, with 15 major pieces of legislation," he conceded. "But leaving aside that impossible comparison, Obama's accomplishments stack up quite well." [66]

Similarly, the scope of the Patient Protection and Affordable Care Act, a 2,073 page law projected to cost $938 billion over its first ten years, amounted to a transformation of American health care. It would be described as "landmark" legislation and compared to laws establishing Medicare and Medicaid in 1965 and Social Security in 1935. [67] In contrast to the earlier measures which passed with bipartisan congressional support, Obama's health reform would receive no Republican votes (and the stimulus, but three GOP senators). Jacobson and others attribute the absence of Republican votes to a combination of GOP cynicism, personal animus towards Obama and a rightward ideological movement by the Republican Party. While there are valid arguments to be made for each, it is also undeniable that health reform (and the stimulus) promulgated a substantial expansion of governmental power and spending. Americans lacking the knowledge of American history and comparative health policy necessary to making more nuanced judgments about each might justifiably conclude that both the stimulus and health care reform were liberal, even radical pieces of legislation.

Deception and Aggressive Tactics

Throughout *A Divider, Not a Uniter*, Jacobson implies that the Bush administration engaged in unprecedented levels of deception and employed an unusually heavy handed approach to achieve its policy goals. By contrast, Jacobson believes that Obama's policies are relatively moderate and consequently is silent regarding the arguments and tactics employed on their behalf. Again, this picture is inaccurate: Bush and his advisers were nowhere nearly as deceptive as Jacobson portrays them while the Obama administration is hardly immune from making specious arguments to justify it policies. Additionally, in pursuing them, Obama and his advisers have been comparably aggressive in playing political hardball.

Bush and Iraq

In his book, Jacobson's harshest criticisms are reserved for the Bush administration's justifications for the Iraq war. Granted this is not the proper forum to relitigate the debate, nor is it possible to address all of his allegations. However, a few points are in order:

First, it bears repeating that before the war, a virtual consensus existed that Saddam Hussein possessed WMD. This extended well beyond the CIA, whose director, George Tenet, famously told President Bush that the evidence was "a slam dunk." It included the intelligence agencies of Britain, Germany, Russia, China, Israel and France. In the U.S. the assertions regarding Saddam and WMD predated the Bush administration and were widely embraced by President Clinton and his advisers. In 1998, it was President Clinton who stated that, "If Saddam rejects peace and we have to use force our purpose is clear. We want to seriously diminish the threat posed by Iraq's Weapons of Mass Destruction program." As the nation prepared for war in 2002 and 2003 this position would be embraced by numerous Democrats including Hillary Clinton and John Kerry. [68]

Even Democrats unwilling to support the congressional resolution authorizing war believed the intelligence about WMD. In 2002, no less than Ted Kennedy would assert: "We have known for many years that Saddam Hussein is seeking and developing Weapons of Mass Destruction." [69] Even Jacobson himself concedes that, "Bush and his advisers were certain that Iraq was hiding WMD as were most experts American and foreign." [70] Thus, the Bush administration's most frequently employed justification for war against Iraq was not the result of lying or deception. While the failure to locate WMD in Iraq was nothing less than an intelligence disaster, criticism of Bush for believing they existed is dishonest. Later when opponents began asserting that "Bush lied" many in the Democratic establishment would hypocritically assert that the president had deceived them too. Interestingly, Jacobson never criticizes this as divisive.

Second, while Iraq did not have an active program for producing a nuclear weapon, Saddam aspired to procure one and maintained an organization dedicated to its production. Further, the CIA believed that had Saddam been able to procure fissile material from, for example, North Korea, his regime possessed the capacity to produce a nuclear weapon in less than a year. After the 1991 Gulf War, weapons inspectors reported that Saddam's regime intended to restart its nuclear weapons program. According to the Iraq Survey Group, between 2001 and 2003, Saddam increased the budget of the Iraqi Atomic Energy Commission (including a 10 fold increase in salaries), directed the agency chief to keep scientists together, and invested in new projects. [71] While the ISG made no assessment as to the time period necessary to produce a nuclear weapon, Douglas Feith, Under Secretary of Defense for Policy in the Bush administration, argues that "it could be cut substantially if Iraq obtained fissile material from an outside supplier such as North Korea, rather than trying to produce the fissile material itself." Under such a scenario, the CIA "estimated that Iraq would require less than a year to produce a nuclear device." [72]

Third, while no link exists between Saddam and 9/11, his regime was connected to numerous terrorist groups including al Qaeda. Although Jacobson insists that the Bush administration repeatedly implied a connection between Saddam and 9/11 [73] defenders of the Bush administration continue to argue that it never asserted such a connection. [74] Regardless of this dispute, American intelligence consistently demonstrated that Saddam had close connections to terrorists. In 2002, the CIA reported that, "Iraq continues to be a safehaven, transit point, or operational node for groups and individuals who direct violence against the United States Israel, and other allies. Iraq has a long history of supporting terrorism." [75] Notably, unlike its faulty assessment of WMD, postwar discoveries would corroborate this CIA finding and perhaps even underestimate the link between Saddam and terrorist groups [76].

Given the criticism surrounding the American government's failure to "connect the dots" before 9/11, the absence of evidence regarding "a meaningful Al Qaeda connection" with Saddam, was unnecessary to justify the Iraq war. Following 9/11 the Bush administration feared that Saddam (the only international figure other than Bin Laden to praise the attack) "might provide terrorists poison gas, anthrax or smallpox weapons and possibly at some point a nuclear weapon." [77] Failure to prevent an attack would lead many to ask why the American government had not responded more aggressively. As Jacobson himself writes, "...Bush and his advisers were far more worried about failing to do enough than about doing too much in defending the nation from further assaults. The worst-case scenarios used to bring Congress on board, however unlikely, were certainly frightening enough to make leaders more cautious than Bush willing to initiate a war." [78] In short, circumstances provided Bush more than a measure of justification for military action to remove Saddam Hussein.

Jacobson is on a bit firmer ground when he criticizes the Bush administration's shifting rationales for the Iraq war. When no WMD were found, Bush and his advisers would begin emphasizing Saddam's brutality against his own people and "that the war had set in motion a movement towards freedom and democracy across the Middle East." [79] Each of these objectives, though laudable, was perceived as unrelated to American security and caused many Americans to turn against both Bush and the war. Jacobson's argument here is sensible and even Feith appears to agree with much of it. [80] However, it might also be argued that events had rendered all justifications for the war unpersuasive. Once no WMD were discovered and a quick victory proved elusive both the war and Bush were destined to become unpopular.

OBAMA'S AFFORDABLE CARE ACT

In contrast to Bush and Iraq, Jacobson has remarkably little to say regarding the arguments and tactics employed by the Obama administration in promoting its agenda. For example, in discussing Obama's most significant achievement, the passage of the Affordable Care Act, Jacobson notes that "both the process and product proved controversial and divisive" [81] but says virtually nothing about the administration's role in either. Instead, he emphasizes "all out opposition" by Republicans who, on occasion resorted to "adopting the Tea Party's apocalyptic rhetoric" in denouncing the legislation. [82] However, an examination of the episode reveals more than a few instances of deception by the Obama administration as well as a willingness to bend the rules when necessary.

Regarding the latter, the methods used to pass health reform were a far cry from Obama's campaign promises of open, ethical government. Whereas Obama had promised during the 2008 campaign to open negotiations on health care reform televised on C-SPAN, the actual process proved extraordinarily opaque. [83] Deals with special interest groups occurred at the White House, negotiations on Capitol Hill in each of the respective leader's offices. In

January, 2010, House Speaker Nancy Pelosi would announce that, "The House and Senate plan to put together the final health care bill behind closed doors according to an agreement of top Democrats." [84] While Obama initially denied he had broken his promise regarding transparency, he ultimately conceded that excluding the public from key discussions was a "mistake." [85]

Public perceptions of the process were further tarnished by a pair of backroom deals. Undoubtedly, the most embarrassing was the infamous "Cornhusker Kickback" struck with Senator Ben Nelson. While the Nebraskan's initial refusal to support the Senate bill was ostensibly related to his opposition to abortion provisions, he agreed to support health reform in exchange for a promise to exempt his state *in perpetuity* from additional Medicaid expenses resulting from the bill. [86] There was also the "Louisiana Purchase" agreement in which Senator Nancy Landrieu agreed to support health reform in exchange for approximately $100 million in additional funding for her state's Medicaid program. [87] While deal making is by no means unusual in the law making process backroom bargains such as these clearly undermined Obama's promise to reform the political process itself.

Also worthy of mention here is Obama's willingness to employ reconciliation. In the Senate, most bills are subject to a filibuster and consequently require 60 votes to pass. The only major exception involves budget matters which are subject to reconciliation. Under this procedure, debate is limited and passage requires only 51 votes. In 1993, President Clinton had sought to employ reconciliation to pass his health plan, only to be rebuffed by Senator Robert Byrd, arguably the Senate's most eminent authority on its rules. The West Virginia senator and author of the "Byrd Rule," believed that Clinton's plan did not qualify for reconciliation because it was not directly related to deficit reduction. The ruling proved pivotal and played a key role in killing the Clinton plan. [88]

In January, 2010 the election of Republican Scott Brown of Massachusetts to the seat held by Ted Kennedy essentially broke the filibuster proof majority Democrats held in the Senate. To pass health reform Obama and Democrats essentially sought to do exactly what Clinton had more than a decade earlier. With an ailing Byrd perhaps too enfeebled to object, Democrats introduced the bill under reconciliation and proceeded to pass it. Viewed narrowly, there was nothing illegal in the Democrats' decision- on paper their bill would actually reduce the deficit over 10 years. Further, other legislation that had not reduced the deficit, including the Bush tax cuts, had been passed under the procedure. [89] Nevertheless, the health reform bill was not primarily budget related and Senate Republicans reacted angrily to this maneuver. Unlike legislation establishing Social Security and Medicare, health reform would pass the Senate with not a single vote from the minority party.

Then there was the Affordable Care Act itself. Health reform was extraordinarily expensive, costing almost $1 trillion over the first 10 years and much more thereafter. With Obama promising that the legislation would not increase the deficit, his advisers and congressional Democrats employed all type of dubious assumptions and sleight of hand in pursuit of this goal. Some examples included:

1. Reducing the law's cost to under $1 trillion by delaying benefits until 2014. In the first 10 years of *full* implementation the legislation would cost $2.3 trillion. [90]
2. Including premiums for the CLASS Act (Community Living Assistance Services and Supports Act). This provision, establishing a massive long-term care entitlement, would collect $70 billion in premiums during the first 10 years. Although the

program would pay no benefits during this period, the revenues were counted for purposes of deficit reduction. [91, 92]

3. Jettisoning the Medicare "Doc Fix": An early version of the legislation proposed to update Medicare's formula for compensating physicians. Otherwise, reimbursement rates would decline by almost 25 percent in the following year with further reductions in subsequent ones. In exchange for agreement from the American Medical Association to support health reform, the Obama administration promised to address the problem. However, as the costs of health reform escalated Obama and Democrats removed it, leaving the increasingly expensive problem unresolved. [93]

Finally, there were the shifting explanations to justify health reform. Just as the Bush administration revised its case for the Iraq war as some became untenable, so too did Obama and Democratic supporters with the Affordable Care Act. First, there was the individual mandate requiring Americans to buy health insurance or pay a penalty. When Congress was considering the provision, Obama denied that it constituted a tax: "For us to say that you've got to take a responsibility to get health insurance is absolutely not a tax." However, when opponents contested the constitutionality of the mandate in court, Obama's Justice Department defended it as one, arguing that the requirement to possess insurance or pay a fine constituted a "'valid exercise" of Congress's power to impose taxes.'" [94]

Second, in the months before the 2010 election, Politico's Ben Smith would report that "Key White House allies are dramatically shifting their attempts to defend health care legislation, abandoning claims that it will reduce costs and the deficit and instead stressing a promise to 'improve it.'" It went on to reveal details of a confidential presentation (including PowerPoints) that counseled Democrats to avoid claiming "the law will reduce costs and the deficit." Supporters were also advised "against the kind of grand claims of change that accompanied the law's passage." [95] While the Obama White House would deny this "messaging shift" [96] most Democratic campaigns in 2010 would abandon full throated defenses of the law.

In sum, there are clear parallels between Bush and Iraq and Obama and health reform. Both involve what are arguably the most significant initiatives of each administration. Both were initially popular but became unpopular over time. To achieve their goals, each administration employed "hardball" political tactics. And finally, when their policies became unpopular both employed shifting arguments to justify them.

RIGHT WING RADICALS

The common factor linking Jacobson's research on the Bush and Obama presidencies is the presence of those he perceives to be extreme conservatives. During the Iraq war they were primarily evangelical Christians who continued to support President Bush when most Americans abandoned him. In the Obama presidency their role has been assumed by the Tea Party which has emerged as the fulcrum of opposition sentiment. However, while evangelicals were merely delusional (supporting the Iraq war long after the rationales for fighting it were exposed as fraudulent) the Tea Party is unhinged, criticizing Obama in the most vitriolic manner and questioning his legitimacy. All the same, Jacobson believes these staunch conservatives are primarily responsible for widening the nation's partisan divide during the Bush presidency and exacerbating it further during Obama's.

A number of points, however, call this critique into question. First, contrary to Jacobson's assertions, a reasonable person could both support the Iraq war and believe the basic rationales for fighting it. Even when the U.S. military failed to find evidence of WMD the fact remained that virtually everyone, including numerous international intelligence agencies and American political leaders from both parties, believed Saddam possessed them. Further, even if no WMD existed in 2003, wasn't the fact that Saddam had previously employed them to devastating effect and possessed the know how to reconstitute such a program relatively quickly reason enough for many to believe the war was justified?

Similarly, even though there was no proven connection between Saddam Hussein and 9/11 an ordinary person might also be forgiven for confusing this point with the fact that any number of links existed between the Iraqi dictator and al Qaeda. Indeed, given that Saddam had been a major sponsor of terrorist groups in general and expressed public support for 9/11 one might rationally believe that even in the absence of a specific connection he presented a dangerous threat and needed to be removed.

Also problematic is Jacobson's attempt to link the beliefs of Iraq war supporters with their tendency to rely on Fox News. In fact, the scholarly article Jacobson cites presents no evidence that Fox News reporters stated any untrue fact about the war. Thus, the inference that a major media outlet was essentially manipulating its conservative viewers with falsehoods is simply not true. [97]

Second, Jacobson's attempt to caricature the Tea Party as a group of kooks guided by authoritarian and racist beliefs is inaccurate and unfair. As discussed earlier, there is a valid argument to be made that Barack Obama is the most liberal president in a generation, and, as such, has pursued liberal policies. Further, one can believe these things without harboring authoritarian or racist sentiments as Jacobson implies. Indeed, the pseudo social science measures he employs to arrive at such conclusions tell us little about anything. A preference for "respect for elders" over "independence" or "being well behaved" over "being considerate" might signal some type of personal shortcoming to Jacobson but to many Americans would not indicate anything unseemly or malevolent. For that matter, in much of the United States, those inclined to "expressions of superpatriotism" and literal interpretations of the Constitution might be described as patriots, not authoritarians.

Additionally, agreeing that black Americans should overcome prejudice and "work their way up" as did other groups suffering discrimination "without any special favors" fits the definition of an opponent of affirmative action, not someone harboring "racial resentment." To cite another example, one is hardly guilty of racial resentment if he disagrees that "Over the last few years, blacks have gotten less than they deserve."

Third, and most importantly, the political right possesses no monopoly on crazy beliefs or incendiary rhetoric. In fact, the political left, a force mysteriously absent from Jacobson's scholarship, is guilty of many of the same sins. Long before critics on the right attacked President Obama as a communist, vitriol from the left compared President Bush to Hitler. Just as opponents of Obama questioned his birthplace in an attempt to undermine his legitimacy, so too did critics on the left attempt to argue that Bush had stolen the 2000 election. In 2004, he would subsequently stand accused of stealing that election too. Indeed, the precedent for the "birther" movement was the "truther" movement which promoted the belief that the 9/11 attacks were "an inside job" carried out with Bush's complicity.

Furthermore, there is evidence that such irrational views were relatively widespread among Democrats. For example, a 2006 Scripps Howard poll asked "How likely is it that people in the federal government either assisted in the 9/11 attacks or took no action to stop the attacks because they wanted the United States to go to war in the Middle East?" Almost 23 percent of Democrats agreed it was "very likely" while another 28 percent called it "somewhat likely." That is, wrote *Politico's* Ben Smith, "More than half of Democrats, according to the survey, said they believed Bush was complicit in the 9/11 terror attacks." [98]

As the Bush presidency wound down in 2008, the left would increasingly focus its fire on Republican vice presidential nominee Sarah Palin. In one of the more bizarre theories that permeated the blogosphere advocates of what became known as "Trig Trutherism" argued, with no truth whatsoever, that Palin was not the mother of her three year old son born with Down syndrome. [99] In short, over the past two presidencies there has arisen an extraordinary degree of malevolence on *both sides* of the political debate, not merely at the behest of one as Jacobson might have us believe.

CONCLUSION

In assessing the political right sole responsibility for the partisan divide, Gary Jacobson essentially adopts the liberal narrative of American politics in the 21st century. Were Jacobson an ordinary partisan his analysis might be dismissed as a mere polemic. However, as one of political science's most respected scholars, his work is likely to be read as a serious, substantive analysis of the nation's political ills. Hopefully the previous discussion provides a persuasive counterargument to Jacobson's distorted picture of the Bush and Obama eras.

A more accurate description, I would offer, might read something like this: Since 2000, American politics have been characterized by a citizenry deeply divided between two fundamentally conflicting visions. In this context, the presidencies of George W. Bush and Barack Obama might be viewed as ideological bookends sharing a number of important characteristics. Both presidents are relatively principled politicians who view themselves as agents of change. Both undertook policies that can be characterized as major, nonincremental, controversial and politically risky- Bush, the Iraq War, and Obama, health reform. Even as both proved divisive, each held fast to his position and believed that he had subordinated political considerations to the national interest. To achieve their respective goals, both administrations demonstrated a willingness to employ political tactics that might be criticized as heavy handed and deceptive. In a deeply divided nation, both presidencies proved divisive, simultaneously defended by like-minded supporters and abhorred by ideological enemies, some of whom embraced beliefs that lacked empirical support. Finally, both Bush and Obama would lose support among independents who provided pivotal votes to remove the party in power (Republicans in 2006, Democrats in 2010) from control of Congress and, in 2008, the White House.

In short, there are many similarities between the Bush and Obama eras, just not the ones Jacobson asserts. Instead of a nation whose politics have been hijacked by the right the United States is a deeply divided country governed in the 21st century by a pair of principled presidents pursuing controversial, transformative policies.

REFERENCES

[1] Gary C. Jacobson, *A Divider, Not a Uniter, George W. Bush and the American People*, 2nd Edition (New York: Longman, 2011), xi.

[2] Gary C. Jacobson, "Polarization, Public Opinion, and the Presidency: The Obama and Anti-Obama Coalitions," in Bert A. Rockman, Andrew Rudalevige, and Colin Campbell, eds., *The Obama Presidency: Appraisals and Prospects (Los Angeles: Sage, 2012), 94.*

[3] Ibid.

[4] In addition to those already cited, they include: Gary C. Jacobson, "George Bush, the Iraq War, and the Election of Barack Obama," Draft of June 28, 2009; Gary C. Jacobson, "Barack Obama and the American Public: The First 18 Months," Prepared for delivery at the 2010 Meeting of the American Political Science Association, Washington, D.C., September 2-5, 2010; Gary C. Jacobson, "The Republican Resurgence in 2010," *Political Science Quarterly*, Spring, 2011, 27-52; Gary C. Jacobson, "The President, the Tea Party, and Voting Behavior in 2010: Insights from the Cooperative Congressional Election Study," Prepared for delivery at the 2011 Annual Meeting of the American Political Science Association, Seattle, WA, September 1-4, 2011.

[5] Jacobson, *A Divider, Not A Uniter*, p. 1.

[6] Ibid.

[7] Ibid., p. 7.

[8] Ibid., p. 8.

[9] Ibid., p. 14.

[10] Ibid., p. 59.

[11] Ibid.

[12] Ibid., p. 60.

[13] Ibid., p. 79.

[14] Ibid., p. 80.

[15] Ibid., 4, 101.

[16] Ibid., pp. 102-107.

[17] Ibid., p. 101.

[18] Ibid., p. 112.

[19] Ibid.

[20] Ibid., p. 97.

[21] Ibid., p. 113

[22] Ibid., p. 74.

[23] Ibid., p. 73.

[24] Ibid., p. 222.

[25] Ibid., p. 118.

[26] Ibid., p. 271.

[27] Ibid., pp. 212-214.

[28] Ibid., p. 268.

[29] Ibid.

[30] Ibid.

[31] Ibid., p. 284.

[32] Jacobson, "Polarization, Public Opinion and the Presidency: The Obama and Anti-Obama Coalitions," p. 96.

[33] Gallup, "Obama Ratings Historically Polarized," January 27, 2012.

[34] Andrew Rudalevige and Bert A. Rockman, "Introduction: A Counterfactual Presidency," in Rudalevige, Rockland and Colin Campbell, *The Obama Presidency, Appraisals and Prospects* (Los Angeles: Sage, 2012), p. 2.

[35] Quoted in James W. Caeser, Andrew E. Busch and John J. Pitney, Jr., *Epic Journey: The 2008 Elections and American Politics* (Rowman and Littlefield: Lanham, MD, 2009), p. 112.

[36] Ryan Lizza, "The Obama Memos," *The New Yorker*, January 30, 2012.

[37] Jacobson, "Polarization, Public Opinion and the Presidency: The Obama and Anti-Obama Coalitions," p. 95.

[38] Ibid., p. 106.

[39] Cited in Jacobson, "The Republican Resurgence in 2010," p. 44.

[40] Jacobson, "Polarization, Public Opinion and the Presidency: The Obama and Anti-Obama Coalitions," p. 111.

[41] Jacobson, "Barack Obama and the American Public: The First 18 Months," p. 2.

[42] Jacobson, "The Republican Resurgence in 2010," p. 44.

[43] Jacobson, "Polarization, Public Opinion, and the Presidency: the Obama and Anti-Obama Coalitions," pp. 108-109.

[44] Ibid., p. 100.

[45] Interestingly, he doesn't link this group to the evangelicals who supported George W. Bush.

[46] Ibid.

[47] Ibid.

[48] Ibid., pp. 100-101.

[49] Ibid., p. 101.

[50] Jacobson, "Barack and Obama and the American Public: The First 18 Months," p. 1.

[51] Jacobson, "The President, the Tea Party, and Voting Behavior in 2010: Insights from the Cooperative Congressional Election Study," p. 14.

[52] Jacobson, "Polarization, Public Opinion and the Presidency: The Obama and Anti-Obama Coalitions, p. 102.

[53] Cited in Jacobson, "Polarization, Public Opinion and the Presidency," p. 119, fn. 24: Donald R. Kinder and Lynn M. Sanders, *Divided by Color*, (Chicago: University of Chicago Press, 1996), chapter 3.

[54] Jacobson, "Obama and the Polarized Public," p. 25.

[55] Jacobson, "Barack Obama and the American Public: The First 18 Months," p. 11.

[56] Ibid.

[57] Indeed, even the *New York Times* David Brooks who originally characterized Obama as "a center-left pragmatic reformer" advocating "a moderately activist government constrained by a sense of tradeoffs" has changed his mind. In January, 2012, Brooks would say of Obama: "He's more liberal than he thinks he is. He thinks he's slightly center-left but when you get down to his instincts their pretty left." Jacobson, "Polarization, Public Opinion and the Presidency," p. 101; Donovan Slack, "Brooks: Obama More Liberal Than I Thought," *Politico*, January 5, 2012. For a more detailed

discussion of Brooks' revised perspective on Obama see David Brooks, "Obama Rejects Obamism," *New York Times*, September 19, 2011.

[58] Nate Silver, "How Liberal Is President Obama?" FiveThirtyEight, *New York Times*, April 29, 2011.

[59] Ibid.

[60] Ibid.

[61] For example, conservative talk show host Mark Levin calls Bush a "moderate conservative." Mark R. Levin, "Ronald Reagan and George W. Bush," HumanEvents.com, Updated August 18, 2011.

[62] Ronald Brownstein on *Meet the Press*, February 15, 2009.

[63] Matthew Benjamin and Julianna Goldman, "Obama's Economic Stimulus Bill Most Ambitious Since Roosevelt," Bloomberg, February 17, 2009.

[64] Allan Lichtman, quoted in Benjamin and Goldman, "Obama's Economic Stimulus..."

[65] Ronald Brownstein on *Meet the Press*, February 15, 2009.

[66] Quoted in Benjamin and Goldman, "Obama's Economic Stimulus..."

[67] Staff of the *Washington Post, Landmark: The Inside Story of America's New Health Care Law and What It Means for Us All* (New York: Public Affairs, 2010).

[68] Norman Podhoretz, "Who Is Lying About Iraq?" *Commentary;* December, 2005. Arthur Herman, "Why Iraq Was Inevitable," *Commentary*, July, 2008.

[69] Quoted in Podhoretz, "Who Is Lying About Iraq?"

[70] Jacobson, *A Divider, Not a Uniter*, p. 82.

[71] Douglas J. Feith, *War and Decision: Inside the Pentagon at the Dawn of the War on Terrorism*, (New York: Harper, 2008), pp. 327-328.

[72] Ibid., p. 328.

[73] Jacobson, *A Divider, Not a Uniter*, p. 96.

[74] Herman, "Why Iraq Was Inevitable."

[75] Quoted in Feith, *War and Decision*, p. 187.

[76] Herman, "Why Iraq Was Inevitable."

[77] Feith, *War and Decision*, p. 215.

[78] Jacobson, *A Divider, Not a Uniter*, p. 82

[79] Jacobson, *A Divider, Not a Uniter*, p. 97.

[80] Feith, *War and Decision*, pp. 521-522.

[81] Jacobson, "The 2010 Mid-Term Elections," p. 45.

[82] Jacobson, "Obama and the Polarized Public," p. 29.

[83] Matt Welch, "Obama and the L-Word," *Reason*, April, 2010; Chip Reid, "Obama Reneges on Health Care Transparency," CBS News, January 7, 2010.

[84] Reid, "Obama Reneges on Health Care Transparency."

[85] Josh Gerstein, "President Obama: Lack of Transparency a 'Mistake,'" *Politico*, January 25, 2010.

[86] Stuart Altman and David Shactman, *Power, Politics and Universal Health Care: The Inside Story of a Century-Long Battle* (Prometheus, Amherst, NY, 2011), pp. 309-311.

[87] Ibid., p. 296.

[88] Haynes Johnson and David S. Broder, *The System: The American Way of Politics at the Breaking Point*, (Little, Brown: Boston, MA), pp. 125-127; Altman and Shactman, *Power, Politics and Universal Health Care*, pp. 125-127.

[89] Altman and Shactman, *Power, Politics, and Universal Health Care*, p. 335.

[90] Douglas Holtz-Eakin, Joseph Antos and James C. Capretta, "Health Care Repeal Won't Add to the Deficit," *Wall Street Journal*, January 19, 2011.

[91] Ibid.

[92] In October, 2011, the Obama administration announced that it was "scrapping" the CLASS act because "it was too costly and would not work." Robert Pear, "Health Law to Be Revised by Ending a Program." *New York Times*, October 14, 2011.

[93] Peter Suderman, "The Doc Fix Dilemma," *Reason*, January 18, 2011.

[94] Robert Pear, "Changing Stance, Administration Now Defends Insurance Mandate as a Tax," *New York Times*, July 17, 2010.

[95] Ben Smith, "Dems Retreat on Health Care Cost Pitch," *Politico*, August 19, 2010.

[96] Ibid.

[97] For a discussion of this issue, see Tim Groseclose, *Left Turn: How Liberal Media Bias Distorts the American Mind*, St. Martins: New York, 2011, pp. 208-211.

[98] Ben Smith, "More than Half of Democrats Believed Bush Knew," *Politico*, April 22, 2011.

[99] Justin Elliot, "Trig Trutherism: The Definitive Debunker," *Salon*, April 22, 2011.

In: Change in the White House?
Editor: Meena Bose

ISBN: 978-1-62948-920-9
© 2014 Nova Science Publishers, Inc.

Chapter 4

OVERCOMING A POLARIZED CONGRESS: THE ECONOMIC POLITICS OF BUSH AND OBAMA[*]

John D. Graham[1] and Veronica Vargas Stidvent[2]

ABSTRACT

This article provides a comparison of domestic policy under the presidential administrations of George W. Bush and Barack Obama. It compares how Bush and Obama addressed polarization on three economic policy initiatives: Bush's tax cuts (2001 - 2006), the Bush and Obama bailouts of industry during the Great Recession (2007 - 2009), and Obama's recovery ("stimulus") packages (2009 - 2010). The fundamental lesson of the case studies is that it is feasible – though certainly not easy − for the White House to overcome partisan polarization in Congress and enact priority legislation. In other words, the gridlock hypothesis found in the polarization literature is not always or necessarily applicable to presidential initiatives.

George W. Bush and Barack Obama shared a similar dilemma: their service in the White House occurred during an era of American politics when the Congress was highly polarized along party lines. When Congress is polarized, members avoid lawmaking cooperation with members of the other party and frown upon collaborative efforts initiated by fellow members of their party. Moreover, party leaders in Congress, aided by party activists, seek to punish rank - and - file members for casting votes contrary to the wishes of the party leadership. Thus, Presidents Bush and Obama confronted members of Congress who were highly likely to vote in accordance with the wishes of their party leadership.

The president cannot escape polarization because the president is typically perceived as the national leader of his party. Indeed, the president may be a strong polarizing influence (Jacobson, 2007). On the other hand, congressional leaders of the opposing party work to

---

[*] This paper was prepared for the symposium, "Change in the White House? Comparing the Presidencies of George W. Bush and Barack Obama," Peter S. Kalikow, Center for the Study of the American Presidency, Hofstra University, April 19, 2012.

unify their members in opposition to the president's legislative agenda. The opposition is triggered partly by ideological differences between the two parties on multiple issues (so - called "conflict extension") but also by the strategic electoral interests of the opposing party, who have strong incentives to thwart the president's efforts to enact his legislative priorities (Lee, 2009). When a president is ineffective in passing his agenda in Congress, the opposing party may be rewarded with diminished presidential approval ratings and political advantage at the next election. Even if a president proposes legislation that is ideologically compatible with the positions of the opposing party, the strategic interests of the opposing party may be sufficient to motivate determined opposition. The phenomenon of party opposition for strategic (as opposed to ideological) reasons should not be overlooked, although the opposing party always runs the risk of being painted as unreasonable obstructionists.

While the polarization thesis predicts gridlock in the Congress (Brady and Volden, 2006; Saeki, 2010), Bush and Obama accomplished significant policy victories in domestic affairs. Some of this success was accomplished through executive action but, due to constitutional constraints, much of their domestic policy agendas required approval by Congress in order to be enacted and implemented. For example, any presidential initiative that requires statutory authorization and/or new public funding must have congressional approval. Thus, an effective president in a polarized era finds a way to overcome the polarization in Congress and obtain congressional approval of his legislative agenda (Mayhew, 2011). A key challenge for presidential scholars – and one of keen interest to future presidents – is to explain how Bush and Obama avoided the perils of gridlock.

In this paper, we compare how Bush and Obama addressed polarization on three economic policy initiatives: Bush's tax cuts (2001 - 2006), the Bush and Obama bailouts of industry during the Great Recession (2007 - 2009), and Obama's recovery ("stimulus") packages (2009 - 2010). "Success" and "failure" in this paper refers not to the merits of the policy initiatives but to whether the White House was effective in persuading Congress to enact the president's proposal.

We use case studies to illustrate the three strategies available to any president: cooperative bipartisanship (where the president engages the leaders of both parties in the Congress in an effort at bipartisan consensus), partisanship (where the president's party seeks to out vote the members of the opposing party), and cross - partisanship or "cheap" bipartisanship (where the president unifies his party and then recruits support from only a limited number of members of the opposing party in order to obtain the required number of votes). Only in the case of cooperative bipartisanship does the president negotiate with the leadership of the opposing party in Congress (Jones, 1995; Jones, 2005).

In the case studies that follow, we examine how well Bush and Obama discouraged defections from members of their own party while attracting cross - over votes from selected members of the opposing party. We highlight how the president and his allies in Congress bypassed or overcame the dreaded filibuster threat in the Senate, which imposes a supermajority requirement of 60 votes on most measures (Arenberg and Dove, 2012; Koger, 2010).

Our focus in this paper is economic policy, as it was certainly one of the defining issues of the Bush and Obama presidencies. The lessons drawn, however, are applicable to a wide range of domestic issues. The lessons may be less applicable to foreign and military affairs because of the stronger constitutional role of the president on these issues and the historical tendency for these issues to have less partisan content.

Overcoming a Polarized Congress

For context, it is useful to remember the changing partisan margins in the Congress from 2001 - 2012. Bush never enjoyed a filibuster - proof margin of Republican votes in the Senate. He started in 2001 with a 50 - 50 margin, achieved peak Republican strength in the Senate in 2005 (56 - 43) but ultimately lost control of the Senate in 2007 - 2008. Obama started 2009 with a brief filibuster - proof margin of 60 Democratic Senators but the 60th vote was lost within a year due to the death of Ted Kennedy and a stunning Republican victory in the race to succeed Kennedy in Massachusetts. Obama's Democratic margin dwindled to 53 - 47 after the Republican landslide at the polls in November 2010. In the House, Bush enjoyed a Republican majority from 2001 to 2006 while Obama enjoyed a Democratic majority for only two years (2009 - 2010). An appreciation of these partisan counts in Congress, and the voting rules imposed by legislative procedures, is necessary to appreciate White House efforts to influence Congress on presidential initiatives.

CASE STUDY # 1: PASSAGE OF THE BUSH TAX CUTS, 2001 - 2006

The seeds of the 2001 recession are found in the late 1990s in the form of the "dot.com bubble", the spectacular failure of a group of internet - based companies that were launched in a period of low interest rates, plentiful venture capital, and exuberant attitudes toward the future of the stock market. The ensuing recession is revealed in the declining rate of GDP growth in mid-2001, and the steady rise of unemployment from 4.0 per cent in 2000 to 6.0 percent in 2003 (see Table 1). During this same period, the terrorist attacks of 9/11 inflicted significant direct damage on the U.S. economy but, more importantly, spawned a new type of uncertainty about America's security and economic future. There was significant concern in 2002 - 2003 about a second recession and/or a jobless recovery.

During the Bush vs. Gore campaign, Bush pledged substantial reductions in the personal income tax and, throughout his two terms, he sought to accomplish permanent tax reductions. While Bush saw tax cuts primarily as a vehicle to spur long - term economic growth, the recession of 2001 provided a more urgent short - term rationale, one that Federal Reserve Board chairman Alan Greenspan embraced.

Due to his fragile political strength and weak party control in Congress (50 - 50 in the Senate and 221 - 214 in the House), Bush elected to use the budget reconciliation procedure as the legislative vehicle for passage of tax cuts. The advantage of this procedure is that only a majority vote in the Senate is required (i.e., the 60 - vote rule to overcome filibuster threats is relaxed), but the disadvantage is that the time frame for legislation cannot exceed 10 years. In other words, tax changes cannot be made permanent under the rules of reconciliation.

With remarkable speed (faster than the Reagan tax cuts of 1981 - 2002), Congress delivered Bush a 10 - year, $1.35 trillion package of income - tax cuts. While the final package was tilted somewhat more to relief for lower - income tax payers than he requested, Bush accomplished the largest tax reduction in a generation.

The Bush White House executed a political strategy on tax cuts that was used repeatedly during his two terms in office (Graham, 2010). The House passed Bush's tax plan without any negotiation with House Democratic leaders. For example, the winning margin in the House conference - report vote was 240 - 154, as 29 rank - and - file Democrats chose to join the unanimous House Republicans. A "cross - partisan" technique was employed in the Senate. Bush lost two Republican votes (Senators John McCain of Arizona and Lincoln

Chafee of Rhode Island), but compensated for these defections by attracting twelve cross - over Democratic votes. The final conference report passed the Senate 58 - 33.

Table 1. Key Economic Statistics: U.S. GDP Growth and Unemployment, 2000 - 2012

Year	% Change in GOP	Unemployment Rate
2000	+4.1	4.0
2001*	+1.1	4.7
2002	+1.8	5.8
2003	+2.5	6.0
2004	+3.5	5.5
2005	+3.1	5.1
2006	+2.7	4.6
2007	+1.9	4.6
2008	- 0.3	5.8
2009	- 3.5	9.3
2010	+3.0	9.6
2011	+1.7	8.9
2012	+2.5	8.0

Source: http://www.bea.gov/national/index.htm; Council of Economic Advisors, Economic Report to the President, 2012, Tables B - 2 and B - 35.
*Note that real GDP growth was actually negative from March to November 2001.

For the remainder of his two terms in office, Bush fought persistently yet unsuccessfully to make these tax cuts permanent. He was successful in adding to them (e.g., reductions in taxes on capital gains and dividends in 2003) and extending some of them for several years, but they were not made permanent. The closest Bush came to achieving permanence was in 2006, when a measure to repeal the estate tax fell three votes short of the 60 required votes in the Senate.

In each successive vote on tax cuts from 2001 to 2006, the Bush position continued to attract some support from cross - over Democrats in the Senate. However, the number of cross - over Democrats was larger in the early Bush years than in the later years of his presidency (Graham, 2010). The diminishing support from Senate Democrats may be attributable to growing concerns about the federal fiscal situation, the improving economy from 2002 to 2007, and Bush's declining popularity. The number of "gettable" Senate Democrats was also diminishing due to Republican successes at the polls in 2002 and 2004, as the number of Senate Republicans grew from 50 to 56.

In summary, cross - over votes from Democratic Senators were critical to Bush's legislative victories on tax cuts. As we shall see, they also help explain Obama's difficulty in repealing the Bush tax cuts.

Obama and the Bush Tax Cuts

Since permanence was not accomplished, a key issue in the presidential election of 2008 was whether the Bush tax cuts should be allowed to expire or whether they should be extended or made permanent. In the Democratic presidential primary, both Hilary Clinton and Barack Obama pledged not to allow taxes to rise on Americans with incomes less than $200,000 per year, but they pledged to raise tax rates on high - income Americans. Republican candidate John McCain reversed his position as Senator (recall he voted against the Bush tax cuts) and campaigned to make all of the Bush tax cuts permanent.

Candidate Obama was particularly insistent that the Bush tax cuts for those with high incomes be rescinded, even before they were scheduled to expire (i.e., at the end of 2009 instead of the end of 2010) (Calmes, 2010). But in the period between his decisive victory in November 2008 and his swearing - in ceremony in late January 2009, Obama changed his mind. He indicated that the tax increase for high - income filers should be delayed until the end of 2010. This unexpected reversal created an early, public disagreement between House Speaker Nancy Pelosi and Obama (Mooney, 2009). In the end, the Obama stimulus plan did not call for repeal of any of the Bush tax cuts, Pelosi's views were overruled, and no changes to the Bush tax cuts were made in 2009.

As the mid - term elections approached in November 2010, Obama and the congressional leadership were acutely aware of the fact that the Bush tax cuts were scheduled to expire soon after the election. Obama began the year taking the position that they should be extended for all families except those whose incomes exceed $250,000 per year (about 2% of tax filers). Recognizing Obama's stance, the Senate Democratic leadership began to plan a floor debate on this issue in the early fall of 2010. And the revenue implications were not trivial: ending the Bush tax cuts for the high - income filers was projected to generate $678 billion in badly needed revenue from 2011 - 2020. In fiscal year 2010 alone, the Obama White House was looking at a federal deficit in excess of $1 trillion.

As the scheduled congressional deliberations approached, a small but growing number of moderate Democrats in Congress began to question the wisdom of higher taxes, even if restricted to high - income taxpayers (Lightman, 2010). Over thirty "Blue Dog" Democrats in the House urged Speaker Pelosi to support extension of the Bush tax cuts for all Americans. One of the earliest signs of public resistance in the Senate came from Senator Evan Bayh (D - Indiana), who had already announced his retirement and was more concerned about the near - term state of the economy than the mounting deficits. Veteran Senator Ben Nelson (D - Nebraska) had voted for all of the Bush tax cuts from 2001 - 2008 and did not believe they should be rescinded. Perhaps most significant was the public stance of Kent Conrad (D - North Dakota), the respected chair of the Senate Budget Committee. As Conrad and other moderates signaled an interest in further extending all of the Bush tax cuts, the Obama White House began to reconsider.

In the summer of 2010 the Democratic candidates for re - election felt tough headwinds on the campaign trail, and thus the Senate Democratic leadership reversed course and postponed the contentious floor fight on taxes until after the elections. The House leadership reluctantly followed suit, seeing little purpose in making vulnerable House Democrats vote on a contentious issue that the Senate would not address until after the election.

A political earthquake occurred in the November 2010 elections: the Democrats lost 65 seats in the House and five in the Senate. Yet a legislative compromise was needed quickly in the lame - duck session, since the Bush tax cuts were scheduled to expire for all Americans starting January 2011. The House leadership quickly passed a tax - relief plan (by a vote of 234 - 188) that extended the Bush tax cuts for all households with incomes under $250,000, as Obama requested (Sonmez, 2010). But this plan fell well short (53 - 36) of the 60 - vote margin in the Senate, in part because five Democratic Senators defected from the White House position (Dayen, 2010). More importantly, all 42 Republican Senators informed the White House in writing that no business in the lame - duck session would be permitted to occur until the Bush tax cuts were extended for all Americans.

The Obama White House promptly flip - flopped. A two - year extension of the Bush tax cuts was negotiated, thereby ensuring that they would not expire until after the November 2012 elections. In exchange for the concession, Obama won a 13 - month extension of unemployment benefits for the long - term unemployed and a temporary cut in payroll taxes from 6.2% to 4.2%. Republicans also won two additional years of relief from the alternative minimum tax, a large reduction in estate taxes, and some targeted business tax cuts. In the end, the plan mushroomed into an $858 billion stimulus package, $700 billion in tax cuts and $158 billion in additional spending (Herszenhorn, 2010). Despite some intense opposition from the far left and far right in both chambers, the package passed the Senate 81 - 19 and the House 277 - 148 (Associated Press, 2010; Hook and McKinnon, 2010). Obama was clearly on the defensive, but displayed considerable agility in this negotiated settlement.

In summary, Obama tried to repeal the Bush tax cuts for high - income filers but could not overcome resistance from moderates in his own party, who were aligned with a unified Republican minority in the Senate. Obama made some progress on this issue after his 2012 re - election but only after the high income threshold was raised from $250,000 to $400,000 per year.

CASE STUDY #2: BUSH AND OBAMA BAILOUT INDUSTRIES, 2008 - 9

The Great Recession of 2007 - 2009 can be traced to the housing boom experienced by the US from the late 1990s to 2006. Real home prices in the USA climbed an average of 85%, while more than doubling in some cities (Minneapolis, Naples, Phoenix, Sacramento, Salt Lake City and Tucson). Rates of homeownership climbed rapidly in this period, often financed through large mortgages with small or zero down payments, weak income verification, and interest - rate schemes that put the squeeze on households a few years after purchase. Mortgage brokers were compensated for the number of mortgages written, not for minimizing risk. Mortgages were bundled together, "securitized", and sold to investors around the world without much disclosure of risk. Many of the transactions occurred at relatively unregulated financial institutions such as investment and commercial banks, real estate investment trusts, hedge funds, and money market funds. Meanwhile, the government - sponsored insurers of secondary mortgages, Fannie Mae and Freddie Mac, were exempt from typical capital - reserve requirements and seemed to be more focused on expanding homeownership rates in low - income and minority communities than in ensuring the safety and soundness of the housing finance system. The rating agencies were not much help. They were assigning triple - A ratings to mortgage securities that were later shown to be quite risky. And they were earning big consulting fees from clients that the rating agencies were supposed to be evaluating for risk.

None of this was widely recognized as a big problem in Washington or Wall Street. Housing prices had increased for decades and were expected to continue to rise.

When the unexpected correction in housing prices began in 2006 - 20077, a rapid proliferation of mortgage foreclosures occurred around the country. Simply put, families could not afford to make their mortgage payments, and the strategy of borrowing against the rising value of their home was no longer available. Losses mounted rapidly at banks and other financial institutions. Before policy makers fully realized it, the entire financial system – in both the US and abroad – came under severe stress, as exemplified by the demise of Lehman Brothers just a few weeks before the 2008 presidential election.

Bush and Obama as Bailout Specialists

Bush and Obama have many philosophical differences but, faced with the prospect of a repeat of the Great Depression of the 1930s, they set aside philosophy in favor of practical steps to avert economic collapse. They actually collaborated on some of these efforts as Bush's second term came to a close and Obama was preparing to take office. Working with a Democratic Congress, Bush and Obama initiated targeted bailouts of the housing, financial, and automotive sectors of the U.S. economy. Fear of a repeat of the Great Depression was powerful enough to motivate some cooperative bipartisanship.

Housing Bailout

Without appreciating the gravity of what was unfolding, the Bush White House started with "FHA Secure", a modest program designed to help homeowners reset the terms of their mortgage. Yet many distressed homeowners could not meet the program's down payment and income requirements. Bush followed with another modest initiative, "Hope Now", aimed at encouraging market actors to set new mortgage terms. But as the recession deepened, it became clear that more potent medicine was required. Bush reversed his earlier stance and supported larger lending authority for the federal government. When it became clear that Fannie Mae and Freddie Mac were going down (both companies lost 80% of their stock value from July 2007 to July 2008), Bush reluctantly asked Congress for unlimited authority to lend them money, including authority to purchase their stock, a position that some Democrats in Congress argued should have been taken much earlier. This housing bailout easily passed the Congress, a rare case of bipartisan collaboration.

In March 2009, Obama announced a $75 billion plan to end the foreclosure crisis by keeping defaulting owners in their homes. The goal was to modify permanently the mortgages of at least 3 million homeowners. Called the "Making Home Affordable Program", the idea was to modestly reward lenders when they modified the terms of mortgages in an effort to assist homeowners. Financing for the program came from Treasury, which was administering the $700 billion Wall Street bailout package (see below).

Obama's plan did not achieve its goal (Streitfeld, 2010). By July 2010, only 390,000 mortgages had been permanently modified. The program was crippled by weak oversight, conflicts of interest, and low rates of bank participation. When banks did participate, they denied participation to many homeowners on the grounds that they are not eligible for the program. After - the - fact studies have found that some of these homeowners were in fact eligible. It is estimated that the program spent only $4 billion of the original $30 billion approved for it. In March 2011 the House of Representatives voted to eliminate the program but Senate Democrats, while irritated with Treasury's incompetent program administration, blocked repeal. In October 2011 Obama announced a new effort to fix the program, including an explicit goal to help an additional one million homeowners who might otherwise foreclose. By late 2011 the slow economic recovery began to curb the number of new mortgage foreclosures.

Wall Street Bailout

As the financial sector collapsed in 2008, the cries from Wall Street were nothing like had been heard since the 1930s. A Wall Street bailout package called Troubled Asset Relief Package (TARP) was hastily put together by the Bush administration. The basic aim was to provide Treasury with liquidity that could be used to rescue otherwise viable financial institutions.

Members of Congress were in no mood to subsidize Wall Street. Initially, the House voted down the rescue package 228 - 205. Republicans voted against the package 133 - 65, and they were joined by all African American members of the House, who were offended by so much money going to protect wealthy organizations that had made bad investment decisions. But on the day of the House vote, the Dow dropped 778 points (7%), and similar losses rippled through stock markets around the world.

Bush and the Democratic leaders in Congress pleaded for a last - ditch effort to avoid complete financial collapse. Four days later the House passed TARP – which had been sweetened with some popular tax relief and spending programs – on a decisive vote of 263 - 171. Action in the Senate was less controversial, as the measure was passed 74 - 25, with opponents comprised of 15 Republican and 10 Democratic Senators. Like the housing bailout, the initial $700 billion TARP package is best seen as a case of cooperative bipartisan legislation.

A key feature of TARP was that monies were to be allocated in two $350 billion chunks, the second chunk to be allocated only after a presidential request of Congress and then only after Congress had fifteen days to deny permission. Implementation of TARP proved to be extremely controversial. Some of the initial monies were simply used by banks to improve their balance sheets, rather than make more loans available to consumers. Claims were made that monies went to many foreign banks. Some members of Congress objected to the fact that tens of billions of dollars were diverted from the TARP program to bail out General Motors and Chrysler (see below). The high levels of executive compensation at some of the recipient institutions also sparked outrage.

Once the initial $350 billion was spent by Treasury, it was not clear whether Congress would approve the second chunk. President Bush, before leaving office, requested release of the second $350 billion installment. The request was made with the support of President - elect Obama, who was also calling Senators to reassure them that the funds would be used responsibly.

Reflecting widespread public discontent with TARP, a measure was introduced in the Senate to deny the second $350 billion. But the measure was defeated 52 - 42 when a majority of Democrats and six Republicans voted to grant the joint request coming from Bush and Obama (ABC News, 2009). Thus, while sufficient bipartisan support for TARP was mustered, the extent of consensus was dwindling.

The legal authority to expend TARP monies expired on October 2, 2010. Treasury never tapped the full $700 billion. While $470 billion was committed, some of this began to be repaid as Wall Street stabilized and the economy began to recover.

The Obama White House was much more interested in new legislation aimed at curbing abusive lending practices and high - risk bets on complex derivative securities. Obama proposed such legislation in June 2009, including a call for a new bureau to protect consumers from financial fraud and mandatory cuts in the fees that banks may charge for debit - credit cards.

A year later Congress delivered "Dodd - Frank", one of the most complex pieces of business legislation in modern American history named for its principal authors: Senator Christopher Dodd (D - CN) and Representative Barney Frank (D - MA). The House and Senate passed different versions of Obama's plan, largely on party - line votes. The final version passed the House in June 2010 on vote of 237 - 192. Only three Republicans voted for Dodd - Frank. Nineteen House Democrats defected. The package was passed through the Senate with the slimmest of margins (60 - 39), aided by three crucial votes from Republican cross - overs: Olympia Snowe and Susan Collins of Maine and Scott Brown of Massachusetts. Senator Robert Byrd (D - WV) passed away before the House - Senate disagreements were resolved and Senator Russ Feingold (E-WI) opposed the measure because it was not strong enough.

Dodd - Frank is so complex that its true meaning will not be appreciated until more than 400 rulemakings are completed. But the Dodd - Frank legislation should be seen as a success in cross - partisanship, as Obama was able to unify his party while attracting three Republican voters in the Senate to accomplish the victory.

Auto Bailout

One of Bush's last acts as president was to respond to the grave financial difficulties faced by the Big Three. Although these companies had been losing market share to Honda and Toyota for decades, a severe credit crunch in the economy followed the correction in the housing sector. Without loans, consumers cannot afford to buy cars. The national rate of car sales plummeted from a peak of 17 million sales in 2006 to 11 million in late 2008.

In the second quarter of 2008 alone, GM reported a loss of $15.5 billion. And GM was rapidly running out of cash. Ford had much more cash on hand (due to asset sales in 2006) but had incurred $26 billion in losses since 2006, including $8.7 billion in the second quarter of 2008. Chrysler was in deep trouble, and was predicted to be the first of the Big Three to declare bankruptcy, although the Wall Street firm Cerberus was striving to rescue it. Even the highly profitable Japanese auto makers were beginning to pile up red ink.

The imminent failure of the Detroit automakers sent shivers through Wall Street because the Big Three owed $100 billion to bankers and bondholders. If the Big 3 collapsed, the potential ripple effects in the economy were sobering: parts suppliers, car dealers, car financing firms, insurance companies, hedge funds and pension funds were all at risk. The United Auto Workers had already made major concessions to the Big Three in 2007 and yet were facing a potentially large loss of members in unstructured bankruptcy proceedings.

In the fall of 2008, the Big Three and UAW requested that Bush and Congress engineer a loan program to help the industry weather the Great Recession. An initial industry request for

$25 billion was later enlarged to $34 billion. And these requests were on top of $25 billion in low - interest loans that Congress had already authorized in 2007 to help finance advances in green engines and fuels. But that money was restricted for use by financially sustainable firms, and the Big Three were not looking very sustainable.

Bush initially expressed skepticism about the merits of a bailout but he ultimately relented in the face of pleas from a wide range of advocates, including President - elect Barack Obama (Hitt, 2008). Bush proposed that some of the $25 billion authorized in 2007 be made available to relieve the cash crunch at the Big Three. House Speaker Nancy Pelosi, backed by environmentalists, objected that these funds were intended for development of green technologies.

As an alternative, the Bush White House worked with congressional leaders on an emergency loan package for GM and Chrysler. A plan passed the House on a vote of 237 - 170 (Herszenhorn and Sanger, 2008), with far more support from House Democrats (205 - 20) than House Republicans (32 - 150). Bush's efforts were aided in the House by a key ally: President - elect Barack Obama.

In the Senate, the resistance was much stronger and 60 votes were required. When the roll - call vote was taken, the plan was eight votes short of the necessary 60 (Herszenhorn and Sanger, 2008). Senate Democrats supported the plan 42 - 4, but Senate Republicans voted it down 31 - 10. Although multiple reasons were cited for opposition, the fact that the plan did not compel significant concessions from the UAW was a contributing factor. And some Republicans felt simply that GM and Chrysler deserve nothing and should fail.

In summary, Bush's legislative effort to rescue the Big 3 failed primarily because he could not discourage mass defections from his own party in the Senate. But Bush did not surrender.

After the Senate blocked the emergency loan package, Bush reluctantly agreed to Pelosi's original suggestion: use of executive powers to provide some TARP monies to GM and Chrysler, thereby ensuring that President Obama had enough time to consider how the dire situation should be handled. The Department of Treasury began with a $13.4 billion loan to GM and a $4 billion loan to Chrysler. Later Bush approved an additional $5 billion and $1.5 billion, respectively, to the lending arms of GM and Chrysler. And before leaving office, Bush's Treasury leadership also started the process of opening up TARP monies to the bleeding suppliers of the Big Three.

As GM and Chrysler were about to enter Chapter 11 bankruptcy proceedings, the Obama White House played an extraordinarily powerful role in defining the terms and conditions of their bankruptcy, who the winners and losers would be, who would lead the companies after bankruptcy, and what kinds of products would be expected of the new companies. The United Auto Workers were a winner in the sense that they were harmed much less significantly than they might have been in an unstructured bankruptcy proceeding. The preferred creditors of Chrysler and GM, on the other hand, suffered unexpectedly high losses.

Obama and the Congress did even more work for Detroit. In Europe several countries responded to the low rate of new car sales with "cash for clunker" programs. Details of the programs vary, but the basic approach is for government to provide a financial incentive for owners of old cars to buy a new one. Sometimes the plans were used exclusively for stimulus purposes; in other cases they were used to clean the environment by replacing old, dirty cars with cleaner ones.

With support from President Obama, the House passed a $1 billion cash - for - clunkers plan by a vote of 298 - 119 (Liberto, 2009). Fifty nine House Republicans defected from their leadership's stance and supported the plan. Only nine House Democrats voted against it.

In the Senate, Obama and the Senate Democratic leadership again faced the 60 - vote hurdle. Republican Senator Judd Gregg of New Hampshire led the opposition, invoking a procedural argument that the plan should not be attached to a $106 billion war - spending plan, as proposed by the Democrats. Exactly enough votes were found to overcome the procedural hurdle, with the final vote total being 60 - 36 in June 2009 (Fox News, 2009). All Senate Democrats except Ben Nelson of Nebraska voted in favor of moving the plan forward. While the Republican opposition was substantial, four Senate Republicans crossed over to support the plan: Kit Bond of Missouri, Tad Cochran of Mississippi, Susan Collins of Maine and George Voinovich of Ohio. This is another illustration of a successful cross – partisan strategy in the Senate.

Once "cash for clunkers" was enacted, a flood of applications was submitted by interested consumers. The $1 billion fund was quickly exhausted, even though many applications remained to be processed. Consequently, Obama and the congressional leadership worked on a measure to expand the program with an additional $2 billion (Healey and Woodyard, 2009).

The expansion passed the House easily (316 - 109), but opposition in the Senate was again strong. The Senate ultimately voted to expand the program, this time on a 60 - 37 vote (Wald, 2009). Although four Democratic Senators defected this time, seven cross over Republicans provided just the margin necessary for passage. Thus, the second cash - for - clunkers vote is best seen as yet another successful use of the cross - partisan strategy.

In summary, Bush may have been a reluctant actor, but he set in motion a wide range of bailout programs in the housing, financial, and automotive sectors of the economy (Graham, 2010). As President - elect, Obama encouraged Bush to move in this direction. Obama then refined, buttressed, and expanded these policies. Thus, both Bush and Obama will be seen in history books as "big government" presidents who strived to prevent the Great Recession from becoming another Great Depression, in part by subsidizing the housing, finance, and auto sectors. They overcame polarization through a mix of bipartisan cooperation and limited party cross – overs.

CASE STUDY #3:
PASSAGE OF THE OBAMA "STIMULUS" PACKAGES, 2009 - 2010

Less than one month after being sworn in, President Obama signed a $787 billion economic - stimulus package aimed at boosting the economic recovery. Approximately 70% of the package was new spending (e.g., Medicaid assistance to the states, grants to schools and colleges, expanded unemployment compensation, bridge and highway repairs, and food/health assistance for low - income families); 30% was tax relief (e.g., general tax credits for individual and businesses and targeted tax relief to promote renewable energy, energy efficiency, clean coal technology, home and vehicle purchases, and plug - in vehicle purchases). Roughly three quarters of the funds were to be spent within eighteen months, the point being to put America back to work ("shovel – ready" projects) repairing the country's infrastructure.

The stimulus package, much to Obama's dismay, was not a bipartisan affair, despite the dire condition of the economy and Obama's big win at the polls in November 2008. The original House package, a bit larger at $819 billion, passed the House 244 - 188 with zero Republican votes. Eleven House Democrats defected. A somewhat different package passed the Senate 61 - 37. Crucial votes from three Republican Senators (Olympia Snowe and Susan Collins of Maine and Arlen Specter of Pennsylvania) were combined with votes from all of the Democratic Senators (Calmes, 2009). Once again, Obama won through a cross – partisan Senate strategy.

When the House - Senate conference submitted the final $787 billion package, it passed the House 246 - 183, again with no Republican votes. Seven Democrats defected. In the Senate, the margin at passage was 60 - 38, with the same three Republican Senators joining all of the Senate Democrats in support of the package (Herszenhorn, 2009). Without those three cross - over Republican votes, the final package may have been quite different.

At the end of 2010, Obama unexpectedly won a second round of stimulus, since the Bush tax cuts were about to expire and several million of the long - term unemployed were about to lose unemployment insurance benefits. As explained above, the Obama White House helped engineer an $858 billion stimulus package, $700 billion in tax relief (comprised largely of a two - year extension of the Bush tax cuts in 2011 and 2012) and $158 billion in new spending (primarily the 13 - month extension of unemployment insurance for the long - term unemployed).

In September 2011, Obama proposed yet a third stimulus effort, a $447 billion "jobs bill" comprised of $272 billion in tax relief (largely payroll tax cuts) and $175 billion in new spending (e.g., public works projects, aid to states for public schools, and extension of unemployment benefits). In order to consider this package on the Senate floor, Majority Leader Harry Reid needed 60 votes for a motion to limit debate. That motion failed 50 - 49, as all 47 Republican Senators joined 2 Democratic Senators (Ben Nelson of Nebraska and Jon Tester of Montana) in opposition to considering the measure. Two more Democratic Senators (Jim Webb of Virginia and Joe Manchini of West Virginia) indicated that, while they voted in favor of the procedural motion, they were opposed to the Obama plan on its merits. Thus, while the Democratic Party was controlling the floor in the Senate, the Obama White House was not able to rally all of the Democrats behind this package, let alone attract some Republican cross - over votes (Pear, 2011). This effort at cross-partisan legislation did not succeed, in part because Obama's favorability ratings were dangerously low and few Republican Senators had incentives to collaborate.

Lessons from the Cases

The fundamental lesson of the case studies is that it is feasible – though certainly not easy – for the White House to overcome partisan polarization in Congress and enact priority legislation. In other words, the gridlock hypothesis found in the polarization literature is not always or necessarily applicable to presidential initiatives. For future scholarly work, we advance some related hypotheses that may shed light on how and when the White House will be successful in domestic legislation, despite polarization.

First, presidents must give careful thought to their first - year priorities, as Bush and Obama seemed to be most successful in Congress during their first year. The honeymoon period for new presidents may have shortened significantly but the White House continues to have a window of legislative opportunity soon after a presidential election. This pattern was evident again after Obama's 2012 re - election.

Second, capitalizing on recent events in the public eye (e.g., the dot - com recession of 2001 and the Great Recession of 2007 - 2009) may provide an umbrella under which larger presidential policy objectives can be achieved. Bush won a large reduction in the tax rate on dividends and capital gains in 2003, even though the long - term virtues of this policy were unlikely to have any near - term effect on the post - 2001 "jobless recovery". Obama's 2009 recovery package became a vehicle to advance liberal objectives ranging from temporary expansion of anti - poverty programs to subsidies for green technology.

Third, presidents should give laser - like attention to the political interests of Senators from the opposing party who are potential cross – over votes. For example, those Senators may represent states that voted for the president or they may have previous voting records that appear sympathetic to the president's initiative. Bush had a focus on Senate Democrats from the south and midwest while Obama courted the dwindling number of Republicans from the northeast (Reiter and Stonecagh, 2011). Despite the pressures for unity from their party leadership in Congress, both Bush and Obama found some crucial cross – over votes in the Senate.

Finally, the limited promise of cooperative bipartisan efforts is amply illustrated by the polarized reaction of Congress to Obama's 2009 "recovery act" proposal. If the biggest downturn in the U.S. economy since the Great Depression cannot generate bipartisan consensus for economic policy, then it seems unlikely that cooperative bipartisanship will be routinely effective during bouts of polarization. The exceptions are the initial housing bailout and the TARP legislation, but they occurred under a lame - duck Republican president facing a heavily Democratic Congress. All things considered, a key lesson from the Bush and Obama years is that the most promising route to success in the Senate is often a form of "cheap bipartisanship": combine virtual unanimity from senators of the president's party with a limited number of cross over votes from the opposing party (Hacker and Pearson, 2006).

ACKNOWLEDGMENTS

I would like to thank Emilce Sanchez and Matt Irick of Indiana University who provided helpful brainstorming, comments, and research assistance.

REFERENCES

ABC News.com. Obama Wins $350 Billion Senate Tarp Vote. January 15, 2009.

Arenberg Richard A., Dove Robert B., *Defending the Filibuster: The Soul of the Senate.* (Indiana University Press, 2012).

Associated Press. *Senate Passes Package Extending Bush Tax Cuts. Mxn.com.* December 15, 2010.

Brady David W., Volden Craig, *Revolving Gridlock: Politics and Policy from Jimmy Carter to George W. Bush. Second Edition.* (Westview Press, 2006).

Calmes Jackie., House Passes Stimulus Plan with No GOP Votes. *New York Times.* January 28, 2009.

Calmes Jackie, Expiring Tax Cuts' Fate Has Parties Strategizing. *New York Times.* April 14, 2010.

Dayen David, Senate GOP Blocks Consideration of Tax Plan Extending Rates on First $250,000 and First $1 Million. Newsfiredoglake.com. December 4, 2010.

Fox News.com. Dodd Resists Tax on Health Care Benefits, Calls Proposal Unnecessary. *Foxnews.com,* June 14, 2009.

Fox News.com. Congress Approves *'Cash for Clunkers' Program.* June 18, 2009.

Fox News.com. Obama: Immigration Reform Requires Changing the Law. *Fox.news.com.* September 13, 2011.

Graham John D., *Bush on the Home Front* (Indiana University Press, 2010).

Hacker Jacob S. and Pierson Paul, *Off Center: The Republican Revolution and the Erosion of American Democracy* (Yale University Press, 2006).

Healey James R., Woodyard Chris, House Adds Cash to 'Clunkers' Program; Senate Vote Needed. *USA Today.* August 2, 2009.

Herszenhorn David M., DE Sanger, Senate Abandons Automaker Bailout Bid. *New York Times.* December 11, 2008.

Herszenhorn David M., Recovery Bill Gets Final Approval. *New York Times.* February 13, 2009.

Herszenhorn David M., House Set to Follow Senate in Approving Tax Deal. *New York Times.* December 15, 2010.

Hitt Greg, House Passes Rescue Plan for Big 3. *Wall Street Journal.* December 11, 2008.

Hook Janet, McKinnon John. Congress Passes Tax Deal. *Wall Street Journal.* December 17, 2010.

Jacobson Gary, A Divider, *Not a Uniter: George W. Bush's Troubled Quest for a Presidential Legacy* (Pearson Education, 2007).

Jones Charles O., *Separate But Equal Branches*: *Congress and the Presidency* (Chatham House Press, 1995).

Jones Charles O., *The Presidency in a Separated System. Second Edition.* (Brookings, 2005).

Koger Gregory, Filibustering: A Political History of Obstruction in the House and Senate, (University of Chicago Press, 2010).

Lee Frances S., *Beyond Ideology: Politics, Principles, and Partisanship in the U.S. Senate.* (University of Chicago Press, 2009).

Liberto Jennifer, House Oks $4 Billion *'Clunker' Bill.* CNN.com, June 6, 2009.

Lightman David, Democrats Unlikely to Repeal Tax Cuts for the Rich. *McClatchy.com,* 9/1/2010.

Mayhew David R., *Congress: The Electoral Connection. Second Edition.* (Yale University Press 2004).

Mayhew David R., *Partisan Balance* (Princeton University Press, 2011).

Mooney Alexander, Pelosi, Obama Disagree on Bush Tax Cuts, Bush Investigations. *CNN.com,* January 18, 2009.

Pear Robert, President's Jobs Measure is Turned Back in Key Senate Test. *New York Times.* October 11, 2011.

Reiter Howard L., Stonecagh Jeffrey M., *Counter Realignment: Political Change in the Northeastern United States.* (Cambridge University Press, 2011).

Sonmez Felicia, House Passes Bill to Extend Bush-Era Tax Cuts to Middle Class. *Washington P*ost. December 2, 2010.

Saeki Manabu, *The Other Side of Gridlock*, SUNY Press, 2010.

Streitfeld David. U.S. Mortgage Relief Effort is Falling Short of Goal. *New York Times.* August 20, 2010.

Wald Matthew L., Senate Adds Cash to 'Clunker' Plan. *New York Times.* August 6, 2009.

PART II:
CHANGES IN THE WHITE HOUSE AND THE WORLD FROM GEORGE W. BUSH TO BARACK OBAMA

In: Change in the White House?
Editor: Meena Bose

ISBN: 978-1-62948-920-9
© 2014 Nova Science Publishers, Inc.

Chapter 5

UNDERSTANDING THE OBAMA DOCTRINE

Stanley A. Renshon

ABSTRACT

This article examines President Obama's foreign policy worldview and its relationship to an emerging "Obama Doctrine." It is a hybrid doctrine, building on the legacy of his predecessor but increasingly making that legacy a smaller and narrower part of his evolving policies. Central to those new policies that constitute the Obama Doctrine is America's redemption and the president as the vehicle for its accomplishment.

Given its unique position, American foreign policy must of necessity encompass the world. It is the indispensable leader of the Western alliance and still the world's predominant power often called upon to use its weight or lend its help in a variety of international circumstances. It is the only power able to mount world-spanning relief efforts. It is the power of last resort, when aspiring hegemons threaten or actually do break free of their constraints. And it is often the international power of choice when domestic groups in other countries ask for either protection or help. [1]

In short, any president faces a world of American involvement abroad. And, more than a decade after the formulation, implementation, successes and setbacks of the Bush Doctrine, President Obama inherited the opportunity and the need to define the nature of American world leadership. This is he done in an evolving series of policies that represent a clear Obama Doctrine.

THE UNIQUE PERSONAL ORIGINS OF THE OBAMA DOCTRINE

To understand the real Obama Doctrine, it is first necessary to underscore the fact that the president has placed himself at the center of his administration's policies He made clear in introducing his senior foreign policy team that, [2]

But understand, I will be setting policy as president. I will be responsible for the vision that this team carries out, and I expect them to implement that vision once decisions are made. So, as Harry Truman said, the buck will stop with me. And nobody who's standing here, I think, would have agreed to join this administration unless they had confidence that in fact that vision was one that would help secure the American people and our interests.

There is nothing unusual about a president wishing to be and be seen as the author of his own administration's policies. In this president's case there is ample evidence that is true as a matter of fact, as well as a reflection of aspirations. [3] The point of noting this is that the Obama Doctrine I am about to analyze is truly the presidents' and springs directly from his views and ambitions.

Moreover, the president sees himself as uniquely qualified for that position. Obama's enormous self-confidence is legendary and has been publically noted by a variety of people who have worked closely with him over the years. [4]

Self-confidence of course is no stranger to presidential ambitions, but the scope of Obama's are somewhat unusual. When Patrick Gaspard interviewed then candidate Obama for the position of the campaign's political director, Obama told him, "I think that I'm a better speechwriter than my speechwriters. I know more about policies on any particular issue than my policy directors." [5] One "senior official" went on record to say, "The truth is that President Obama is his own Henry Kissinger—no one else plays that role. Every administration reflects the personality of the president. This president wants all the trains routed through the Oval Office." [6]

These are of course the words of others, but they reflect words that Obama has said himself. At one point during the presidential campaign he asserted that in picking a vice presidential nominee he didn't have to worry about foreign policy experience because, "Ironically, this is an area—foreign policy is the area where I am probably most confident that I know more and understand the world better than Senator Clinton or Senator McCain." [7]

The point here is not raise the question of whether the president's high level of self-confidence is in danger of sliding over into arrogance, or can lead to policy misjudgments, although both are clearly dangers. Rather, the point is that the president's high self-confidence and strong beliefs in the correctness of his own views make this a presidency where those views carry a great deal of policy weight. Therefore the president's foreign policy beliefs, understandings, and perspectives are not merely background factors that inform the specifics of his case- by- case approach to foreign policies. They are front and center.

It remains to analyze just what those beliefs are and to analyze the extent to which they are coupled with the president's transformational ambitions.

The President's Foreign Policy Worldview: Liberal Internationalism

The president's basic approach to American foreign policy is to be found in both his worldview and the transformative ambitions that underlie them. His worldview is easily stated. Secretary Clinton, clearly reflecting her boss' view stated it quite succinctly (emphasis added):

President Obama has led us to think outside the usual boundaries. He has launched a new era of engagement based on common interests, shared values, and mutual r=espect. Going forward, capitalizing on America's unique strengths, *we must advance those interests through partnership, and promote universal values through the power of our example and the empowerment of people.* In this way, we can forge the global consensus required to defeat the threats, manage the dangers, and seize the opportunities of the 21st century. *America will always be a world leader as long as we remain true to our ideals and embrace strategies that match the times.* [8]

The president himself has written that, "it was in America's interest to work with other countries to build up international institutions and promote international norms. Not because of a naïve assumption that international laws and treaties alone would end conflicts among nations or eliminate the need for American military action, but because the more international norms were enforced and the more America signaled a willingness to show restraint in the exercise of its power, the fewer the number of conflicts that would arise –and the more legitimate our actions would appear in the eyes of the world when we did have to move militarily." [9]

These views describe a well-establish viewpoint in international relations theory--liberal internationalism. [10] The tenants of this foreign policy viewpoint were detailed sometime ago in Oli Holsti's classic study. [11] Examining a variety of survey data going back decades, Holsti confirmed that generally Republicans took positions consist with national assertiveness, while Democrats took positions consistent with cooperative internationalism.

Holsti wrote that, "Liberalism denies that conflict is an immutable element of relations between nations." [12] And, "it emphasizes the potential for cooperative relations among nations; institutional building to reduce uncertainty and fears and antagonisms based on misinformation and misperception, and the positive sum possibilities of such activities...[to] mitigate, if not eliminate, the harshest features of international relations emphasized by the realists." [13]

So the liberal internationalist view might well be summed up as follows: America's strength rests on its relationships with its allies and in building strong international institutions; America might take the lead, but always as a member in good standing of its alliances and international obligations, and force is a last resort and must be used sparingly, precisely, and legitimately. Talking and reaching agreements are always preferable.

If Obama's Doctrine were simply a reflection of a Democratic Party president's preference for a liberal international perspective on foreign policy, it would be of some interest, but not exactly startling. That is, after all, Democratic Party's modern post Cold War core view of American foreign policy.

What makes the Obama Doctrine unique is that it is not so much aimed at foreign rivals or opponents, but at the behavior of the United States itself.

THE OBAMA DOCTRINE AND AMERICA'S NEED FOR REDEMPTION

Redemption is a term more frequently heard in theology than psychology or political science, but its basic dynamic would be familiar to any psychoanalyst. It begins with a transgression in which the person or object, in this case a country, violates either personal or "international community" norms that either exist or those President Obama hopes to help establish and feels (or ought to) guilt or remorse. Redemption is the vehicle through which the person or a president's country reacquires standing and legitimacy in the community. It begins with public atonement, a promise to do things differently, and efforts to live up to that redemptive promise.

My working theory is that the president entered office having struggled through his personal life and political career with a set of redemption issues [14] including the larger issue of America's ideals and its failure to live up to them at home and abroad. It is the president's intention to reclaim, through example, policy and the force of his moral vision, America's legitimacy in the world.

Obama's redemptive ambitions bear a strong resemblance to his presidential initiatives in both domestic and foreign policy.

Obama's Redemption and America's

In a 2008 interview, Mr. Obama clearly linked the theme of his redemption with that of the country. The interview was about his *Dreams* book and Obama was asked about racial progress in the country since Dr. King and the civil rights movement. Obama replied, [15]

> I worked as a community organizer in Chicago, [and] was very active in low-income neighborhoods working on issues of crime and education and employment, and seeing that in some ways certain portions of the African-American community are doing as bad, if not worse, and recognizing that my fate remained tied up with their fates. *That my individual salvation is not going to come about without a collective salvation for the country. Unfortunately, I think that recognition requires that we make sacrifices, and this country has not always been willing to make the sacrifices necessary to bring about a new day and a new age. (emphasis added)*

In this quote we find two themes. The first is that Obama believes that his and all Americans' salvation is dependent on the collective salvation of the country. Embedded in that view is the assumption that the country and its citizens need salvation. Why? Because they failed to make the sacrifices that Obama views as necessary. And in that view lie the seeds of Obama's transformative ambitions.

Of these ambitions there can be little doubt. In announcing his presidential campaign he said, "let us transform this nation." [16] Campaigning in Iowa he said directly "I want to transform this country" [17]. Campaigning in New Hampshire, he told those assembled, "we're going to change the country and change the world." [18] In his inaugural address, he called on his fellow citizens to help "remake America"—not change mind you, but remake. [19]

That this is not solely political rhetoric was evidenced in Obama's relentless pursuit to transform American domestic policy though both his health care and stimulus initiatives. The first involves the expansion of the federal government into the American heath care system to a new and unprecedented degree. The second raises the level of government baseline spending to new unprecedented levels, a reflection of the fairer redistributive policies at the heart of the president's domestic policy premises.

In retrospect, these policies ought not to have been surprising. Transforming America had always been at the heart of the Obama presidency and his policy ambitions.

In a 2006 interview, Obama had said that if he ran he "wanted to be a great president." [20] He was asked about his during a *Meet the Press* interview: [21]

> **MR. RUSSERT**: You told *Men's Vogue Magazine*, that if you wanted to be president, you shouldn't just think about being president, that you should want to be a great president. So you've clearly given this some thought.

> **SEN. OBAMA**: Yes.

> **MR. RUSSERT**: And what would, in your mind, define a great president?

> **SEN. OBAMA**: But I think, when I think about great presidents, I think about those *who transform how we think about ourselves as a country in fundamental ways* so that, that, at the end of their tenure, we have looked and said to ours—that's who we are. And, and our, our—and for me at least, that means that we have a more expansive view of our democracy, that we've included more people into the bounty of this country. ... *And they transformed the culture and not simply promoted one or two particular issues.(emphasis added)*

The exchange makes Obama's view of transformation as involving remaking America's basic culture and identity quite clear. Transformation, in the president's stated view, is the political vehicle of his historical "greatness."

Even ordinary large-scale accomplishments would not suffice. The *New York Times* reports that Timothy Geither, his Secretary of the Treasury, trying to council moderate policy initiatives in the first part of Obama's presidency and said to the president "Your legacy is going to be preventing the second Great Depression," to which the president, vexed, replied "That's not enough for me." [22]

AMERICA'S FOREIGN AND DOMESTIC POLICY FAILINGS

Redemption requires the acknowledgement of moral, ethical, or behavioral failures.

It is clear that the president thinks that the United States has not lived up to its foreign policy ideals and responsibilities. In a series of highly public venues abroad, the president has called attention to the errors and arrogance of this country's foreign policy.

This is not merely an "apology tour" as the president's critics contended. His purpose was both strategic and redemptive. The strategic aspect of his calling attention to the errors he sees is clearly intended to reset America's relationships with the world and herald the arrival of Obama's new approach to American foreign policy.

The assumption behind doing so is that the United States should admit error and turn over a new foreign policy leaf. Then, our allies and our competitors will take note and perhaps our enemies will feel that they may be able to reach accommodation with a new, less belligerent and more honest America. However smart these strategic calculations are, Obama's criticisms, reported and analyzed below, mark an extraordinary public announcement of error and contrition on the part of an American president. In their number, range, and sharpness they are simply unprecedented.

America's Foreign Policy Faults: A Bill of Particulars

Obama explicitly chastised the United States in a 2009 Prague speech, "as having a moral responsibility to act to abolish nuclear arms because it was the only nuclear power to have used a nuclear weapon." [23] Clearly that decision was morally tainted in Obama's view and calls for redemptive, policies including unilateral deep cuts in the American nuclear arsenal, [24] and the eventual abolition of those weapons, "Global Zero," [25] followed.

In a European town hall meeting, President Obama said that the United States had "failed to appreciate Europe's leading role in the world" and that "there have been times when America has shown arrogance and been dismissive, even derisive." [26] Perhaps Mr. Obama was referring to his view that, "we dismissed European reservations about the wisdom and necessity of the Iraq war." [27] Obama had also written," In Asia, we belittled South Korean efforts to improve relationships with the North." [28]

At the Summit of the Americas Obama said, "we have at times been disengaged, and at times we sought to dictate our terms. But I pledge to you that we seek an equal partnership." [29] And in the president's first interview with an Arab newspaper he said of the United States, "all too often the United States starts by dictating … " [30] He went on to say, "the same respect and partnership that America had with the Muslim world as recently as 20 or 30 years ago, there's no reason why we can't restore that." [31]

In a speech to the Turkish Parliament, President Obama said, [32]

> The United States is still working through some of our own darker periods in our history. Facing the Washington Monument that I spoke of is a memorial of Abraham Lincoln, the man who freed those who were enslaved even after Washington led our Revolution. Our country still struggles with the legacies of slavery and segregation, the past treatment of Native Americans.

And he also noted in the same speech that, "in the United States, we recently ordered the prison at Guantanamo Bay closed. That's why we prohibited—without exception or equivocation—the use of torture." The implication of this statement is that the United States had, until he prohibited it, practiced and condoned torture and tried to obfuscate its role in doing so.

Obviously, a number of these criticisms are debatable, but that is not the point. For a president to go abroad and criticize his country so repeatedly and directly clearly reflects a deeply held view that the United has not lived up to its ideals in its dealing with other countries, and that these transgressions must be admitted, and policies premises changed, if redemption is to be possible.

The policy vehicles though which the president hopes to engineer America's redemption are at the core of the real Obama Doctrine.

THE REAL OBAMA DOCTRINE

A number of people have put forward their views of the Obama Doctrine. Some doubt he has a grand strategy at all [33]. Others think they have found the key to his doctrine and are critical of it. Fouad Ajami has written that, "In the Obama world, the tendency to wait has become official policy." [34] Elliot Abrams has written, "President Obama has never summarized the Obama Doctrine with such clarity, but here is what it would look like: 'I will undertake any military attack against our enemies, regardless of the risks and collateral damage, so long as it is over by the time I have to announce it.'" [35]

On the other hand a supportive *New York Times* columnist writes, "The Obama Administration has a doctrine. It's called the doctrine of silence... There has seldom been so big a change in approach to U.S. strategic policy with so little explanation." And what is this new policy that silence masks? Obama, "has gone covert." [36] And Ryan Lizza in a much-discussed *New Yorker* article on the president's foreign policy wrote, "Obama may be moving toward something resembling a doctrine. One of his advisers described the president's actions in Libya as "leading from behind." [37]

Each of these observers, and others, put their fingers on an element of Obama's foreign policy thinking and the Doctrine that is emerging from it, although not always accurately.

The broad contours of the Obama Doctrine—a lighter military footprint, a reliance on coalitions are easily discernable. [38] But such analyses error in not stepping back and noticing the broader transformational and redemptive origins of what the president is trying to accomplish both at home and abroad because the two are very much related.

Doing so leads to focusing on three major elements of the Obama Doctrine [39]:

1. *Redemptive transformation*: The president wants to transform both U.S. foreign and domestic policy in the service of redeeming America's past failures to live up to its promises and premises. However, domestic transformation is primary and foreign policy redemption is in the service of domestic transformation.
2. *Managing diminished primacy*: American primacy is receding and this requires a new emphasis on liberal international tenants of international cooperation. Fortunately, the necessary adjustments to American primacy are consistent with a focus on rebuilding America at home.
3. *"Hidden-hand" International Leadership*: In cases where American power is used abroad it may involve military power, so long as it is limited and preferably masked or embedded in a collective endeavor.

Redemptive Transformation

The president's view of the ways in which the United States has failed to live up to its promises has led the president to the conviction that it must do so. In his view American policies much be reformed both at home to be become "fairer" and abroad to become more cooperative. *And the latter is a major vehicle to insure the former.*

The president's perspective is clear in his public statements. In his speech announcing the drawdown of American military troops from Iraq he said, ".. after a decade of war, *the nation that we need to build -- and the nation that we will build -- is our own*; an America that sees its economic strength restored just as we've restored our leadership around the globe." [40]

Eight months later in his speech announcing the phasing out and withdrawal of American troops from Afghanistan, he said, "Above all, we are a nation whose strength abroad has been anchored in opportunity for our citizens here at home. Over the last decade, we have spent a trillion dollars on war, at a time of rising debt and hard economic times. Now, we must invest in America's greatest resource — our people. We must unleash innovation that creates new jobs and industries, while living within our means. We must rebuild our infrastructure and find new and clean sources of energy….. *America, it is time to focus on nation building here at home."* [41] (emphasis added) He added a long list of what he considered necessary domestic investments in his State of the Union Address. [42]

Even before the president assumed office, he had made this linkage clear. In an interview he was asked why he didn't support the surge in Iraq when he was a Senator. He replied, "..us putting $10 billion to $12 billion a month, $200 billion, that's money that could have gone into Afghanistan. Those additional troops could have gone into Afghanistan. *That money also could have been used to shore up a declining economic situation in the United States. That money could have been applied to having a serious energy security plan so that we were reducing our demand on oil, which is helping to fund the insurgents in many countries."* [43] (emphasis added)

Obama's theme of national building at home directly echoes the George McGovern's 1972 call during his presidential campaign, to "Come Home, America." [44] And whatever strategic reasons there might be for winding down the wars Iraq and Afghanistan, it is very clear that one cardinal virtue of doing so, in the president's view, is that money allocated for the war [45] can be spent on domestic "investments." The president has a long list of large-scale government initiatives that he wishes to undertake, [46] which he compares to building the Hoover Dam, the Golden Gate Bridge and our national highway system. One mainstream media story summed up the president's budget and political approach with the aptly descriptive story title "Obama gambles on costly initiatives." [47]

Managing diminished primacy: American primacy in the international system, as both the leader of the Western alliance and de facto power of last resort in the event of natural disasters or strategic calamities has been an article of faith and expectation since the end of the Cold War. And as Robert Kagan has recently reminded us, [48] "The present world order was largely shaped by American power and reflects American interests and preferences. If the balance of power shifts in the direction of other nations, the world order will change to suit their interests and preferences."

Kagan's observation is in the service of a larger debate about American "decline." That decline has been alternatively: as being a byproduct of imperial overreach, [49] a result of having too much power, [50] the fact that American power is seen as a threat, [51] having too much debt, [52] the likelihood of budget retrenchments, [53] or the "rise of the rest" in which theory the United States becomes one of a large group of world-class powers. [54] Whatever the purported causes the theorized results are the same—diminished primacy and the admonition to practice "self-restraint." [55]

Discerning the president's position on this issue requires one to look beyond his rhetoric. After being relentless criticized for what conservatives dubbed his "apology tour" in which the president openly criticized past American domestic and foreign policy behavior (see above), and giving equivocal support to the idea of American exceptionalism, [56] he has come out as a firm believer in it and American primacy, [57] and his own role in restoring them [58] He has said, "The United States of America is the greatest force for freedom and security that the world has ever known. And in no small measure, that's because we've built the best-trained, best-led, best-equipped military in history -- and as Commander-in-Chief, I'm going to keep it that way." [59]

This is entirely expected. No president can go on public record as disowning American primacy. And no president can be on public record as disowning American exceptionalism. It is the president's early deviation from this norm, not his subsequent embrace of it that is the surprise.

Hidden-Hand International Leadership and the Downsizing of American Primacy

In a path-breaking book on the Eisenhower presidency, Fred Greenstein characterized him as a "hidden hand president." [60] His point was that behind the genial, sometimes verbally challenged façade, there was an incisive experienced decision maker steering American foreign and domestic policy. I adapt the adjective here not to suggest that President Obama himself is playing a somewhat hidden behind the scenes role in his administration. Far from it; the president is clearly the embodiment of his own administration.

I borrow the adjective because it seems to best describe President Obama's approach to the exercise of American power. That approach, is most vividly displayed, in the American role in the Libyan operation that forced Muammar Gaddafi from power, but it is also present as well, in the administration's general approach to Middle Eastern turmoil, including that in Syria, and beyond.

As noted earlier, Ryan Lizza in a widely discussed story quoted one administration official as describing "the president's actions in Libya as 'leading from behind.'" [61] The term stuck, especially among administration critics, [62] but it is a misnomer. A better, more accurate description would be American leadership that is *minimized, embedded*, and *unobtrusive.*

The *minimized* nature of American power in Obama's Doctrine is the preference for American power to provide the minimum of what is needed. It might well be called the "just enough" approach. The *embedded* nature of American power is that American leadership is undertaken within contexts of others acting in concert with the United States and even seeming to take a publically leading role. And the *unobtrusive* nature of the exercise of American power in the Obama Doctrine reflects a preference for a small footprint and if possible one that is publically opaque, if not invisible to the outside world.

These elements are found in a variety of examples, large and small. Its most obvious exemplar was the American role in Libya. Reports on the pre-intervention debates in the White House, suggested that the president, "set two clear parameters for his top advisers: he didn't want to use military force if the U.S. had to be in the lead and he had no intention of sending American ground troops." [63] As a result, Great Britain and especially France took the lead in calling for armed intervention. [64] The president waited a week before publically commenting on the events in Libya and then refused to call for Gaddafi's removal until after France did. [65] A *Washington Post* headlined summed up the approach: "On Libya, Obama willing to let allies take the lead." [66]

Obama's "just enough" approach was reflected in what the American military actually did. The president ordered cruise missile strikes against Libyan air defenses and his administration provided the following explanation: "We're the only nation with the capacity to fire that many," a military official said, explaining why the U.S. was taking the lead for now." [67] That same report indicated that Mr. Obama's goal was to create conditions quickly that would allow the U.S. to step back and assume largely a backup role. Washington wanted France, Britain, Canada and other coalition partners to take responsibility for day-to-day enforcement of the no-fly zone over Libya. Officials described America's longer-term role as providing logistical support, such as refueling allied planes and provide intelligence from drones."

The president's view, directly stated by his deputy national security adviser for strategic communications, was "This is the Obama conception of the U.S. role in the world - to work through multilateral organizations and bilateral relationships to make sure that the steps we are taking are amplified. Maybe this is a different conception of U.S. leadership. But we believe leadership should galvanize an international response, not rely on a unilateral U.S. response." [68] Absent that, the administration is not disposed to act. In the case of Syria, Hillary Clinton resisted calls for American leadership and intervention because, "we don't have the United Nations Security Council approval, legitimacy, credibility that comes with the international community making a decision." [69]

Libya provides a clear illustration of the Obama Doctrine's preference for the *minimized, embedded*, and *unobtrusive* exercise of American power, but these terms allow us to see a broad continuity in the president's approach to foreign policy. The determined winding down of the wars in Afghanistan and Iraq obviously will result in a reduced foreign footprint of American power. Yet, it is the risks involved in the administration's decision of post-withdrawal American involvement in Iraq and Afghanistan underscores just how much that involvement has been minimized.

The change in American post- cold war strategy reflected in the administration's strategic review is another indication of its preference and planning for a reduced American international footprint. The substantial military budget cuts the administration has imposed not only reflect this preference, but also make it more likely.

The administration's emphasis on embedding the exercise of its power in collective initiatives, with its attendant advantages and limitations is easily seen in Libya, but elsewhere as well. It can easily been seen in the administration's approach to Iran and the increasing use of sanctions by American allies. It has been the American Congress and European allies that have been pushing the hardest for sanctions, [70] understandably in view of their preference for diplomacy. That approach has yielded results, biting sanctions are in place, but they leave unanswered the chief question of the embedded approach: What happens if sanctions don't dissuade Iran from becoming a nuclear power? Burden sharing is always prudent when possible, but the chief question of American primacy is what happens when collective action fails to accomplish its purposes.

And what happens if our allies preclude specific actions, at the start, their involvement? Regarding Syria, NATO Secretary-General Anders Fogh Rasmussen said NATO assets won't be used to deliver any military, humanitarian, or medical assistance there, because any type of Western intervention is not likely to help solve the crisis. [71] He went on to note," in an environment of declining defense budgets, how can we assure that we have the necessary military capabilities in the future. To that end, we need a smarter way of spending defense money. And a smarter way of doing that is by going to the model of a multinational corporation instead of purely national solutions." [72] Again, this raises the question for the United States of what happens when our chief allies subscribe to the "multinational corporation" aka international community model of intervention and there are few that step up or can do so effectively?

The administration's preference for the unobtrusive exercise of American power can be seen not only in Libya and Syria but also in its increasing reliance on special operations forces on the ground [73] and reliance on drone warfare in the skies. [74] These are the perfect embodiment of unobtrusive power, and they fit as well with administration plans to downsize American involvement and military budget expenditures. They are deadly. They are relatively cheap, especially compared with fielding an invading army. The scope of the activity is shielded. And the public's knowledge, world wide, is limited.

It is here, at this specific juncture, that the Bush and Obama Doctrines both meet but then go their separate ways.

CONCLUSION: THE REAL OBAMA DOCTRINE IN PERSPECTIVE

The world can often be a dangerous place and the president recognizes this. That recognition has led him to embrace critical elements of the Bush Doctrine and even led to an expansion of some aspects of it. But that expansion has, paradoxically been very narrow, applying military force in short bursts or in small, sharp doses not easily seen by the outside world.

The far larger part of the part of the president's foreign policy agenda is to downsize American primacy, reducing worldwide expectations for American action and leadership in every problem that others want addressed. In that stance lies redemption for America's past sins—its arrogance, unilateralism, and occasional determined military assertion of its own national interests. The downsizing of American international primacy is also instrumental in other absolutely core presidential ambition—transforming American domestic policy and culture in line with Obama's view of our past failures to live up to our ideals.

Obama is not an Eisenhower, Nixon or G.H.W. Bush who were foreign policy presidents. He is by inclination and preference a domestic president. In foreign policy, and especially in those areas bequeathed to him by America's 9/11 experiences and the Bush Doctrine's response to them, President Obama has been a reluctant, but effective follower of his predecessor's policies. In most other areas of American foreign policy though, his reluctance regarding American primacy and power has become administration policy, enshrined in the Obama Doctrine.

This president aspires to greatness and for him that means successful transformation of America's role abroad and the nature of its political identity at home. The real Obama Doctrine is the president's vehicle for transforming America's primacy abroad to more closely resemble the tenants of liberal internationalism. Exercising limited, embedded and unobtrusive primacy frees the president to pursue what are clearly his most cherished presidential ambitions, domestic "national building" consistent with the president's view of America's past political and moral failures and the policies needed to redeem its moral legitimacy and promise.

REFERENCES

[1] Stephan Glain, "Muslim Brotherhood official says West is neglecting Egypt," *Washington Post*, February 3, 2012.

[2]   "President-elect Obama fifth press conference. Transcript," December 1, 2008. At:http://blogs.suntimes.com/sweet/2008/12/presidentelect_obama_fifth_pre.html (Accessed February 5, 2012), emphasis added.

[3]   *Cf.*, Michael Grunwald, "Obama Power Will be in the White House, Not Cabinet," *Time,* December 16, 2008; see also Jonathan Martin, "West Wing on Steroids in Obama W.H.," *Politico*, January 25, 2009; Gerald F. Seib, "Obama Will be a Hands-On Chief," *Wall Street Journal*, January 13, 2009.

[4]   Obama's very close friend and confidant, Marty Nesbitt, spoke of Obama's "supreme confidence." Quoted in David Mendell, *Obama: From Promise to Power* (New York: Harper Collins, 2007), p.154.

Peter Rouse, a thirty-year veteran of Capitol Hill recruited by Obama to organize his Senate office and who served as his chief of staff and is now Counselor to the President said, "that in his thirty years on Capitol Hill, he had never seen anyone with more faith in himself." Quoted in Jonathan Alter, *The Promise: President Obama, Year One* (New York: Simon and Schuster, 2010), p. 140.

[5]   Quoted in Alter, *The Promise*, p. 140.

[6]   Quoted in. Edward Luce and Daniel Dombey, "US Foreign Policy: Waiting on a Sun King," *Financial Times,* March 30, 2010.

[7]   Quoted in Mayhill Fowler, "Obama: No Need for Foreign Policy Help from V.P.," *Huffington Post*, April 7, 2008 (emphasis in original). Miss Fewer recorded candidate Obama's talk before a group of San Francisco supporters.

[8]   Clinton, "Foreign Policy Address... (emphasis added).

[9]   Barack Obama. *The Audacity of Hope* (New York: Three Rivers Press, 2006), p. 285.

[10]   For an argument that liberal internationalism is evolving see G. John Ikenberry, " Liberal Internationalism 3.0: America and the Dilemmas of Liberal World Order," *American Political Science Review*, (March 2009) 7:1, 71-87.

[11]   Oli R. Holsti. *Public Opinion and American Foreign Policy* (Ann Arbor, MI: University of Michigan Press, 1997), p. 139.

[12]   Holsti. *Public Opinion and American Foreign Policy*. p. 49.

[13]   Holsti. *Public Opinion and American Foreign Policy*. pp.49-50.

[14]   The analysis of redemption issues that follows draws on Stanley A. Renshon, *Barack Obama and the Politics of Redemption* (New York: Routledge Press, 2012).

[15]   "An authorized transcript of an Eye on Books author interview": "Barack Obama 'Dreams From My Father,'" Interview recorded 8/9/1995. Available at: http://www.eyeonbooks.com/obama_transcript.pdf (emphasis added) (accessed January 7, 2013).

[16]   "Senator Barack Obama's Announcement for President," Springfield, IL., February 10, 2007. Available at: http://www.barackobama.com/2007/02/10/remarks_of_senator_barack_obam_11.php (accessed July 14, 2010).

[17]   Quoted in Richard Wolffe, *Renegade: The Making of a President* (New York: Crown, 2009), p. 67.

[18]   Toby Harnden, "Barack Obama vows to 'change the world,'" *Telegraph*, October 17, 2008.

[19]   "President Barack Obama's Inaugural Address," January 21, 2009. Available at: http://www.whitehouse.gov/blog/inaugural-address/ (accessed June 28, 2010).

Understanding the Obama Doctrine

[20] Quoted in Robin Givhan, "Mussed for Success: Barack Obama's Smooth Wrinkles," *Washington Post*, August 111, 2006.

[21] Transcript, "Meet the Press," NBC, October 22, 2008 (emphasis added). Available at: http://www.msnbc.msn.com/id/15304689/# (accessed February 15, 2012).

[22] Quoted in Jackie Calmes, "Spotlight Fixed on Geithner, a Man Obama Fought to Keep," *New York Times*, November 12,2011.

[23] Barack Obama, "Remarks by President Barack Obama, Prague, Czech Republic, April 5, 2009." At: http://www.whitehouse.gov/the_press_office/Remarks-By-President-Barack-Obama-In-Prague-As-Delivered (accessed February 19, 2012).

[24] Robert Burns, "U.S. weighing steep nuclear arms cuts," Associated Press, February 14, 2012.

[25] Obama, "Remarks by President Barack Obama, Prague, Czech Republic.."

[26] Remarks by President Obama at Strasbourg Town Hall, April 3, 2009. Available at: http://www.whitehouse.gov/the_press_office/Remarks-by-President-Obama-at-Strasbourg-Town-Hall/ (accessed May 2, 2010).

[27] Barack Obama, "Renewing American Leadership," *Foreign Affairs*, July/August 2007, p.11.

[28] Obama, "Renewing American Leadership," p. 11.

[29] "Official Remarks of the United States President Barack Obama at the Opening Ceremony of the Fifth Summit of the Americas, Port of Spain, Trinidad & Tobago," April 17–19, 2009. Available at: http://www.summitamericas.org/V_Summit/remarks_usa_en.pdf (accessed May 9, 2010).

[30] "Transcript: Obama's Interview with Al Arabiya," January 27, 2009. Available at:http://www.alarabiya.net/articles/2009/01/27/65087.html (accessed May 9, 2010).

[31] Transcript: Obama's Interview with Al Arabiya."

[32] "Remarks by President Obama to the Turkish Parliament," Turkish Grand National Assembly Complex Ankara, Turkey. April 6, 2009. Available at: www.whitehouse.gov/the_press_office/Remarks-By-President-Obama-To-The-Turkish-Parliament (accessed May 9, 2010).

[33] Daniel W. Drezner, "Does Obama Have a Grand Strategy?," *Foreign Affairs*, July/August, 2011.

[34] Found Ajami, " A Kosovo Model for Syria," *Wall Street Journal*, February 10, 2012.

[35] Elliot Abrams, "The Obama Doctrine, *The Weekly Standard*, February 13, 2012.

[36] Roger Cohen, "Doctrine of Silence,"*New York Times*, November 28, 2011; conservative critics have also noticed this element, see Thomas Donnelly, " The Obama Way of War," *The Weekly Standard*, January 30, 2012.

[37] Ryan Lizza, "The Consequentialist: How the Arab Spring remade Obama's Foreign Policy, *The New Yorker*, May 2, 2011.

[38] David E. Sanger, *Confront and Conceal: Obama's Secret Wars and Surprising Use of American Power*. New York Crown, 2012.

[39] These three elements considered together raise the issue risk permissiveness/acceptance that space limitation preclude from treating in detail in this analysis.

[40] Barack Obama, "Remarks by the President on Ending the War in Iraq," The White House, October 21, 2011 (emphasis added). At: http://www.whitehouse.gov/the-press-office/2011/10/21/remarks-president-ending-war-iraq (accessed February 11, 2011.

[41] Barack Obama, "Remarks by the President on the Way Forward in Afghanistan," The White House, June 22, 2011 (emphasis added). At : http://www.whitehouse.gov/the-press-office/2011/06/22/remarks-president (accessed February 11, 2012.

[42] Barack Obama, "Remarks by the President in State of the Union Address," U.S. Capitol, January 27, 2010. At: http://www.whitehouse.gov/the-press-office/remarks-president-state-union-address (accessed February 11, 2012).

[43] Katie Couric, "Obama: Surge Doesn't Meet Long-Term Goals," CBS News, July 22, 2008 (emphasis added). Available at: http://www.cbsnews.com/stories/2008/07/22/eveningnews/main4283623.shtml (accessed July 31, 2010).

[44] George McGovern, "Acceptance Speech-Democratic National Convention," Miami, Fla., July 14,1972. At: http://www.4president.org/speeches/mcgovern1972acceptance.htm (accessed February 13, 2012.

[45] *The Washington Post* notes, "To achieve his debt-reduction goal, Obama would rely on an accounting maneuver that permits him to claim about $850 billion in savings over the next decade by ending the wars in Iraq and Afghanistan, a move Republicans have rejected as a gimmick. Obama would use a portion of those savings to finance new road and rail projects, rather than dedicating the full sum to lower deficits." See Lori Montgomery, "Obama's 2013 Budget Proposal Looks to Tame National Debt," *Washington Post*, February 10, 2012.

[46] In his 2012 State of the Union the president mentioned the grand projects like the "great projects that benefited everybody" he went on to say, "In the next few weeks, I will sign an executive order clearing away the red tape that slows down too many construction projects. But you need to fund these projects. Take the money we're no longer spending at war, use half of it to pay down our debt, *and use the rest to do some nation-building right here at home.*" See Barack Obama, "Remarks by the President in State of the Union Address," U.S. Capitol, January 27, 2012 (emphasis added). At: http://www.whitehouse.gov/the-press-office/2012/01/24/remarks-president-state-union-address (accessed February 11, 2012).

[47] David Rogers, "Obama gambles on costly initiatives, Politico, February 12, 2012.

[48] Robert Kagan, "Why the World Needs America," *Wall Street Journal*, February 11, 2012; see also Robert Kagan, *The World America Made.* New York: Alfred Knopf, 2012.

[49] Martin Jaques, "Imperial overreach is accelerating the global decline of America, *the guardian*, March 27, 2006.

[50] Christopher A. Preble, *The Power Problem.* Ithaca, NY: Cornell University Press, 2009.

[51] Christopher Layne, "The Unipolar Illusion: Why New Powers Will Rise," *International Security*, 17:4 (Spring 1993), pp. 5-51.

[52] Joel Achenbach, " Is debt downgrade an alarm bell for a great nation in decline?," *Washington Post*, August 10, 2011.

[53] Michael Mandelbaum, "America's Coming Retrenchment," *Foreign Affairs*, August 9, 2011; see also Michael Mandelbaum, *The Frugal Superpower: America's Global Leadership in a Cash Strapped Era* (New York: Public Affairs, 2010).

[54] Fareed Zakaria, *The Post-American World* (New York: Norton, 2008).

[55] Christopher Layne, "The Unipolar Illusion Revisited, *International Security*, 31:2 (Fall 2006) p. 9.

[56] When asked during a trio abroad in 2009, whether he believed in American exceptionalism, Obama said, "I believe in American exceptionalism, just as I suspect that the Brits believe in British exceptionalism and the Greeks believe in Greek exceptionalism." See "Transcript: President Obama News Conference," Strasbourg, France April 4, 2009. Available at: http://www.whitehouse.gov/the_press_office/News-Conference-By-President-Obama-4-04-2009 (Accessed February 13, 12).

[57] *Cf.*, "anyone who tells you that America is in decline, or that our influence has waned, doesn't know what they are talking about." See Barack Obama, "Remarks by the President in State of the Union Address, United States Capitol, Washington, D.C. January 24, 2012. At: http://www.whitehouse.gov/the-press-office/2012/01/24/remarks-president-state-union-address (accessed February 13, 2012).

[58] *Cf.,* "And America's moral example must always shine for all who yearn for freedom and justice and dignity. And because we've begun this work, tonight we can say that American leadership has been renewed and America's standing has been restored." See Barack Obama, "Remarks by the President in State of Union Address," United States Capitol, Washington, D.C. January 25, 2011. At: http://www.whitehouse.gov/the-press-office/2011/01/25/remarks-president-state-union-address (accessed February 13, 2012.).

[59] Barack Obama, "Remarks by the President on the Defense Strategic Review".

[60] Fred I. Greenstein, *The Hidden-Hand Presidency*. Baltimore, Md.: Johns Hopkins University Press, 1984.

[61] Ryan Lizza, "The Consequentialist: How the Arab Spring remade Obama's foreign policy," *The New Yorker*, May 2, 2011.

[62] Charles Krauthammer, "The Obama doctrine: Leading from behind," *Washington Post,* April 28, 2011.

[63] Adam Entous and Laura Meckler, "Libyan Raids Show Obama Doctrine in Action," Wall Street Journal, March 20, 2011.

[64] Edward Cody, "France pleads for military intervention as Gaddafi forces attack Libyan rebels," *Washington Post*, March 16, 2011.

[65] Scott Wilson and Karen DeYoung, " President Obama points to value of collective action," *Washington Post*, October 20, 2011.

[66] Scott Wilson, "On Libya, Obama willing to let allies take the lead," *Washington Post*, March 10, 2011.

[67] Quoted in Entous and Meckler, "Libyan Raids Show Obama Doctrine in Action"

[68] Ben Rhodes quoted in Wilson, "On Libya, Obama willing to let allies take the lead".

[69] Hillary Clinton, "Interview With Kim Ghattas of BBC," Rabat, Morocco February 26, 2012. At: http://m.state.gov/md184659.htm (accessed February 29, 2012)

[70] Paul Richter, "Obama administration takes back seat on Iran sanctions," *Los Angeles Times*, February 17, 2012.

[71] Rosh Rogan, "NATO Chief: Intervention Won't work in Syria," *Foreign Policy*: *The Cable*, February 29, 2012.

[72] Rasmussen quoted in Rogan.

[73] Shanker and Schmidt, "U.S. Plans Shift to Elite Units as It Winds Down in Afghanistan."

[74] Greg Miller and Julie Tate, "CIA shifts focus to killing targets," *Washington Post,* September 1, 2011.

In: Change in the White House?
Editor: Meena Bose

ISBN: 978-1-62948-920-9
© 2014 Nova Science Publishers, Inc.

Chapter 6

GEORGE W. BUSH AND BARACK OBAMA: FOREIGN POLICY DECISION MAKING

John P. Burke

ABSTRACT

This article compares the national security decision-making of Presidents George W. Bush and Barack Obama. Since the late 1980's, the "Scowcroft Model" for organizing that process has been utilized by all administrations, whether Democratic or Republican. It has provided the foundation for a well-organized deliberative process. But are its recommendations enough? The article seeks to explore what additional considerations might inform effective decision making. Attention focuses on the role of the national security advisor, the dynamics of key "principals," and presidential attention to and management of the national security system. Additional suggestions for effective decision making are explored.

Beginning with the National Security Act of 1947 and the creation of the National Security Council (NSC), a dilemma arose concerning how to organize the flow of advice and information to the NSC principals and the president and how to manage the NSC's deliberations. The 1947 act was largely silent with regard to what went on below the level of the Council; the process and the flow of information and advice did not figure into congressional and presidential input as legislation was crafted. President Harry Truman especially failed to fill in the void: he regarded the NSC as an intrusion on his decision-making prerogatives, had two weak "executive secretaries" of the NSC with an ineffective staff largely "detailed" from agencies and departments, and met infrequently with the Council until the onset of Korean War. His foreign policy deliberations were informed, essentially, by his close relationship to and trust in his savvy and knowledgeable secretary of state, Dean Acheson.

During the presidency of Dwight D. Eisenhower, a more effective system was put in place. It emerged with the creation, in 1953, of what came to be termed "policy hill": an inter-departmental Planning Board to vet policy options, followed by weekly NSC meeting presided over by the president, and then oversight of policy implementation by the Operations Coordinating Board. As well, the position of "NSC advisor" was created; that person played a key role in the Planning Board and as an "honest broker" in the deliberations of the NSC. [1] However, at the onset of the John F. Kennedy administration, these inter-agency planning and implementation efforts were viewed with suspicion and abolished; policy hill no longer existed. [2] Subsequent presidencies struggled with various arrangements to secure appropriate policy analysis and vetting below the level of the NSC principals. None proved very successful.

In 1987, the Iran-Contra scandal marked a low point in post-World War II foreign policy making, and it almost brought down Ronald Reagan's presidency. But it did lead to a series of recommendations for reform based on the analysis of the Tower Commission. One of its three principal members, former NSC advisor Brent Scowcroft (at that point, he had only served under Gerald Ford; he would serve again under George H. W. Bush) played the leading role. The "Scowcroft Model" proved enduring and has been essentially adopted by subsequent administrations whether Republican or Democratic. Its most notable features are meetings of the principals chaired by the NSC advisor in the absence of the president. Below that level, and informing its deliberations, are deputies' meetings chaired by the deputy NSC advisor and composed of department, agency and NSC staff representatives (much like the Eisenhower Planning Board). Their work, in turn, is assisted by a variety of working groups, again drawn from NSC staff and departmental personnel. Another component of the model, also derived from the lessons of Iran-Contra, concerns how roles are defined. The Tower Commission emphasized the need for presidential attention to and management of the deliberative process. Most importantly, it embraced the notion that the NSC advisor should act as an honest broker, attentive to full and fair policy analysis and deliberation and concerned with the quality of advice reaching the president and the effectiveness of procedures producing it.

Both the George W. Bush and Barack Obama presidencies provide evidence that while the Scowcroft model may solve some organizational difficulties—overcoming the haphazardness of Lyndon Johnson's Tuesday lunches or the isolation of the Kissinger-Nixon years—other factors remain in play that can be consequential for presidential decision making. The main body of this article will explore these. In sum, the model seems necessary but not sufficient. What do Bush's and Obama's decision making processes tell us about what else contributes of effective decision making? This will serve as my lens of analysis.

ADOPTING THE "SCOWCROFT MODEL"

It is important to note that the basic Scowcroft model has endured, starting from steps taken by Reagan's two post-Iran Contra NSC advisors—Frank Carlucci and Colin Powell— and by Scowcroft under G. H. W. Bush. It survived under Bill Clinton and G. W. Bush and now through the Obama presidency.

As his predecessors had done, Obama's basic structure was presented in a presidential directive, in this case Presidential Policy Directive #1 issued on February 13, 2009. Interestingly, it was made public on the same day--eight years earlier--that Bush had issued his, although for Bush it had a slightly different nomenclature: National Security Presidential Directive #1). [3] Statutory membership in the National Security Council had evolved a bit over Bush's two terms: the director of National Intelligence replaced the CIA director as statutory adviser to the NSC in late 2004 when that position was created, and the secretary of energy was added as a statutory member in 2007. [4] Designation of non-statutory NSC members and others invited to attend NSC meetings was slightly different than in the Bush years [5]. The Bush directive also specified that the vice president shall preside *at NSC meetings* in the president's absence and at his direction; similar language was not present in the Obama directive. [6]

Beyond membership in the Council, the basic structure of the NSC process remained the same: a principals' committee chaired by the NSC advisor, a deputies' committee below that chaired by the deputy NSC advisor, and a variety of working groups (now dubbed "Interagency Policy Committees"--IPCs) as the initial "main day-to-day fora for an interagency coordination of national security policy."[7] The Obama directive did not spell out the organization of these IPCs, rather they would be established at the discretion of the deputies' committee, and would be chaired by a staff member of the NSC (or National Economic Council—NEC--if appropriate).

Although some media commentary saw the 2009 directive as a major change in how foreign and national security policy would be formulated under Obama (e.g., a "sweeping overhaul of the National Security Council" according to the *Washington Post* [8]), in reality the shifts in NSC membership were not all that significant or atypical. More importantly, formal meetings of the NSC as the president's chief deliberative forum for decision making continued to remain largely a thing of the past. Instead, the president's meetings with the "principals" (sometimes smaller but also sometimes larger than the formal NSC membership, but largely overlapping nonetheless) and the meetings of the principals themselves that became the critical venues. Adoption of this meeting structure plus the rest of the Scowcroft model was the centerpiece of the February 13 directive. Organizational continuity rather than change was the more important order of the day.

THE ROLE OF THE NSC ADVISOR

One of the chief lessons that the Tower Commission drew from its analysis of Iran-Contra was that the role of the national security advisor was consequential in creating an effective deliberative process (and, likewise, if ill-defined could lead to scandal and peril, as had occurred under NSC advisors Robert McFarlane and Admiral John Poindexter, who were Iran-Contra's chief architects). The decision-making needs and predilections of the president do matter. (According to the Tower Commission, "Because the system is the vehicle through which the president formulates and implements his national security policy, it must adapt to each individual president's style and management philosophy"). [9] But the duties of the NSC advisor should not just be defined as simply someone doing the presidents bidding: a president may have poor decision-making instincts, which may need to be checked or otherwise compensated for. Nor, as in the case of Iran-Contra, should it be a matter of doing what a NSC advisor *believed* the president wanted (especially in Adm. Poindexter's role in the diversion of funds from the arms sales to Iran to the Contras in Nicaragua), while keeping the president and the other principals in the dark [10] Instead, while sometimes serving as a source of policy advice, the NSC advisor needs to be concerned with the full, fair, and balanced presentation of information and advice to the president and in the deliberations of those advising the president, as well as giving due attention to and management concern for the organizations and processes that bear upon foreign and national security policy decision making. This is what has come to be termed the "honest broker" role.

For both presidencies, that role proved difficult to achieve. Condoleezza Rice's tenure as Bush's first NSC advisor seemed promising at the start. She was a veteran of the Scowcroft NSC staff. At least initially, she seemed to embrace the idea of serving as an honest broker. In fact, the chapter in her memoirs, *No Higher Honor*, describing the operations of the NSC system and her job is titled "Honest Broker." [11] Moreover, the broker role was in Bush's mind when he picked Rice for the post in December 2000; she was, in his words, "both a good manager and an honest broker of ideas." [12] Yet, Rice's activities as a broker varied enormously during her tenure. At some decision points, the degree of brokerage was high. At others, it was low or absent. As well, Rice operated within a context of experienced and bureaucratically skilled players: Vice President Richard Cheney, Secretary of State Colin Powell, and Secretary of Defense Donald Rumsfeld. They would prove, at times, a difficult mix. None had future political ambitions, but all had policy stakes and the skill to pursue them.

Clearly, Rice enjoyed a close personal relationship to the president and was an important source of counsel. She does not seem to have exploited this relationship to her own benefit, and she was especially diligent that any advice she gave the president was done confidentially. In Rice's own words, "I have a very strong view about this, which is that the President does not need to read my views in the newspaper. Our discussions about my views are private." [13]

The early record of the Bush presidency through the events of September 11 and the early months of the war in Afghanistan often illustrates Rice's concern about the quality of the deliberative process. As Bob Woodward relates, for example, Bush began to grow impatient and wanted quick action and results: "Rice knew this characteristic. Yet doubt could be the handmaiden of sound policy. Careful reconsideration is a necessary part of any decision-making process. Rice felt it was her job to raise caution flags, even red lights if necessary, to urge the president to rethink." [14]

However, once war with Iraq loomed, Rice's role seemed to change. The decision process seemed less deliberative and more akin to a choice that was "slipped into," with deliberations quickly turning to issues of "how" and "when," not "why" or "whether." [15] CIA Director George Tenet would later write that, "There was no serious debate that I know of within the administration about the imminence of the Iraqi threat. . . . Nor was there ever a significant discussion regarding enhanced containment or the costs and benefits of such an approach versus full-out planning for overt and covert regime change." [16]

Planning for the reconstruction of a post-war Iraq and then putting those plans into action once Saddam Hussein's regime fell were particularly problematic. According to Tenet, "The president was not served well, because the NSC became too deferential to a postwar strategy that was not working. . . . the NSC did not fulfill its role. The NSC avoided slamming on the brakes to force the discussions with the Pentagon and everyone else that was required in the face of a deteriorating situation." [17]

As Bush's first term evolved, a number of accounts suggested that the NSC system—the Scowcroft machinery--was not working well. At lower-level interagency meetings, according to one report, "the Defense Department sometimes doesn't even bother to show up." [18] According to *several* reports, some State and Defense Department officials complained that the situation had become "dysfunctional." "Decisions go unmade at the deadlocked deputies' meetings or get kicked back or ignored by the president's principals, his top advisers." [19] Other accounts, it should be noted in fairness, discern a more effective process, especially through the efforts of Rice's deputy (and eventual successor as NSC advisor) Stephen Hadley. [20] But Hadley also was subject to the criticism that deputies' meetings were too inconclusive and that he was too compliant with Defense's bureaucratic tactics. [21]

From time to time, reports surfaced indicating that Rice had difficulty managing the higher levels of the process. Some examples:

> Officials who have left the administration have said she was a loose administrator, allowing disputes to fester within the National Security Council. [22]

> Her inability to rein in other powerful advisers, critics say, has helped lead to little planning for the occupation in Baghdad, stalled negotiations between the Israelis and Palestinians, and no success in stopping North Korea from making nuclear weapons. [23]

> Many experts consider her one of the weakest national security advisers in recent history in terms of managing interagency conflicts. [24]

Rumsfeld is quite explicit in his memoirs about Rice's shortcomings. He especially notes "issues with Rice's management of the NSC process." Meetings "were not well organized." "Frequent last-minute changes to the times of meetings and to the subject matter made it difficult for the participants to prepare…" NSC staff "often was late in sending papers for meetings…" Summaries of discussion prepared by NSC staff "were often sketchy and didn't always fit with my recollections." [25]

Rumsfeld especially was unhappy about Rice's attempts to achieve consensus among the principals rather than bring their diverging policy views directly to the president: "The most notable feature of Rice's management of the interagency process was her commitment, whenever possible, to 'bridging' differences between the agencies, rather than bringing those differences to the President for decisions." [26] In his view, "Rice seemed to believe that it was a personal shortcoming on her part if she had to ask the President to resolve interagency differences. She studiously avoided forcing clear-cut decisions that might result in one cabinet officer remerging as a 'winner' and another as a 'loser.' By taking elements from the positions of different agencies and trying to combine them in one approach, she seemed to think she could make each agency a winner in policy discussions." [27]

Yet, to be fair to Rice, others felt that she handled the situation well given the circumstances, especially in dealing with a tough and experienced cast of characters. In the view of Vice President Cheney, "This is not a shy, retiring group, but that's good. The challenge for Condi and the task that she handles very well is to referee that group and that process and deliver to the President their best thinking and see to it that everyone gets an opportunity to be heard." [28] So too for Treasury Secretary Paul O'Neill, according to his biographer: "He liked Rice and trusted her. She was clearly doing her best to be an honest broker in foreign affairs—a role desperately needed in economic affairs and domestic policy." [29] Nor did O'Neill share Rumsfeld's view that Rice was overly pre-occupied with consensus: "She doesn't drive to consensus. Rather she drives toward clarity. Then he [Bush] decides what the consensus is." [30] In short, fulfilling the role of honest broker proved a challenge for Rice.

In the early Obama presidency, difficulties also arose for the NSC advisor, but of a different sort. General James L. Jones, who served until October 2010, brought to the position a strong military background. He had been Commandant of the Marine Corps and Supreme Allied Commander to NATO. He had also served during the G. W. Bush presidency as a special envoy to the Mid-East and as head of a non-partisan commission that examined the effectiveness of Iraq's police forces in 2006. At least initially, he seemed to embrace the role of honest broker. His first appearance on the Sunday talk shows did not occur until May 10, 2009; his first major public address was on May 27, before the Atlantic Council. He worked behind the scenes to bring climate and energy issues within the purview of the NSC's deliberations. But he also appeared to be less a policy advocate, at least to the extent that he did not bring a broader geopolitical vision of national security and foreign affairs to the job, compared to some of his predecessors. Had the election of 2008 gone otherwise, he might have emerged as a key figure in a John McCain administration (with whom he had long-standing ties).

Jones's tenure in the job proved to be a bit rocky from the start. Reports repeatedly surfaced in the media that he was likely to leave the administration. Most telling was commentary concerning his standing with President Obama. Two of Jones's key aides, Tom Donilon and Denis McDonough, were perceived as having a closer relationship to the president. Jones was portrayed as the "outsider" in the tightly knit community of Obama advisers. [31] Donilon would eventually succeed him.

This latter dynamic seems particularly important and it contrasts with Rice's close ties to Bush. Donilon, Jones's chief deputy, had been Secretary of State Warren Christopher's chief of staff and then assistant secretary of state for public affairs during the Clinton years. He was at the center of the 2008 foreign policy team, and he also had ties to Vice President Joe Biden. [32] He was also close to Rahm Emanuel, Obama's first White House chief of staff who strongly urged Jones to select Donilon as his deputy. [33]

McDonough, who initially served as the NSC's director of strategic communications and then as NSC chief of staff, had been a longtime staffer to Senate Majority Leader Tom Daschle (D-S.D.). He had worked in John Podesta's Center for American Progress think-tank before joining the Obama campaign as a top foreign policy adviser. Podesta, Clinton's last chief of staff, was placed in charge of Obama's 2008 presidential transition. Both Donilon and McDonough had extensive connections to congressional and Democratic Party circles. Both became part of the tight inner circle of the Obama campaign team.

But their appointments to the NSC staff did not necessarily serve Jones well. According to one account, while Jones "has been the official head of the president's White House foreign policy team, in practical terms that role has been filled in many ways for the past two years by Mr. Donilon and Mr. McDonough."[34]. According to another, Jones's "condition for initially taking the job—that he would be the last one to see Obama on the most pressing national security issues of the day—was often unmet." [35]

Jones's frequent trips abroad also were a contributing factor that weakened his influence. As the *New York Times* noted at the time of Jones's resignation, he "spent a lost of time wrangling with allies and adversaries alike on Mr. Obama's behalf. . . but wielded less influence in the White House, where Mr. Donilon and Mr. McDonough spoke more regularly with Mr. Obama and served as the go-to aides for staff members trying to gauge where the president stood." [36] Diplomatic activity on the part of the NSC advisor has often been problematic for the NSC advisor. In Jones's case, his trips abroad often removed him from the center of action, day-to-day operations often fell to Donilon; Jones "never seemed to click" with the president. [37]

Although Jones proved to an influential adviser to the president during the period when troop increases in Afghanistan were under consideration, he may have been more a weak—and even detached--coordinator in other areas. At the 100-day mark, *Time*'s Joel Klein noted that sources indicated that Jones seems to "attend meetings rather than lead them" and that he "needs to drive the agenda." Moreover, with a high powered team—Hillary Clinton at State, Robert Gates continuing at Defense, and envoys George Mitchell and Richard Holbrooke—Jones was failing to establish himself as "first among equals." [38] Similarly, in the view of David Rothkopf, "The national security adviser needs to be behind the president," however Jones is not "seen as a guy in the room." [39] Bob Woodward would later write that "If Obama wanted something followed up after meetings, he turned to Donilon not Jones. Donilon was the go-to guy, answering the calls that came from the Oval Office." [40] Likewise, according to Woodward, Jones "often felt sidelined" by then chief of staff Emanuel who often dealt directly with Donilon. Jones once told Emanuel, "I'm the national security adviser. . . . come see me." "Jones hadn't realized what a clique the White House was," Woodward notes. [41] As a result, according to Kevin Marsh, the author of one of the first scholarly assessments of Jones's tenure as NSC advisor, Donilon "quickly, and quietly, supplanted Jones as the primary national security and foreign policy advisor at the NSC." At best, Jones was a weak" administrator." [42]

Jones's tenure also is important in understanding the role of the deputy NSC advisor, particularly as the chair of the deputies' committee. Donilon was perceived as very cognizant of the importance of the position and its part in the NSC process. He was apparently tough and effective at the deputy job.

But his activities were not without criticism, especially as the debate over policy in Afghanistan and Pakistan took center stage in the fall of 2009. Donilon was a policy advocate and not just a manager. Secretary of Defense Gates even warned Jones that the possibility of Donilon replacing him would be a "disaster." According to Woodward, "Gates felt that Donilon did not respect the military or treat its senior leadership with sufficient respect." [43]

Jones may have shared similar concerns. At one point, Woodward relates, he was thinking about his successor and discussed with his deputy "what you are doing right and what you may be doing wrong." Jones valued Donilon's managerial skills, but felt that he had lacked needed experience: "You have no direct understanding of these places. You have no credibility with the military. You should go overseas." Jones, like Gates, may also have felt that Donilon was too impetuous in his judgments. After the January 2010 earthquake in Haiti, Donilon felt the military response was too slow and rushed to advise Jones to relieve the commanding general. Jones told him to "calm down." He knew the general and he would get the job done; by the end of the month over 20,000 troops were in Haiti. [44] Later Jones would tell him, "you frequently pop-off with declarations about places you've never been, leaders you've never met, or colleagues you work with." [45]

Gates's and Jones's concerns may illustrate a flip-side of Donilon's experience. .

He was long on politics but perhaps short on policy substance and needed demeanor. Not only was his work in the 1990s in the State Department managerial and often focused on media communications, prior to that he had been a campaign aide to Jimmy Carter in 1980, Walter Mondale in 1984, and Biden in 1988. His DNA was strongly political. As well, Donilon had unprecedented power in the deputy job. As one official noted, "Operationally

Tom has been the National Security Council since the start. Jones was kind of a CEO and Tom has been the COO." [46] While there have been important deputies: Gates under Scowcroft and Sandy Berger under Anthony Lake, none was ever touted as the NSC's chief operating officer.

McDonough, the first prominent NSC chief of staff, was also a powerful player. His relationship with the president was especially important during Jones's tenure. As one profile piece in the *New York Times* observed in July 2010, "Forget Secretary of State Hillary Rodham Clinton or Defense Secretary Robert M. Gates. When it comes to national security," it is McDonough "who is so close to the president that his colleagues—including his superiors—often will not make a move on big issues without checking with him first." Even Jones noted, "It is a big asset for all of us to have Denis, who has known the president for so long. He knows how he thinks about issues." [47] But McDonough's clout, like Donilon's, may have had a downside for Jones. As James Mann notes, "If you got a request from Jim Jones, he might or might not be speaking for the president. If you got a request from Denis McDonough, he's asking on behalf of the president himself." [48]

Since Jones's departure, Donilon's elevation to his job, and McDonough's replacement of Donilon in the chief deputy position, media accounts of the internal workings and dynamics of the NSC system have been few. But the available evidence seems to indicate significant change once Jones was out of the picture. That Donilon proved to be a different kind of NSC advisor than Jones is clear. Some evidence indicates that he has been as attentive to process as he was in the deputy position. While not a grand strategist in the mold of a Henry Kissinger or Zbigniew Brzezinski, "Donilon is a master of process, enforcing order and structure for a president who deeply values both." According to Ben Rhodes, one of the deputy NSC advisors along with McDonough, "He's very devoted to a rigorous process. When things are chaotic in the world, the first thing he'll do is set up a process." [49] According to David Axelrod, one of Obama's chief political advisors, "Tom is completely about the job itself and serving the president, and that creates a lot of comfort." [50] Another account notes that participants "must come to meetings prepared to speak for their bosses. Meeting summaries are typed up and circulated to participants. Assignments are handed out; dissenting opinions are taken to Obama for a final airing, if need be." [51]

Other accounts, however, indicate problems. According to Rosa Brooks, who served as a counselor in the Defense Department early in the Obama presidency, the situation remains "dysfunctional." The NSC staff "is squabbling and demoralized," "strategic planning shops. . .have been marginalized and disempowered," and "the interagency process is in a state of permanent crisis." [52] In her view, Donilon's tenure has proven problematic.

Donilon's personal closeness with Obama is notable and clearly different from what Jones experienced. But the question that remains unresolved is whether Donilon has served as an honest broker. Enforcing order in the NSC system may be a positive sign (it eluded Rice at times). But is it order for the sake of personal control? Or is it order to ensure that the NSC process is effectively developing, vetting, and bringing appropriate options to the highest levels? Formulating the substance of Obama's foreign policy is another issue. As one profile piece in the *Los Angeles Times* noted, "To the degree that he [Donilon] has a foreign policy vision, it has to do with priorities." [53] But are priorities enough? How are they defined? And by whom? According to Brooks, both process and strategic outcome have suffered; "President Obama should find some decent managers. . .honest brokers who are capable of listening, prioritizing, delegating, and holding people accountable for the results." [54]

On July 1, 2013, Susan Rice replaced Donilon as NSC advisor. Rice, who had served as U.S. ambassador to the United Nations during the first term, was yet another longtime associate of the president. Like her predecessors, she too will face the challenge of serving as an honest broker and an effective NSC advisor.

THE ROLES AND INTERPERSONAL DYNAMICS
OF THE PRINCIPALS

Defining the roles of the other key players is also consequential. There are a number of issues here with bearing on broader decision making. What experience does the president bring to the table? If that is slim in the area of foreign policy (a possible similarity here for both Bush and Obama, both of whom had little prior foreign policy experience before assuming office [55]), stronger and more experienced principals may be needed to compensate at State, Defense, and elsewhere. But a strong team may call for more vigilance on the part of the NSC advisor, lest the playing field become unbalanced. It also likely leads to a more difficult job for the NSC advisor.

The personalities of key players matter, especially how they might affect their interactions with each other and the president. G.W. Bush surely brought knowledge and experience on board with his selection of Cheney as vice president, Rumsfeld at Defense, and Powell at State. But it was often a troubled mix: Powell was often the odd-man out, especially as the Iraq war loomed. Most notably, he failed to develop a close relationship with Bush. Recall that Powell had to resort to back-channel efforts—arranged through Rice in the summer of 2002—to press his case with Bush that deliberations were too focused on war plans not the basic case for war, that a United Nations resolution was needed resuming inspections, and that a post-war Iraq might bring negative consequences—the so-called Pottery Barn rule of "You break it, you own it." [56]

Cheney and Rumsfeld were powerful and bureaucratically-skilled actors who made NSC advisor Condoleezza Rice's job as a coordinator and honest broker especially difficult. Her generational and experiential differences with the other principals were marked. In her memoirs, Rice especially notes that "I am convinced that Don simply resented the role I had to play as national security advisor." [57] Moreover, "This animosity toward my role resulted in complaints about the NSC process." But "Don wasn't party to my conversations with the President about matters before the NSC." On occasion, it was Bush who "directed me to try one more time to find common ground." And she sometimes bore the blame for a decision that had been made by the president: sometimes "it is preferable for the national security advisor to deliver the news that a Cabinet secretary had been overruled than to have the President do it." [58]. The length to which both Rice and Rumsfeld go in detailing their criticisms of each other in their respective memoirs (both of which appeared in 2011, Rumsfeld's first) is quite notable.

In addition to his criticisms of Rice, Rumsfeld's problems with Powell are also aired in his book, although at much lesser length. One example: "Though Powell and the other members of the NSC received numerous policy memos from me, I rarely received memos from him suggesting approaches or providing insights into his thinking." Memos from State "were largely process-oriented and rarely laid out concrete policy recommendations." [59]

According to Rice, the Rumsfeld-Powell relationship was very problematic: there was a basic "distrust" between them. And it had serious impact on lower-levels of the NSC system, making them "largely incapable" of functioning effectively. Rumsfeld was "secretive," and claimed to delegate, but

> then didn't always ratify what his lieutenants had done. The people who worked for him were fearful of his wrath. The atmosphere in the Pentagon was one where nothing was really settled until the secretary had opined. That handicapped the Deputies Committee. . . and made necessary the very Principals meetings that Don detested. [60]

"We managed the tensions between us," Rice notes, "But we did clash with increasing frequency as time went on." On the other hand, Powell "always seemed very comfortable with my role and our personal relationship." [61] A final Rice observation, looping back to Rumsfeld: Powell "asked me many times why I didn't go to the President to 'discipline' Defense for any number of sins of omission or commission, some imagined, some not." [62]

On the positive side, Rice did develop a close relationship with the president. As Bush would later write, "I had grown very close to Condi Rice. She could read my mind and my moods. We shared a vision of the world, and she wasn't afraid to let me know when she disagreed with me." [63] A close relationship also existed between the president and Vice President Cheney. Still, there were dyads of conflict. These interpersonal tensions, differing understandings of others' roles, and at times a failure to "buy-in" to the workings of the NSC process had effects at a number of levels. At the top, according to one account, the principals "tend to revisit unresolved issues or reopen decisions already made by the president." [64] Interpersonal tensions among the principals also were noted in the media, although accounts of the degree of tension vary. [65] Some reports indicated that disagreements "have been allowed to spin out of control." [66] Yet, in Rumsfeld's view, personal tensions were "were no more pronounced and the debates were no more epic or intractable in the Bush administration than I had seen in previous administrations. Indeed, if anything, the tensions were noticeably less." [67]

Obama's team appears to have been less problematic in terms of the relationships among key players (National Security Advisor Jones perhaps the exception). However, caution must be a guide: less is currently known at this point in time. Although Gates often disagreed with the White House position during the 2009 contentious debate over Afghanistan, he remained at the Pentagon until his 2011 replacement by CIA Director Leon Panetta. Hillary Clinton's appointment at State could have been a disaster in the making, given the strained relations from the 2008 presidential race and her own political stature. However, nothing of the sort developed to a significant degree. Disagreements remained largely internal, even when she favored a different policy course. As one early account noted, she "has shown no daylight from the foreign policy inclinations of the president she agreed to serve, from supporting engagements with Iran to his earlier tough stance on Israeli settlements." "Clinton has quieted most of the doubters, forged strong alliances with the key department under secretaries and assistant secretaries, pursued an exhausting travel schedule with no sign of sweat, and most of all proven herself loyal to a president she once ran against." [68] Most notable was the lack of conflict and tension between Clinton and Gates. As one account concluded, "Clinton's advisers told me that, during her first two years at Foggy Bottom, Clinton agreed with Gates on every major issue." [69] The two differed, however, on the proper U.S. response to the Libyan uprising in 2011.

Still, there were areas where tension was present. One was between the director of national intelligence, Adm. Dennis Blair, and the CIA. There were clashes over their respective bounds of authority, an intelligence-sharing agreement with France, and Blair's efforts to trim the CIA's covert action programs. Blair was replaced in May 2010. [70] Richard Holbrooke, the special envoy to Pakistan and Afghanistan, also clashed with the Obama inner circle. [71] Another problematic area arose between some of Obama's civilian advisers, especially Donilon and some of the NSC staff, and his military commanders. There were strong differences, especially over the latter's request for increased military forces in Afghanistan and then, later, on the pace of their withdrawal in 2011 and 2012. It will be interesting to see what further light is shed on the internal dynamics of the Obama presidency once their memoirs begin to appear in print.

Finally, James Mann notes an important difference in tenure between the Bush and Obama foreign policy teams. By the end of Obama's third year in office only Hillary Clinton remained among the top eight foreign policy officials. By contrast, at the same point in the Bush presidency, all eight continued in office. This should not be taken to suggest that stability is better, according to Mann. Rather, the tenure of the team posed different dilemmas for each president. For Bush, longer service may have worked against a fresh look at policy and a lack of attention to what was not going well. For Obama, the problem was adjusting to a continually changing stream of key advisors. [72] It may have further bolstered his reliance on his NSC team of Donilon, McDonough, and Rhodes. According to Mann, Obama has "relied heavily upon his own small, informal network of close aides." Trust had been formed in the 2008 campaign, but "They had no previous experience in carrying out foreign policy at the State or Defense Departments, although some had worked on Capitol Hill." This is in marked contrast to the campaign advisers in the area of foreign policy of Obama's predecessors—Zbigniew Brzezinski for Jimmy Carter, Scowcroft and James Baker for G. H. W. Bush, Anthony Lake for Clinton, and Rice for G.W. Bush. All were deeply experienced and then held key positions after Inauguration Day, Mann notes. [73]

In fact, the contrast in backgrounds with the Bush team is quite notable on this score: all of Bush's key principals came to their posts with significant prior experience in foreign and national security affairs. Some had even served in each other's positions. Cheney had been secretary of defense, as well as White House chief of staff. Rumsfeld had served in both of those positions as well as ambassador to NATO. Powell had been NSC advisor and then chairman of the Joint Chiefs of Staff. Rice had served on the NSC staff. Hadley had been an NSC staff member, an assistant secretary of defense, and a staff member of the Tower Commission. For Obama, the one comparable figure was Gates, a holdover from Bush at Defense.

PRESIDENTIAL MANAGEMENT

Each of these presidents differed in their favored patterns and proclivities for making decisions. Both were inclined to delve into matters when they arose; I don't think it is fair to regard either as disengaged or unconcerned. However, Bush was more prone to delegate and to rely upon his subordinates. Obama seems to press more often for details and to be more proactive in exploring alternatives. Bush favored oral briefings, while Obama seems more inclined to supplement them to a greater degree with written material for background and with memoranda laying out clear policy options [74].

Still, both turned mostly to those whom they knew and with whom they were comfortable and familiar; both increasingly came to favor their own policy instincts. There is an element of isolation and insularity for each, albeit slightly different in origin and practice. Interestingly, for neither of them was foreign and national security policy a knowledgeable terrain pre-presidential wise, at least in comparison to some of their predecessors.

Both exhibit a shared shortcoming in managing their deliberative processes that is of utmost importance: domestic policy concerns were initially more primary and weighed more heavily than foreign affairs. And here we find common but not successful similarity in terms of managerial outcome.

Let us return to the Tower Commission, "A president must at the outset provide guidelines. . . . If his advisors are not performing as he likes, only the president can intervene." "The president is ultimately responsible for the operation of this system. If rancorous infighting develops...only he can deal with them." [75] In the view of Walt Rostow, Lyndon Johnson's second NSC advisor, "it takes a very strong president to insist that these people get along. It's only with a very strong president that these clashes you have described can't happen." [76] For Colin Powell, if the president "finds himself not getting the right advice, then he ought to fix the people or the processes that are at work." [77] And here we find a challenge that was problematic to both of these presidents. While effective management must pervade any organization at a number of different levels, it is also one that rises to the very top. In the case before us, it is often a *presidential* responsibility, not just one for administrative subordinates.

For G.W. Bush, discipline and order prevailed in meetings with his advisers (he would often tap his watch if someone arrived even a minute or two late). But other problems remained. Most notably, he did not effectively "ride herd," on some of his principals, especially when some, like Rumsfeld, sought to circumvent the system. Tellingly, he later recounts, "At times, Don frustrated me with his abruptness toward military leaders and members of my staff." "Still, I liked Don." [78]

According to Rice, Bush knew that "Don and Colin did not get along, and decision making was difficult." [79] As Bush himself recounts, while the two were "respectful to each other in my presence. Over time I realized they were like a pair of old duelers who kept their own pistols in their holsters, but let their seconds and thirds fire away." Bush was "irritated" at press leaks detailing the in-fighting. "I announced at NSC meetings that the squabbling and leaks were damaging our credibility. . . I spoke to Don and Colin individually. I asked Dick and Condi to work behind the scenes. I instructed Condi's skillful deputy, Steve Hadley, to tell the seconds and thirds to cool it." But, as Bush concedes, "Nothing worked." [80] In Rice's view, "My task was to work around the personal distrust between the two men, a task that became harder as the problems became more difficult." [81] All failed at addressing the problems at hand.

For Obama, while the details of his managerial practices are somewhat less well-known, there are glimpses indicating similar problems. According to Marsh, Jones's difficulties as national security advisor were not just those of his own making: "Obama's presidential management style was critical to relegating Jones to a weak administrator." [82] Just as Bush never "clicked" with Gen. Powell, Obama never did with Gen. Jones. Moreover, despite his promise to Jones that he would be the last one to see the president on pressing issues, it was the president's preference to consult directly and extensively with Jones's subordinates. Obama's trust in those familiar to him mattered greatly: the campaign team and his senatorial staff associates were more favored and familiar sources of information and advice. This pattern clearly occurred with Donilon and McDonough during Jones's tenure as NSC advisor. But it also reappeared during Richard Daley's tenure as chief of staff. Commentary following Daley's resignation in January 2012 often stressed his difficulty fitting in with the president's inner circle. The common denominator was the president and his lack of ease or, perhaps, trust with unfamiliar outsiders. As well, although a "hands-on" decision maker, Obama sometimes performed poorly in managing his policy team. There were no honest brokers and much fell on Obama's own shoulders: as Pfiffner notes, "he chose to control the details of policy-making himself." [83] In Brooks' view, Obama "is the author of his own lackluster foreign policy. . . he has presided over an exceptionally dysfunctional and un-visionary national security team." [84] Her critique may be too tough. Still, proper presidential management of the policy team and interest in the workings of the broader policy system remained problematic in both presidencies.

CONCLUSION

Utilization of the Scowcroft model seems to resolve some of the organizational difficulties present in pre-Tower Commission presidencies. But it only takes effective national-security decision making so far. Both the G. W. Bush and Obama presidencies indicate that much remains unattended to that may have a significant effect on performance and, ultimately, policy. Properly defining the role of the NSC advisor is central. The roles and interpersonal dynamics of the principals are equally consequential. The presidential task of managing the system and securing allegiance to the workings of the system matters. Presidential efforts in fostering the cooperation of key players in making the system work is also paramount. In a way, both are the glue that makes the process work effectively. Only the president has the power and authority to make the system function for the best; the president is the team leader.

Finally, most elusive of all is determining the substance of foreign policy ideas and a broader vision of national goals. Substance and vision are especially needed when the foreign policy context dramatically shifts and evolves, as the international challenges following 9/11 most recently and readily attest. Determining a wise course has been a continuing problem for both of these presidents. For G.W. Bush, the cautious realism of his father's presidency shifted in a more idealist direction after 9/11. For Obama, there has been more of a delicate balance between the two, but with the public rhetoric often cast in idealist tones.

The Scowcroft model is organizational in its essence and provides guidance on process. It resolves some of the organizational difficulties that vexed earlier presidencies; it appears to have withstood the test of time. But it does not necessarily provide substance and content in its own right, as I suspect he would agree. It can sift and refine, but it is dependent upon its participants to bring to it policy substance, strategy, and vision. It seems to work best when there is president in power and key players who already possess that deep experience. (i.e., G. H. W. Bush and Scowcroft). But it becomes more problematic when a president enters office lacking foreign policy experience and enlists aides who are drawn from his/her pre-presidential jobs or from the political campaign—or both.

There are remedies: even the defense and national security-policy informed Eisenhower convened a number of teams at the start of his presidency—"Project Solarium"—to fundamentally re-examine the foundation of strategies and tactics for dealing with the Cold War. But, in Eisenhower's case, the nation was benefited by a president and a secretary of state, John Foster Dulles, who had deep experience. Where that is lacking, effective organization is helpful, but not definitive. Vision, ideas, strategy, and tactics matter—they are the substance for policy choice. Plus, they are also difficult to define early on in a new presidency: contemporary presidential transitions leave many sub-cabinet positions unfilled. On the eve of September 11, 2001, roughly fifty percent of the sub-cabinet had not yet been confirmed; so too for Obama in 2009.

These are realities of presidential politics and leadership. They present challenges--beyond organizational design and "Scowcroftian" models--with which presidents must cope, manage, decide, and hopefully move successfully forward.

AUTHOR'S NOTES

John P. Burke is the John G. McCullough Professor of Political Science at the University of Vermont. His most recent book is *Honest Broker: The National Security Advisor and Presidential Decision Making* (2009).

REFERENCES

[1] I will follow the White House spelling convention of NSC "advisor" rather than "adviser," which is commonly used in media accounts, save where source material differs. White House usage, however, favors "adviser" for other positions. On the role of the NSC advisor as "honest broker," see John P. Burke, *Honest Broker: The National Security Advisor and Presidential Decision Making*, (College Sta., Tx: Texas A&M University Press, 2009).

[2] On the changes in the national security system from Eisenhower to Kennedy, see Meena Bose, *Shaping and Signaling Presidential Policy: The National Security Decision Making of Eisenhower and Kennedy*, (College Sta., Tx: Texas A&M University Press, 1998).

[3] For whatever reason (largely "territorial" I suspect), these presidential directives and other parts of the memoranda process are given different labels from one administration to another.

[4] The current statutory members are the president, vice president, secretary of state, secretary of defense, and secretary of energy; the chair of the Joints Chiefs of Staff and the director of National Intelligence serve as statutory advisers.

[5] Both presidents included, as non-statutory NSC members, the secretary of the treasury, the secretary of homeland security, the White House chief of staff, and the NSC advisor. Obama also included the UN ambassador and his attorney general (Bush only authorized attendance for the latter when matters of constitutional or legal import

arose). Under the Obama directive the White House legal counsel could attend any meetings, as could the deputy NSC advisor, who shall "serve as secretary." When international economic issues were on the agenda, the secretary of commerce, the U.S. trade representative, the director of the National Economic Council, and the chair of the Council of Economic Advisers were specified as regular attendees. When matters of homeland security or counter-terrorism were on the agenda, the White House homeland security adviser was invited, as was the president's science adviser when science and technology issues were under discussion. Under Bush, the White House legal counsel was invited to meetings at the discretion of the NSC advisor. The director of the Office of Management and Budget was also invited to attend when budgetary matters were under discussion. Both directives specified that other officials shall be invited to attend when appropriate.

[6] It is not clear whether this provision for the vice president to preside at NSC meetings in the president's absence proved at all consequential over the course of the Bush presidency. It may have simply reflected an early attempt by Vice President Cheney to control the NSC process, one which he quickly lost in practice when Rice was designated to preside at meetings of the NSC principals in the president's absence (the difference being whether such meetings were NSC meetings or principals' meetings).

[7] Under Bush, these were dubbed "Policy Coordination Committees" (PCCs) and served- -note the identical language in the Obama directive-- as the initial, "main day-to-day fora for an interagency coordination of national security policy." Under Bush, six regional PCCs were established by the directive, with each to be chaired by an official at the rank of under secretary or assistant secretary, as designated by the secretary of state. Eleven functional PCCs were established, with their chairs determined by the NSC advisor, NEC advisor, State, Treasury, or Defense, depending on the policy area.

[8] Karen DeYoung, "Obama's NSC Will Get New Power," *Washington Post*, February 8, 2009.

[9] John Tower, Edmund Muskie, and Brent Scowcroft, *The Tower Commission Report: The Full Text of the President's Special Review Board.* (New York: Random House, 1987), 88.

[10] I should note that this "in the dark" comment is more true for Poindexter than for McFarlane. The initial arms for hostages piece of the scandal, which McFarlane originated, is more complicated than can be analyzed here. But, suffice it to say, it was presented to the president and the principals, albeit not with deliberative rigor. On McFarlane as NSC advisor and his role in Iran-Contra, see Burke, *Honest Broker*, 212-218.

[11] Condoleezza Rice, *No Higher Honor: A Memoir of My Years in Washington*, (New York: Crown, 2011).

[12] Elaine Sciolino, "Compulsion to Achieve," *New York Times*, December 18, 2000.

[13] Nicholas Lemann, "Without a Doubt," *New Yorker*, October 14, 2002, 167.

[14] Bob Woodward, *Bush at War*, (New York: Simon & Schuster, 2002), 256.

[15] According to James Fallows, "The three known exceptions to this pattern actually underscore the limits on top-level talks. One was the discussions at Camp David just after 9/11: they led to 'Afghanistan first,' which delayed rather than forestalled the concentration on Iraq. The second was Colin Powell's 'You break it, you've bought it' warning to the president in the summer of 2002; far from leading to serious questions

about the war, it did not even persuade the administration to use the postwar plans devised by the State Department, the Army, and the CIA. The third was a long memo from Rumsfeld to Bush a few months before the war began, when a campaign against Iraq was a foregone conclusion....its only apparent effect was that Bush called in his military commanders to look at the war plans" (James Fallows, "Bush's Lost Year," *Atlantic Monthly*, October 2004, 79).

[16] George Tenet, *At the Center of the Storm: My Years at the CIA*, (New York: HarperCollins, 2007), 305, also see 308.

[17] Tenet, *At the Center of the Storm*, 447-448.

[18] Evan Thomas, "The 12 Year Itch," *Newsweek*, March 31, 2003, 64-65.

[19] Evan Thomas, "The Quiet Power of Condi Rice," *Newsweek*, December 16, 2002, 28; also see Glenn Kessler and Peter Slevin, "Rice Fails to Repair Rifts," *Washington Post*, October 12, 2003, Bob Woodward, *Plan of Attack*, (New York: Simon & Schuster, 2004), 175-176, 415. DeYoung especially notes Deputy Secretary of State Richard Armitage's use of the word "dysfunctional," and also that terms use by one former Republican cabinet official (Karen DeYoung, *Soldier: The Life of Colin Powell*, (New York: Simon & Schuster, 2004), 477). According to Risen, Rumsfeld was a prime source of his subordinates' behavior at the deputies' meetings and other lower-level groups: within the NSC staff a strong belief developed that "Rumsfeld had told his aides at the Pentagon that they too could ignore directions from the NSC" (James Risen, *State of War: The Secret History of the CIA and the Bush Administration*, (New York: Free Press, 2006), 161, 163).

[20] Hadley, like Rice, faced a room full of heavyweights as chair of the deputies' committee: Deputy Secretary of Defense Paul Wolfowitz and Armitage from State most notably. According to one participant, one of Hadley's tasks is "reining in some of the right-wing ideologues who can get the president in trouble. He's methodical. He runs meetings like an orchestra conductor. But when they are over, he's quietly tossed some pretty extreme ideas overboard." He also served, in Rice's words, as her "alter ego. I can sometimes jump from A to F. He backs me up to B and C, makes me think through implications" (David Sanger, "Missile Shield Point Man Does Not Shy From Tough Fight," *New York Times*, February 16, 2001). Interestingly, Hadley's activities—if this account is correct--indicate his own brokerage role, as well as the applicability of the role at other points in the policy-making process. But Rothkopf notes later problems in Hadley's coordination: "one senior official told of 'fairly regular' instances in which, after a deputies meetings, notes would be adjusted on the basis of comments that that appeared to come from the Department of Defense." On one occasion, a Defense official tried to amend conclusions "that had been collectively reached by the group. Hadley obliged" (David Rothkopf, *Running the World: The Inside Story of the National Security Council and the Architects of American Power*, (New York: Public Affairs, 2005), 414).

[21] De Young, *Soldier*, 335, 398, 477-478; Rothkopf, *Running the World*, 414.

[22] Mike Allen, "Rice is Named Secretary of State," *Washington Post*, November 17, 2004.

[23] Elisabeth Bumiller, "A Partner in Shaping an Assertive Foreign Policy," *New York Times*, January 7, 2004.

[24] Glenn Kessler and Thomas E. Ricks, "Rice's NSC Tenure Complicates New Post," *Washington Post*, November 16, 2004.

[25] Donald Rumsfeld, *Known and Unknown: A Memoir*, (New York: Sentinel, 2011), 327.

[26] Rumsfeld, *Known and Unknown*, 325.

[27] Rumsfeld, *Known and Unknown*, 326.

[28] Michael Elliott and Massimo Calabresi, "Is Condi the Problem?" *Time*, April 5, 2004, 37.

[29] Ron Suskind, *The Price of Loyalty: George W. Bush, the White House, and the Education of Paul O'Neill*, (New York: Simon & Schuster, 2004), 256.

[30] Thomas, "The Quiet Power of Condi Rice," 29.

[31] See, for example, Karen DeYoung, "In Frenetic White House, A Low-Key 'Outsider'," *Washington Post*, May 7, 2009.

[32] His wife, Catherine M. Russell, served as Jill Biden's chief of staff, while his brother Michael served as counselor to the vice president.

[33] Bob Woodward, *Obama's Wars*, (New York: Simon & Schuster, 2010), 40.

[34] David E. Sanger and Helene Cooper, "Civilian Replaces General in Key Foreign Policy Job," *New York Times*, October 9, 2010.

[35] Scott Wilson, "Jones to Step Down as National Security Adviser," *Washington Post*, October 8, 2010.

[36] David E. Sanger and Helene Cooper, "Civilian Replaces General in Key Foreign Policy Job."

[37] David E. Sanger, "National Security Adviser to Resign, Officials Say," *New York Times*, October 8, 2010.

[38] Joel Klein, "The Rock Builder," *Time*, May 4, 2009, 32.

[39] Helene Cooper, "National Security Adviser Tries Quieter Approach," *New York Times*, May 7, 2009.

[40] Woodward, *Obama's Wars*, 343.

[41] Woodward, *Obama's Wars*, 138.

[42] Kevin Marsh, "The Administrator as Outsider: James Jones as National Security Advisor," *Presidential Studies Quarterly*, 42 (4: 2012), 828.

[43] Woodward, *Obama's Wars*, 343. Woodward recounts that Gates almost even walked out of a meeting following Donilon's "sound-offs and strong spur-of-the moment opinions, especially about one general" (200).

[44] Woodward, *Obama's Wars*, 342.

[45] Woodward, *Obama's Wars*, 199-200.

[46] Scott Wilson, "Jones to Step Down as National Security Adviser."

[47] Helene Cooper, "The Adviser at the Heart of National Security," *New York Times*, July 10, 2010.

[48] James Mann, *The Obamians: The Struggle Inside the White House to Redefine American Power*, (New York: Viking), 10.

[49] Peter Nicholas and Christi Parsons, "National Security Chief Keeps a Low Profile," *Los Angeles Times*, May 3, 2011.

[50] Nicholas and Christi Parsons, "National Security Chief Keeps a Low Profile."

[51] Peter Nicholas and Christi Parsons, "National Security Chief Keeps a Low Profile."

[52] Rosa Brooks, "The Case for Intervention," *Foreign Policy*, October 18, 2012, http://www.foreignpolicy.com/articles/2012/10/18/the_case_for_intervention?page=full (accessed November 1, 2012).

[53] Peter Nicholas and Christi Parsons, "National Security Chief Keeps a Low Profile."

[54] Brooks, "The Case for Intervention."

[55] Obama, however, had been a member of the Senate Foreign Relations Committee.

[56] Woodward, *Plan of Attack*, 149-50.

[57] Rice, *No Higher Honor*, 18.

[58] Rice, *No Higher Honor*, 19.

[59] Rumsfeld, *Known and Unknown*, 324.

[60] Rice, *No Higher Honor*, 20.

[61] Rice, *No Higher Honor*, 20-21.

[62] Rice, *No Higher Honor*, 21.

[63] George W. Bush, *Decision Points*, (New York: Crown, 2010), 90.

[64] Thomas, "The Quiet Power of Condi Rice," 28.

[65] See: John P. Burke, *Becoming President: The Bush Transition, 2000-2003*, (Boulder, Colo.: Lynne Rienner, 2004), 170; Steven Weisman, "What Rift?" *New York Times*, June 1, 2003.

[66] Thomas, "The 12 Year Itch," 64; also see Kessler and Slevin, "Rice Fails to Repair Rifts."

[67] Rumsfeld, *Known and Unknown*, 330.

[68] Laura Rozen and Ben Smith, "Scoring Obama's Nat'l Security Team," www.politico.com, December 13, 2009 (accessed December 14, 2009).

[69] Ryan Lizza, "The Consequentialist," *New Yorker*, May 2, 2011, 48.

[70] On Blair, see Mann, *The Obamians*, 213-21, Woodward, *Obama's Wars*, 370-74.

[71] On Holbrooke, see Mann, *The Obamians*, 231-38.

[72] Mann, *The Obamians*, 338.

[73] Mann, *The Obamians*, xviii.

[74] See: Ryan Lizza, "The Obama Memos," *New Yorker*, January 30, 2012, 36-49. According to Lizza, "Obama likes his advice in writing. He marks up the decision memos and briefing materials with notes and questions in his neat cursive handwriting." Materials are returned to the staff secretary then distributed to key aides, "A single Presidential comment might change a legislative strategy, kill the proposal of a well-meaning adviser, or initiate a bureaucratic process to answer a Presidential question. If the document is a decision memo, its author usually includes options for Obama to check at the end" (42). To be fair to Bush, reports during his presidency also indicated a propensity to mark up written material with comments and questions using a "Sharpie" pen. Unfortunately, comparison of their respective efforts awaits a future generation of scholars, once the twelve year period has passed after their presidencies have ended and documents start to become available.

[75] Tower, Muskie, and Scowcroft, *The Tower Commission Report*, 88, 92.

[76] Daalder and Destler, "The Role of the National Security Adviser," *The National Security Project: Oral History Roundtable,* Washington D.C.: Center for International and Security Studies and the Brookings Institution, 1999, 14 (http://www.brookings.edu/fp/research/projects/nsc/transcripts/19991025.htm.

[77] Daalder and Destler, "The Role of the National Security Adviser," 53.

[78] Bush, *Decision Points*, 92.

[79] Rice, *No Higher Honor*, 22.

[80] Bush, *Decision Points*, 88.

[81] Rice, *No Higher Honor*, 22.

[82] Marsh, "The Administrator as Outsider," 840.
[83] James P. Pfiffner, "Decision Making in the Obama White House," *Presidential Studies Quarterly* 41 (2: 2011), 244.
[84] Brooks, "The Case for Intervention."

In: Change in the White House?
Editor: Meena Bose

ISBN: 978-1-62948-920-9
© 2014 Nova Science Publishers, Inc.

Chapter 7

EVALUATING AFGHANISTAN AND IRAQ IN THE GEORGE W. BUSH AND OBAMA PRESIDENCIES: CHANGE WE CAN BELIEVE IN?

Carolyn Eisenberg

ABSTRACT

This essay argues that President Bush and President Obama had in common the view that the problem of "terrorism" needed to be handled through military means. This fundamentally flawed approach has led to a succession of policy failures in both Iraq and Afghanistan. US soldiers and civilians in these countries have experienced enormous hardship for elusive goals. Apart from the human costs and the steady drain on the American treasury, there is little reason to think that the United States is any less vulnerable to terrorism. The rising tide of hostility in the Muslim world poses considerable danger. While President Obama has changed the tone of US foreign relations and has exhibited increasing reluctance to pursue ground wars, his continued reliance on military means, as exemplified by his use of drones, continues to multiply enemies of the United States. The choices of both Presidents are less a reflection of their intellect and character, than of a disposition towards militarism embedded in American institutions.

The war in Iraq will soon belong to history. Your service belongs to the ages.
Never forget that you are part of an unbroken line of heroes spanning two centuries-
from the colonists, who overthrew an empire, to your grandparents and parents who faced
down fascism and communism, to you—men and women who fought for the same
principles in Fallujah and Kandahar, and delivered justice to those
who attacked us on 9/11.[1]
(President Barack Obama, Fort Bragg, December 12, 2011).

For many parents in the Iraqi city of Fallujah, the President's soaring words would have resonated poorly. The site of some of the war's most bitter fighting, its hospitals were reporting a dramatic rise in child mortality, cancer, leukemia and other birth defects that may have exceeded the rates found among survivors at Hiroshima and Nagasaki. [2] Widely reported in the British press, physicians at the Fallujah General Hospital, funded by American dollars, claimed to be seeing an average of two cases of birth defects a day, as compared with a pre-2003 rate of one case every two months. [3] Some children were exhibiting grotesque malformations –missing arms and legs, cleft palates, elongated heads, malformed ears, noses and spines. Mothers were being warned not to become pregnant. The source of all this misery had not been reliably identified. But among residents of Fallujah, it was widely assumed that the American use of depleted uranium and phosphorus, when they retook the city in November 2004, was the cause.

An ambiguous story perhaps. But also a reminder of how the vision of our policymakers can be so profoundly at odds with the experiences of people on the ground. In examining the transition between Presidents Bush and Obama in their handling of Iraq and Afghanistan, one common feature is the failure to acknowledge or even recognize the far-reaching human tragedy that has accompanied the American "war on terrorism."

One beautiful September morning, nineteen men armed with box-cutters and knives boarded planes and crashed them into the World Trade Center and the Pentagon. More than 3000 Americans died in that attack. The response in Washington was to launch two major wars and smaller military operations around the world. In the aftermath of these decisions, more than 6000 American soldiers were killed, another 100,000 were wounded or returned home with post -traumatic stress disorder. According to the most conservative estimates, 125,000 Iraqi civilians perished in the wars, along with 20,000 innocent Afghans, many of them children. From these two countries, an excess of 6 million people were displaced. To this point, the United States has spent $1.4 trillion, not counting the past or future cost of veterans' medical and disability benefits. On September 12, 2001 sympathy for the United States and admiration for the police and firemen, who rushed into burning buildings in order to save lives was near universal. Today in many parts of the world, this good will has turned to rage.

In the immediate aftermath of 9-11, President Bush made what was perhaps his single most important decision by defining the attacks on our shores by a non-state actor "as an act of war against our country." [4] In his address to the Congress, still steeped in the grief and anger of the moment, he proclaimed, "a war on terror, which begins with Al Qaeda, but it does not end there." Indeed, "it will not end until every terrorist group of global reach has been found, stopped and defeated."

Although little noticed at the time, this approach was a radical departure from the usual practice of the United States and other countries to treat acts of terrorism, even when launched from inside another country, as a crime rather than a war- an event to be handled through investigation, arrest and criminal prosecution. In the short term, this meant that the United States would be attacking the country of Afghanistan, rather than seeking out a specific group of perpetrators.

The President's first action was to offer an ultimatum, which demanded that the Taliban deliver all leaders of Al Qaeda to the United States, "to close immediately and permanently every terrorist training camp in Afghanistan" and to give the United States "full access to these camps, so we can make sure they are no longer operating." [5] When no satisfactory response was forthcoming, on October 20 United States and Britain began a military campaign designed to overthrow the Taliban, and to capture or kill members of Al Qaeda- an effort, which enjoyed substantial moral and material support from other countries, as well as NATO.

Operation Enduring Freedom. as it was grandly called, relied heavily on air-strikes, supported by Special Operations troops and highly trained CIA teams on the ground. In addition to gathering intelligence and identifying targets for the planes, some American operatives in Afghanistan were carrying large quantities of cash, to be distributed to local warlords and tribal leaders for help in identifying terrorists and joining the fight. [6] The main burden of combat was entrusted to the Northern Alliance, a loose coalition of Afghan warriors, who had been fighting the Taliban for years. Few Americans were actually involved in battle and not until year's end were significant numbers on the ground. [7]

Despite the absence of American troops, the Taliban was quickly outmatched and as of mid-November had retreated from Kabul. Three weeks later, they surrendered in their southern stronghold of Kandahar. By the time this occurred, representatives of different Afghan groups had already met in Bonn, under United Nations auspices, and established an Afghan Interim Authority to be headed up by Hamid Karzai, a prominent Pashtun, who had been living in Pakistan. [8]

During the weeks of preparation for *Enduring Freedom,* bin Laden and his confederates clearly understood that the Americans were coming after them, giving them time to plan their escape. As the fighting proceeded, they made their way into the elaborate complex of caves in the mountainous territory of Tora Bora, 20 miles from the Pakistan border. Although the US Commanding General Tommy Franks was aware that hard-core Al Qaeda fighters had moved into this area, he left primary responsibility for hunting them down to the Afghan militia, supported by American air-strikes. Back in Kabul, the CIA team leader Gary Berntsen was pleading for more help. "We need Rangers now," he implored. "The opportunity to get bin Laden and his men is slipping away." [9] Hundreds of miles to the east, Brigadier General James Mattis, who was commanding 1100 Marines, requested that his men be transported to the Pakistan border, so they could seal off the escape routes. Franks turned him down. In Washington, the CIA had briefed Bush and Cheney about the situation in Tora Bora, but the President was strangely unwilling to send more troops. [10]

The Afghan warlords, upon whom Bush was relying, proved less than zealous. While they engaged in negotiations about a possible cease-fire, bin Laden, his family and other Al Qaeda fighters seized the opportunity to cross the border into Pakistan [11] Despite the significance of this development, at the time few Americans were aware of it. During the latter months of 2001, the most visible occurrence was the overthrow of the Taliban, which had happened rapidly with only a handful of US casualties. Television and newspapers featured stories of happy Afghans flying kites, playing music, shaving their beards and enjoying what appeared to be "enduring freedom." [12]

With the ostensible "defeat" of the Taliban, the Administration rapidly turned its attention away from Afghanistan. As of 2003 US troops levels, never high to begin with, stood at 13,600 for a country of 26 million people. The Administration seemed content to give NATO prime responsibility for security. And despite early intimations of a Marshall Plan scale assistance, US economic aid hovered around $1.75 billion a year, a comparatively low figure. In view of the Bush Administration's stated aversion to "nation-building," this neglect was not surprising. From the outset, its objective in Afghanistan had been limited to driving out the Taliban and Al Qaeda.

As has been widely discussed, the Bush Administration's more pressing interest was in going to war with Iraq. In its hurry to move on, it attached little significance to the fact that most Taliban members had simply melted back into their home villages to await more auspicious circumstances. And they also discounted the unknown clusters of men from Al Qaeda and the Taliban, who were now in Pakistan waiting to return. To Secretary of State Colin Powell and some others in the State Department and CIA, this emphasis on Iraq seemed misplaced. As observed by counter-terrorism coordinator Richard Clark, "Having been attacked by al Qaeda, for us to go bombing Iraq would be like our invading Mexico after the Japanese attacked us at Pearl Harbor." [13]

The dissenters in the Administration were easily marginalized. By the beginning of 2002, military planning for the invasion of Iraq was already underway. Top officials had begun whipping up the public's fears about "weapons of massive destruction," now alleged to be in Saddam Hussein's hands. And while they did not directly blame the Iraqi leader for the events of 9-11, Americans were repeatedly told that Saddam had a connection to "terrorists" and if given the opportunity might share his "weapons of mass destruction," with them.

In September 2002, the Administration released its new National Security Strategy paper, articulating a doctrine of "pre-emption:"

> Traditional concepts of deterrence will not work against a terrorist enemy whose avowed tactics are wanton destruction and the targeting of the innocents... ...*The greater the threat, the greater the risk of inaction-and the more compelling the case for taking anticipatory action to defend ourselves, even if uncertainty remains as to the time and place of the enemy's attack....* [14] (ed. Italics added)

This formulation went well beyond the right of pre-emptive action, recognized in international law. Moreover, in its bold assertion that America had the right to attack another country because it posed some undetermined threat at some indefinite time was a significant departure from previous Presidential utterances.

As Bush moved towards war, he faced a storm of opposition abroad and even at home. Around the world millions of people marched to US Embassies, protesting what they perceived as a planned act of aggression against another country. And in the United States, a reinvented peace movement sprang up seemingly from nowhere —with hundreds of thousands of people in the streets of New York City on a bitter February day. [15]

An immediate problem for the Administration was corralling support in the UN Security Council. As of November 2002, the Council had unanimously passed Resolution 1441, which gave Baghdad "a final opportunity" to demonstrate to the world that it was ridding itself of all "weapons of mass destruction." Towards that end, it required Saddam Hussein to give unrestricted access to international weapons inspectors, who would file a report within sixty days. Saddam had complied, allowing two teams of inspectors to roam freely through the country: a group from the International Atomic Energy Commission (IAEA) seeking evidence of a nuclear program and a separate group under Hans Blix looking for chemical and biological weapons. For the Bush Administration, which had already decided on war, this was a charade chiefly designed to pacify international opinion. However, much to its dismay, after two months the head of the IAEA was reporting, "No prohibited nuclear activities have been identified." [16] And while the findings of the second team were less definitive, its chief Hans Blix was asking for more time to look. [17]

President Bush was unwilling to delay. Already tens of thousands of US troops were deployed in Kuwait and in the region. The longer they waited, the more problematic the weather in Iraq would become. Even more serious, with each passing day there was growing skepticism in the international community as to the actual existence of these weapons. For months, Secretary Rumsfeld and others had maintained that they knew where the weapons were located, yet curiously whatever intelligence they were passing to the UN inspectors was yielding nothing [18] Although the Bush Administration believed that Security Council Resolution 1441 provided a sufficient basis for an invasion, in deference to British Prime Minister Tony Blair they sought a second resolution. After many days of cajoling and pressure, only two other countries (Bulgaria and Spain) on the Security Council were reliably in favor. [19]

Abandoning the effort to secure UN backing, Bush chose to proceed. The domestic peace movement was growing larger with each passing day. Nevertheless, a majority of Americans had been convinced that the menace of Saddam Hussein warranted immediate war. [20] And while Congress was restive, the previous October 2002 it had forfeited its leverage by authorizing the use of force in Iraq, if the President deemed this necessary "to defend the security of the United States." That vote had been cleverly scheduled in advance of elections to maximize pressure on legislators, who did not wish to appear weak on national security. There was widespread skepticism even then, but a majority of Democrats in both Houses had voted in favor, [21] including the four Senators who planned to run for President in 2004- Joseph Biden, John Edwards, John Kerry and Hilary Clinton.

On March 17, 2003 the President informed the world that for Iraq time was up. "Intelligence gathered by this and other governments leaves no doubt that the Iraq regime continues to possess and conceal some of the most lethal weapons known to man." [22] American patience had run out. Saddam Hussein and his sons would have 48-hours to leave Iraq. If they failed to do so, military conflict would begin "at a time of our choosing." On March 19, the first US Tomahawk missiles struck Baghdad. The Iraq war, which had so tantalized members of the Administration, even before the attack on 9-11, [23] had finally begun.

By contrast with Afghanistan, the American invasion of Iraq elicited massive criticism from around the world, with many warning of dire results. Yet as the American army advanced into Baghdad, Saddam's armies failed to offer significant resistance. Within three weeks, the main fighting had subsided and a hated dictator was driven from power. It seemed a remarkable achievement at the time. However, before his first term in office was complete, this Bush adventure would bring embarrassment to its perpetrators and misery to millions of people – a cascade of sorrows, which even today afflicts new generations in Fallujah and elsewhere.

The numerous missteps have been widely discussed and analyzed. [24] The most serious occurred before the actual invasion, when the Bush Administration prevented the UN weapons inspectors from completing their work. Had they been less eager for war, they and the rest of the world might have learned that there were no weapons of mass destruction in Iraq. Since that discovery only emerged after the war had commenced, when hundreds of Americans and thousands of Iraqis were already dead, this presented a shameful spectacle in the eyes of people around the world and among large swathes of the American public. Left unanswered was the question of whether members of the Bush Administration were deliberately deceptive or were simply so determined to find proof of their beliefs that they failed to objectively evaluate the existing evidence.

Whatever the reason, it was an egregious error which bordered on the macabre when President Bush used the occasion of the annual Radio and Television Correspondents Dinner, to present a humorous slide show on the topic [25] In a sequence of photos, he could be seen looking under furniture of the Oval Office, "These weapons of mass destruction have got to be somewhere. Nope no weapons over there…Maybe under there?" For friends and relatives of young men and women risking their lives in Iraq, it was hard to see the joke.

Yet as damaging as it was to discover the non-existence of Saddam Hussein's terrifying weapons, the effect might have dwindled over time had the American and British presence in Iraq proved more salutary. Underlying a multitude of problems was the simple fact that prior to the war, the Bush administration had not devoted the resources or developed the plans for the post-hostilities period. This was neither oversight nor mere incompetence. Mobilizing the needed resources would have required a delay and made it clear to a wavering public that the war in Iraq might prove costly. Moreover, serious planning would have required greater influence for the Middle East experts in the State Department. Yet it was precisely these specialists who were assailed by doubt about the entire project.

Over the ensuing weeks and months, the American military proved incapable of providing security to the Iraqi people or of ensuring an adequate supply of food, clean water and electricity. And having punted on the arrangements for a transfer of political power, they established a Coalition Provisional Authority that for a period claimed absolute authority over the country. [26] For all the excited rhetoric about liberating the Iraqi people, during the next four years, under a variety of makeshift arrangements, American officials intervened massively in the economic and political affairs of the country, trying to mold it to US predilections, while still failing to keep the population safe.

The waves of violence that swept over Iraq were of varying character. Shortly after the invasion, there was the surge of criminality, first manifest in widespread looting, but later morphing into kidnappings, armed robbery and murder. [27] By the summer of 2003, a Sunni insurgency had emerged, directed primarily at the Americans, but also targeting some local officials and international actors. In one horrifying moment a suicide bomber driving a cement truck managed to blow up the UN headquarters in Baghdad, killing its highly respected mission chief Sergio Viera de Mello and twenty-three others.

Contributing to the chaos was an uprising of the Mahdi army, the private militia of the Shiite cleric Muqtadr al Sadr, who was demanding the removal of American troops. [28] During one especially bleak period in 2004, US soldiers found themselves battling Sadrist forces in Baghdad, Najaf and Basra, while other American units fought with Sunni insurgents in Samara, Ramadi and Fallujah. Fighting was especially intense in Fallujah as American marines tried to assert control over the rebellious city. Many civilians were caught in the crossfire and pictures of the destruction circulated widely across the Middle East, attracting foreign warriors, notably including the terrorist leader Abu Musab al-Zarqawi. Perversely then a war that had ostensibly been undertaken to avert a terrorist danger was providing them with a new base of operations. [29]

By 2004, the various enemies had launched over 26,000 attacks. In 2005 the number had risen to 34,000, including scores of bombings every week. With so much bloodshed it was difficult to determine who was murdering whom and for what reason. [30] Associated with these killings was a pattern of ethnic cleansing, even in urban neighborhoods where Shia and

Sunni had mingled peacefully for decades. While there was no precise information about the extent of displacement, it was clear that in Baghdad alone hundreds of thousands of Sunnis were driven from their homes. [31]

As the catastrophe in Iraq unfolded world opinion, which had been unfavorable to begin with, became even harsher. Judgments about the war faded imperceptibly into anger over what were widely viewed as US violations of international law and disregard for human rights, A BBC World Service Poll in January 2007 found that 73% of people in 25 different countries disapproved of how the United States government was dealing with Iraq. [32] Over two-thirds (68%) believed that the US military presence in the Middle East provoked more conflict than it prevented, while only 17% viewed US troops there as a stabilizing force.

In the United States, there was also growing disapproval of the Iraq War. However without a draft or an increase in taxes, this remained a secondary concern for many. In the 2004 Presidential election, the Democratic challenger John Kerry did not offer a clear alternative on Iraq, enabling Bush to label him a "flip-flopper" and to eke out a narrow victory despite the debacle. Having defeated Kerry, the President quickly authorized a second assault on Falluja. The previous April he had yielded to international pressure that included entreaties from normally docile Iraqi leaders, to pull the troops back [33] thereby frustrating his Generals. But with the election behind him, Bush was emboldened. Residents of Falluja were urged to leave the city, as US marines, accompanied by newly formed Iraqi security forces began the attack.

In Fallujah the marines faced the largest concentration of insurgents in the entire war and some of the most ruthless foreign fighters. Forced to proceed block-by-block, the ground troops were supported by a rain of bombs and artillery fire. Within a week, they had achieved control of the city, but the victory had come at a price. At least 10,000 homes were totally destroyed, along with mosques, schools and local businesses. The insurgents had used civilian facilities to make their stand and the Americans had been indiscriminate in response. There were a stream of reports that in their effort to flush out the enemy, the Americans had used cluster bombs and white phosphorus. According to independent journalist Dahr Jamail, who had been interviewing refugees coming out of the city:

> The consistent stories I have been getting have been refugees describing phosphorus weapons, horribly burned bodies, fires that burn on people when they touch these weapons and they are unable to extinguish the fires even after dumping large quantities of water on people. [34]

After initially denying these charges, a Pentagon spokesman acknowledged that phosphorus had been used against enemy combatants, but not civilians [35]. And contrary to what was being claimed, this should not be considered a chemical weapon.

Despite the marine triumph in Fallujah, American disillusionment with the war continued to mount. While the plight of the Iraqis was arguably of less concern than the cost to the United States, disturbing reports about the behavior of American soldiers were taking a toll on national pride. There were appalling pictures from Abu Ghraib, showing naked prisoners being tortured by American guards, and photos from Haditha in 2005, where a group of US soldiers had mowed down 24 unarmed Iraqis. Incrementally, all of these events tarnished the sense of achievement, associated with the overthrow of Saddam Hussein.

The most pressing public concern was the rise in American casualties. By 2007, more than 3900 US soldiers had been killed in Iraq, surpassing the number of deaths that had occurred on September 11. Advances in medical technology had made it possible for injured soldiers, who might have died in earlier wars, to survive. But often, they were sitting in hospitals or perhaps even at home with gruesome wounds and grave handicaps. Moreover, as the American economy sunk into recession, the costs of the war to the United States seemed more significant. Before the invasion Bush officials were blithely assuring each other and the public that given Iraq's oil revenues, the war would pay for itself. That quixotic notion had disappeared within the first year. By 2008, conservative estimates of US expenditures on Iraq stood at $648 billion, taking no account of the future skyrocketing health care costs of returning veterans. [36]

Against this grim backdrop, Barack Obama began his candidacy for the White House. Unlike his rivals, who were in the United States Senate at the time the President asked for an authorization for the use of force, Obama was spared the difficult political choice. While all of these competitors had voted in favor, his own involvement came at a 2002 protest rally in Chicago, where he gave a rousing speech, deploring this "dumb and rash war." [37] Whatever political future State Senator Barack Obama was envisioning at the time, six years later when he was running for President that Chicago speech proved to be an asset rather than a liability, enabling him to successfully challenge Hillary Clinton, who had given her "aye" vote on the invasion. [38]

Once he was facing John McCain in a general election, Obama's position on Iraq became more sharply focused and was re-woven into a broad critique of the Bush "war on terrorism." He now offered a plan, under which the United States would immediately start drawing down two combat brigades a month, with the expectation that after sixteen months all combat troops would be out of Iraq. [39] But there was also fine print: the United States would not be departing completely but should leave a "residual force" for the limited purposes of hunting down the remaining terrorists, protecting US service members and training Iraqi security forces. Obama framed his critique of the Iraq War within the context of the Bush Administration's failure to capture bin Laden and to defeat Al Qaeda in Afghanistan. By adopting this stance, he was able to appeal to his party's antiwar base, which had prioritized US withdrawal from Iraq, at the same time projecting himself as a leader, who would be tough and smart in defending the nation's security [40] "We took our eye off the ball," Obama lamented.

For those Americans, who wished to know more about Barack Obama before casting their vote, his books were omnipresent. In the *Audacity of Hope*, which lingered for thirty months on the *NY Times* best- seller list, he laid out his vision for the American role in the world. Obama called for a "revised foreign policy framework that matches the boldness and scope of Truman's post-World War II policies... one that guides our use of force and expresses our deepest ideals." At times the United States would have to act as a "reluctant sheriff," using its military power if directly threatened and acting unilaterally if other countries failed to help. However, the main thrust of his writing was to emphasize peaceful solutions, the observance of international law and the desirability of acting in concert with other nations. "I'm convinced," he asserted "that it will almost always be in our strategic interest to act multilaterally, when we use force around the world. [41] The reason was simple:

> Because nobody benefits more than we do from observance of 'the rules of the road.'
> We can't win converts to these rules if we act as if they apply to everyone but us.

Barack Obama's stated views on national security were complicated and at times contradictory. While making broad promises, he was careful to include many qualifications and loopholes. However, on November 2, 2008 when voters went to the polls and elected him President of the United States, there was a powerful feeling of hope both at home and abroad that this new leader would take a different direction, reversing what were widely perceived as the incompetent, bullying actions of the Bush Administration.

A remarkable expression of that excitement was the unprecedented decision of the Nobel Peace Prize Committee to grant the President this award after less than a year in office, explaining that, "Obama has as President created a new climate in international politics," in which "dialogue and negotiations are preferred as instrument for resolving even the most difficult international conflicts." [42] This extraordinary honor placed Obama in a delicate position. It was obviously important to accept the prize graciously and to embrace the values, which it represented. Yet he could not afford to convey the impression at home that he was some kind of wooly-eyed pacifist, unwilling to use military power.

In his much awaited speech at Oslo, he acknowledged the awkward fact that he was coming there as "the Commander-in-chief of a nation in the midst of two wars." [43] Playing homage to the inspirational ideals of Martin Luther King and Mahatma Gandhi, he also clarified that "as a head of state sworn to protect and defend my nation, I cannot be guided by their examples alone. I face the world as it is and I cannot stand idle in the face of threats to the American people. For make no mistake, evil does exist in the world." Because members of Al Qaeda could not be lured into negotiations, they had to be handled with military force. But to say "that force is sometimes necessary is not a call to cynicism," but "a recognition of history; the imperfections of man and the limits of reason."

For invoking philosophy, the new American President was without peer. Yet the real test of his leadership was whether he could deliver "the change you can believe in," which had been his campaign mantra. A revealing sign of his intentions had come during the transition period, as he searched for people to fill the key national security posts. Early in the process, he had admonished his transition director John Podesta that, "I don't want the same old crowd in Washington, who do the same old things, the same old way." [44] Yet by choosing Podesta, the former Chief of Staff in the Clinton White House to implement this task, he had virtually assured the selection of familiar people.

The most telling appointment was the decision to maintain Robert Gates as the Secretary of Defense. Gates had served for decades in the National Security Council and the CIA, where he had ultimately become its Director. Known as a die-hard Cold Warrior, who during the 1980s had exaggerated the Soviet arms build-up, he still referred to the old USSR as the "Evil Empire." It was the measure of the right-wing zealotry of the George W Bush administration, that Gates had been curiously resurrected as a responsible moderate. How much of this history was known to Obama is unclear. But he was more than grateful when the Secretary of Defense agreed to stay on. Other appointments- including Hillary Clinton as Secretary of State, Leon Panetta as head of the CIA and Richard Holbrooke as special emissary for Afghanistan and Pakistan, suggested nothing more unorthodox than a possible reversion to the principles of the Clinton White House. Moreover, with General Petraeus remaining as Commander at CENTCOM and Admiral Mullen continuing as Chairman of the

Joint Chiefs of Staff, the composition of the Obama national security team looked very much like "the same old crowd. " Whether or not they "they would do the same old things the same old way" as they managed two wars had yet to be determined.

For Iraq, change had become inevitable. In the very last month of the Bush Presidency, he was compelled to sign a Status of Forces Agreement (SOFA) with the Iraqi government, committing the United States to remove all combat troops from Iraqi cities by June 2009 and to withdraw all American armed forces no later than December 2011. The road to that agreement had been oddly circular and subject to diverse interpretations. In early 2007, President Bush had defied his critics and approved "a surge" of 30,000 US troops into Iraq, charged with the specific task of getting control of the violence there. He also accepted the advice of General Petraeus, who urged him to strike a deal with the Sunni insurgents, to put them on the payroll and enlist their help with fighting the increasingly despised *Al Qaeda in Iraq*.

By September of 2007, the Iraq Ministry was reporting a dramatic decrease in the level of violence. [45] Among experts, there were different interpretations as to whether this decline was attributable to the arrival of the new troops, the belated outreach to the Sunnis or to the fact that so much ethnic cleansing had taken place, there were fewer occasions for conflict. [46] Whatever the reasons, there was greater stability in Iraq than at any time since the Americans had invaded. As the worst violence subsided the Shiite government of Prime Minister Nuri al-Maliki felt emboldened to push the American troops out, or at least speed their exit.

The focal point became the negotiations on the Status of Forces Agreement, which would provide the Bush administration and its successor with the legal foundation to keep their troops in Iraq. Once Obama had become the president-elect this task became even more urgent, if only to forestall any precipitous decision on his part. Recognizing an opportunity and pressed by his own supporters, the Iraqi Prime Minister drove a hard bargain, extracting a commitment from Bush that by the end of 2011 all American troops would be gone.

Once the deal became public, there were many Iraqis, who were enraged by the prospect of another three years of American soldiers in their country. Thousands expressed their dissatisfaction by demonstrating in Central Baghdad and burning George W. Bush in effigy. The depth of the resentment received shocking expression on December 14, when the President came to Baghdad for a final signing of the SOFA. During a joint press conference with Maliki in the heavily guarded Green Zone, an Iraqi journalist stood up in the crowd and threw two shoes at the American leader. "This is a farewell you dog," he shouted. And, "this is for the widows, the orphans and those who were killed in Iraq," came his final words. [47]

In theory, the Status of Forces Agreement should have been a great boon to President Obama, given his famed opposition to the American presence there. However, Obama was surrounded by people, who assumed that before the three years had elapsed, a new agreement would be negotiated. That was certainly the perspective of Secretary Gates, who publicly conjectured that there would be "several tens of thousands of American troops" retained as a residual force. In line with the SOFA, the Obama Administration began drawing down troops and changing the mission of those that remained. The soldiers now stayed closer to base and were allowing Maliki's military to do most of the fighting. However, as the 2011 deadline approached, the Obama Administration pressed the Iraqi Prime Minister to re-negotiate an agreement that would allow at least ten thousand US troops to stay. When that was ruled out, they proposed to keep 3000 troops in Iraq to strike at terrorists and to protect the US Embassy in Baghdad.

Maliki seemed personally amenable to the lower number. However, negotiations broke down over the volatile issue of "immunity from persecution." In every country in the world, where the United States had stationed troops, this was a required safeguard. To members of the Iraqi parliament, including those from Maliki's own coalition, there had been too many years in which American military personnel and private contractors had committed crimes against their people with apparent impunity [48] But without the assurance that American soldiers would not be prosecuted in Iraqi courts, Obama recognized that he could not leave any troops there. So to the surprise of official Washington, the 2008 Status of Forces agreement held sway after all and the President gave the order to bring everyone home by year's end.

Once this was settled, Obama made a virtue out of necessity, claiming credit for ending the Iraq War: [49] "As promised," he announced, "the rest of our troops will come home by the end of the year. After nearly nine years, America's war in Iraq will be over." For the small number of people, who were closely tracking the subject, this presentation strained credulity because the President's efforts to keep troops in Iraq had been openly discussed. It was no small irony that a man whose bid for the Presidency had been facilitated by his early opposition to the war had struggled in the end to keep the troops there.

One of Obama's particular talents was the ability to cloak painful events in an uplifting narrative. For obvious reasons, he chose Fort Bragg, South Carolina as the place to relate an inspirational story:

> As your Commander-in-Chief, I can tell you that it will indeed be a part of history. Those last American troops will move south on desert sands, and then they will cross the border out of Iraq with heads held high. One of the most extraordinary chapters in the history of the American military will come to an end. Iraq's future will be in the hands of its people. [50]

"Iraq is not a perfect place," he reflected, thereby obscuring with a phrase all the inconvenient facts: the three million Iraqis still without homes, the collapse of the economy, the unnecessary deaths of 100,000 or more people, the tens of thousands of Sunni prisoners now transferred to Maliki's jails, where torture was endemic. [51]

As Commander-in-Chief addressing men and women of the armed forces of whom many had served multiple tours in Iraq and seen friends killed or wounded there, such reticence was understandable. But if the harsh realities of the Iraq experience were obscured, what were the prospects for wiser choices in the more difficult terrain of Afghanistan? Obama had arrived in the White House at a point when the situation there was deteriorating rapidly. The government of Ahmed Karzai, upon which the Bush Administration had invested such high hopes, had failed to consolidate its control of the country and was mired in corruption. Outside of Kabul and other cities, the rule of law was non-existent. Millions of dollars in international aid had been pledged, but almost none of it had reached the people. [52] Afghanistan remained one of the very poorest countries in the world, with many of its farmers turning back to poppy-growing as a their only way to make a living. [53]

As early as 2006, it had become clear that the Taliban had returned, along with a small number of Al Qaeda operatives and other foreign terrorists. In the Pashtun areas of southeastern Afghanistan, some Taliban courts were back in business and "shadow governments" were already operating. [54] There were other signs of trouble. Suicide bombing was rising precipitously, as well as IED attacks on American and NATO forces.

During the last two years of the Bush Administration these developments had become a serious concern, but it could not easily respond because of the chaotic situation in Iraq. It was not until 2008 that the situation there had quieted sufficiently, enabling the President to raise the American troop levels in Afghanistan to 38,000 men and women and placing on the table a possible change of strategy.

On the campaign trail, Obama had flayed the previous administration for its failure to eradicate Al Qaeda and to consolidate control over Afghanistan. If elected, he promised to step up the American presence there and to offer a realistic plan for winning. Liberal supporters might hope this was electoral posturing designed to assure worried voters about his "toughness," but if so they were rapidly disappointed. Faced with a deteriorating situation on the ground and pressure from his own appointees and the military that rapid steps be taken, Obama was determined to act.

To figure out a strategy, Obama tapped the services of Bruce Riedel, another Washington insider, who had worked for 29 years in the CIA, the Pentagon and the Clinton National Security Council. Riedel was given sixty days to complete a review of the situation and to make the appropriate recommendations. [55] However, this schedule was too slow for General Petraeus at CENTCOM and for Admiral Mullen, Chairman of the Joint Chiefs of Staff. Both men insisted that the President needed to decide immediately on the dispatch of 30,000 new troops into Afghanistan. Their ostensible reason for stepping up the process was the urgency of providing more security for Afghan elections, scheduled in the summer. [56] Yet for Petraeus, the more compelling motive was to rapidly obtain a large increment of troops in order to apply "counter-insurgency" doctrine in Afghanistan, as he had done in Iraq.

Within the Administration, the only serious opponent of this hasty decision was Vice President Biden, who thought it absurd to send more troops without any agreement on future strategy. Also skeptical, President Obama asked the Pentagon to explain why 30,000 additional soldiers were needed to insure an election. Under more scrutiny than usual from the man in the White House, the military paired down the request to 17,000 fresh troops.

Still bothered by the idea of sending more soldiers in advance of a strategic review, Obama pushed back with an instruction to the NSC to present him with a range of options. They came up with four, but in a longstanding bureaucratic ploy, only one of these was plausible. [57] Moreover, apart from Biden, all of the principals -Gates, Clinton, Mullen, Petraeus and National Security Advisor James Jones-were agreed that 17,000 was the right number to pick. Obama pressed Reidel: did it make sense to dispatch more troops, when his review was not complete? In "a perfect world," the latter replied, it might be wiser to wait," [58] but the President should not take a chance on Afghan elections being sabotaged. The 17,000 troops would give him "an insurance policy" and greater flexibility down the road.

Yet having granted the Pentagon its troop request, their pressure was unrelenting. In May 2009, Secretary Gates yielded to the advice of General Petraeus by firing the US commander in Afghanistan General David McKiernan and replacing him with General Stanley McChrystal, who had previously been the Director of the Joint Special Operations Command in Iraq. [59] This appointment gave Petraeus an important new ally in his campaign to institute a counter-insurgency strategy and to enlarge the US military presence there.

Evaluating Afghanistan and Iraq in the George W. Bush and Obama Presidencies   123

By mid-August General McChrystal had completed his own survey of the situation on the ground and was calling for another 40,000 soldiers. Although presented in a classified memorandum to Secretary Gates, it was quickly leaked to the press. And from unidentified sources, warnings circulated in Washington that if the President failed to provide the forces, which the military said it needed, then the Taliban could win, with disastrous consequences for America's global standing and his own.

The White House political team was enraged by these obvious end-runs. [60] And this time around Obama was unwilling to be rushed. Instead he set in motion an elaborate process for decision-making, with months of meetings in which the principals went around the same issues. What were the goals in Afghanistan? Was it to defeat Al Qaeda? To beat the Taliban or "degrade" it? To stabilize the Karzai government or to produce a diplomatic solution? And once the objectives were finally settled, what kind of implementation should there be? How many Afghan security forces would need to be trained? Would it be better to send a smaller number of US troops, with "up-ramps" for later on? Or would it be wiser, to dispatch a larger number of troops with provision for "off-ramps" should things go better than expected? Finally, how many brigades would need to go? And was there any hope that NATO countries would increase their contribution?

For all the complications, the issue ultimately boiled down to one core question: would President Obama agree to send tens of thousands of new American troops into Afghanistan? Once again, it was Biden who dissented. He maintained that the gains Petraeus and McChrystal were envisioning were fantasy. As a member and then Chariman of the Senate Foreign Relations Committee, he had been listening to overblown military promises for years. And in his mind, there were major contradictions in what the Pentagon was now proposing. What sense did make to keep 100,000 plus troops in Afghanistan when according to the best estimates there were at most 100 Al Qaeda operatives in the whole country? And if the real aim was to beat the Taliban, which was clearly the case, how could this be done when their members were finding sanctuary in Pakistan? Furthermore, how would the additional troops there ameliorate the problem of Karzai and the monumentally corrupt, ineffectual government in Kabul? Was it reasonable for US soldiers to risk their lives to build good government in Afghan villages, when the center was so rotten?

Still nobody in these meetings, including Biden, was willing to say that the United States should withdraw its military from Afghanistan. [61] And so long as the troops remained, neither he nor the President could easily dismiss the warning that without 40,000 more soldiers their mission would fail. During these many sessions, Obama's unhappiness was palpable, as he repeatedly pressed for some viable alternative to McChrystal's recommendation. Perhaps seeking a reality check, at the end of October he and Michelle flew privately to Dover Air Force base in Delaware to quietly observe the arrival of the bodies of the last eighteen Americans to die in Afghanistan and to meet their families. As a community organizer, state legislator and US Senator, Obama had never been directly responsible for the death of anyone. Now he was.

There were also political considerations. As the weeks went on, the President was under increasing attack by Republicans and members of the press for his slowness in deciding. And he was once again faced with a unified military –Generals Petraeus and McChystal, Admiral Mullen—all strongly supported by Secretary of Defense Gates. As on the previous occasion, Secretary of State Clinton had teamed up with Gates. "If we go half-hearted we will have achieved nothing," she maintained. "We must act like we are going to win." To CIA Director

Leon Panetta, this was a no-brainer: "No Democratic President can go against military advice, especially if he asked for it…Just do as they say," he opined. [62]

On December 1, the President announced his decision at West Point. Responding to complaints of delay, he assured the cadets that "there has never been an option before me that called for troop deployments before 2010, so there has been no delay or denial of resources" during the review period." He had used the time "to ask the hard questions and to explore all the different options, along with my national security team." Based on their findings, he was now ordering an additional 30,000 soldiers to Afghanistan, which he intended to deploy at the "fastest possible pace so that they could target the insurgency and secure key population centers" He was also asking NATO partners to contribute thousands of their own troops and had made it clear to the government of Pakistan that the United States "cannot tolerate a safe-haven for terrorists, whose location is known." To these commitments he added a caveat, which had privately disturbed General Petraeus and his other military advisors. The U.S. soldiers would move in swiftly but after 18 months "our troops will begin to come home"

Obama emphasized that this was not a decision he had taken lightly. He was "convinced that our security is at stake in Afghanistan and Pakistan." While insisting on a time limit, the President appeared to embrace the counter-insurgency doctrine advocated by Petraeus and many of his subordinates. The goal of US troops was to ferret out the insurgents, while remaining long enough to insure the safety and well-being of the populace. As life improved, the Americans and their coalition allies would accelerate the training of the Afghan security forces so that by July 2011 they could begin to assume responsibility for their own country.

Despite its seeming logic, by December 2009 the plan proffered by the President had little chance of succeeding for all the reasons put forward by Biden: the Karzai regime had won a fraudulent election and had alienated much of the populace; counter-insurgency couldn't work if the Pakistanis were unwilling or unable to halt the flow of Taliban across the border; and, despite eight years of NATO efforts, the Afghan Security Forces had shown few signs of motivation or competence. There were other negatives that Biden did not mention: the natural antipathy of villagers, when foreign soldiers marched through their lands; the differences of cultures, religion and language that made cooperation tenuous; and perhaps most important, the fear and rage of American soldiers, who were far from home and subject to unpredictable attacks by apparent civilians.

Over the next three years, as the Petraeus plan was implemented, the results were decidedly mixed. [63] In places where the Americans established a significant and extended beachhead, they succeeded in driving the Taliban out of the area and improving the quality of daily life. However, while enemy forces disappeared from one location, they reappeared in others. There were notable gains in the south of Afghanistan, but new challenges from the Haqqani network in the east. And despite a massive infusion of American material assistance, the Karzai government had achieved no greater legitimacy or control of its own society, while faulting Washington for policy failure [64]. After three more years of war and approximately two hundred and fifty billion dollars spent, only one brigade of Afghan Security Forces could reliably fight on its own, without NATO support and backup. [65]

Added to this were the periodic horror stories, which alienated the local populace. In March 2012 in the Panjawi province near Kandahar, US Staff Sergeant Robert Boles, attached to "a village stability" program in the area, left his base in dead of night. He allegedly entered the homes of three Afghan families and executed thirteen people, including nine children. In at least one of the homes, observers claimed that he poured chemicals on the

Evaluating Afghanistan and Iraq in the George W. Bush and Obama Presidencies 125

bodies and set them on fire. A Mr. Samar, age 60 had been away with his teen-age son. When they returned the next morning, an elderly neighbor Anar Gula claimed to have "heard an explosion, screaming and shooting, as the soldier broke down the door of Mr. Samad's house and chased his wife and two other female members from room to room before he shot them." [66] Among the slain females were Mr. Samar's wife and four daughters between the ages of 8 and 12.

President Obama was understandably appalled by this massacre and quickly conveyed his apologies and condolences to the Afghan people, emphasizing that this tragedy "does not represent the exceptional character of our military and the respect that the United States has for the people of Afghanistan." Coming as it did in the aftermath of two recent episodes in which Americans had been discovered burning Korans and US soldiers were pictured urinating on Afghan corpses, this characterization was unconvincing.

Furthermore, the unraveling of this one sergeant was not idiosyncratic. Reports from the Fort Lewis-McChord military base in Washington State, where Sergeant Boles had been previously stationed, revealed a pattern of violent activity. [67] According to the local Sheriff's office, there had been a rising tide of suicides, domestic violence, drunken driving and malicious mischief by soldiers who had done multiple tours of duty. Moreover, during the previous year, four members of a platoon from the base's 5th Stryker Brigade had been found guilty of the "joy killing" of three unarmed Afghan civilians. Two other soldiers were accused of "water-boarding" their own children- in one case because the child couldn't recite his ABC's and in the other because a foster son had wet his bed. There was also the case of David Stewart, age 38, who shot himself after killing his wife and five-year old child.

These were of course sensational stories. Not many American soldiers went home and water-boarded their own children. Nor was it common for a US soldier to enter an Afghan home, murder the youngsters and set the building afire. But while American officials might prefer to deny this, these events were emblematic of wider phenomena, which were characteristic of the two wars. From the very beginning, the US "war on terror," specifically aimed Osama bin Laden and his associates, had "terrorized" foreign civilians, who were just as dead when an American plane bombed their house as when a single staff sergeant burst into their living quarters with a gun. And for more than ten years, there were countless examples of American military families, who welcomed home a returning soldier so full of unexplained anger and despair that they were a danger to themselves and those they live with.

These human tragedies had as their source, a fundamentally flawed decision by President Bush and then perpetuated by President Obama, to respond to terrifying criminal acts directed towards the United States by waging war in other countries. Bush had seemed eager for a fight in both Afghanistan and Iraq, whereas Obama was the "reluctant sheriff," who had uneasily acquiesced to the military's demand for more troops in Afghanistan. Yet the fact remained that during months on the campaign trail and thereafter, he had personally insisted that, by contrast to Iraq, Afghanistan was "the right war," which needed to be fought.

Three years later, he was less enthusiastic. And as he had promised at West Point, he had begun to bring the troops home. But as Obama began his second term, there were still significantly more US soldiers in Afghanistan than had been there when he took office. And despite promises of changing the mission and transferring complete authority for security to the Afghan forces by the end of 2014, there was no commitment to bringing them all home.

While losing faith in the efficacy of large land wars, the President had not lost confidence in the use of military force to eradicate terrorism and to exert greater US control in the Middle

East and elsewhere. Most startling in this regard was his embrace of drones (unmanned aerial vehicles) for hunting down suspected terrorists in Afghanistan, Pakistan, Yemen and Somalia. President Bush had been the first to introduce this new technology for purposes of surveillance and "precision" killings. But while the Bush administration had authorized several dozen strikes, President Obama had approved hundreds of drone attacks in an expanding list of countries. According to the Bureau of Investigative Journalism, in Pakistan alone 2152 people had been killed, including 290 civilians of whom 64 were children. [68] Most remarkable was the President's direct participation in the program. According to an extensively sourced feature in the NY *Times,* every Tuesday Obama sat down with his national security team and reviewed a list of people, whom the Predator drones would kill [69]

Back in 2008, when Barack Obama was seeking the Democratic nomination for President, he had repeatedly asserted, "I don't want to just end the war, but I want to end the mindset that got us into war in the first place." [70] This promise was "dead on arrival." Indeed, the continuity of so many Obama policies with that of President Bush is testament to the powerful grip of military thinking and military institutions on American political life. It is perhaps the most durable legacy of the Cold War: this habit of threatening or using military force in the service of an ambitious foreign policy. Associated with that propensity were some weighty consequences: an unprecedented centralization of power within the executive branch, a sprawling "military-industrial complex" which fused old-fashioned profiteering with the art of war-making, and an apolitical parochial culture that glorified American supremacy. [71] Each of these elements was present on the bright September morning, when terrorists with box-cutters and knives attacked the United States. And all were in place, on that much colder morning in January 2009, when a new President who had made "change you can believe in," the centerpiece of his campaign, ascended to the White House.

The human costs of that continuity were immense: millions of displaced people, tens of thousands of dead civilians in several countries, vast numbers of American soldiers, who returning from Iraq or Afghanistan would never be normal again. Accolades to the contrary, Iraq was in the hands of an authoritarian Shiite ruler, who imposed his will through violent security forces and whose political sympathies lay with Teheran. [72] Despite public assurances that the Afghanistan surge was working, the Taliban was still alive and showing momentum. [73] Many thousands of Afghan security forces had been trained, but as exemplified by ongoing attacks on American and NATO troops, their loyalty to the Karzai government and to the United States was doubtful.

More impressive certainly is the record against al-Qaeda. In the most dramatic achievement of his Presidency, the elusive bin Laden was found in Pakistan and killed. The Predator drones were highly effective in taking out the higher echelons of the organization and disrupting its internal functioning. Between President Bush and President Obama, the original band of "evil-doers" had been decimated. Yet as they disappeared, new "terrorist" formations were springing up in the Middle East, Africa and elsewhere.

Indeed, if the events of 9-11 had taught any lessons, it was that furious people enraged by American foreign policy could find ways to strike back. [74] Twelve years later, such enemies had multiplied. No matter how flat or flowery the Presidential rhetoric, or how different in temperament, there was reason to suspect that the "pragmatic" choice of war and assassination had left the American people less secure.

REFERENCES

[1]   Transcript, President Obama's Speech, Fort Bragg,, *New York Times (NYT)*, 12/14/2011.

[2]   Patrick Cockburn, "Toxic Legacy of US Assault on Fallujah 'Worse Than Hiroshima'," *The Independent*, 7/24/2010.

[3]   "Research Links Rise in Falluja Birth Defects and Cancers to US Assault," *The Guardian*, 12/30/2010; BBC, "Disturbing Story of Falluja's Birth Defects," 3/4/2010; "Birth Defects Soar in Fallujah," United Press International, 11/14/2009; "Huge Rise in Birth Defects in Falluja," *The Guardian,* 11/13/2009; BBC, "US Used White Phosphorus in Iraq," 11/16/2005; Democracy Now, US Broadcast Exclusive, "Fallujah: the Hidden Massacre-on the US Use of Napalm-Like White Phosphorus Bombs," 11/8/2005. http://archive.org/details/dn2005-1108 : Jonathan Steele, "This is Our Guernica," *The Guardian*, 4/27/2005; " Film Reveals True Destruction to Ghost City Falluja," *The Guardian,* 05/10/2005.

[4]   Transcript of President Bush's Address, *CNN*.com 9/20/2001; Michael Howard, "What's in a Name*?" Foreign Affairs*, Jan/Feb, 2002.

[5]   "Bush Delivers Ultimatum," *CNN World*, 9/20/2001.

[6]   Terry A. Anderson, *Bush's Wars* (New York: Oxford University Press) 86.

[7]   *Ibid*, 87.

[8]   *Ibid,* 90-91; Peter L. Bergen, *The Longest War* (New York: Free Press) 63.

[9]   Cited in Anderson, 81.

[10]   Anderson, 86; Bergen, 74-78.

[11]   Bergen, 79.

[12]   "The Fall of Kabul, " PBS, 11/13/2001, http://www.pbs.org/newshour/bb/asia/july-dec01/kabul_11-13.html; "Celebration: First day of Muslim Eid al-Fitr holiday is marked by kite flying, music and other simple joys banned by the Taliban," *Los Angeles Times,* 12/17/2001.

[13]   Richard A. Clarke, *Against All Enemies* (New York: Free Press, 2004), 30-31.

[14]   White House. National Security Strategy of the United States 2002, www.whitehouse.gov/nsc/nssall.html.

[15]   Micah Sifry, "The Second Superpower," in Sifry and Christopher Cerf (eds) *The Iraq War Reader* (hereafter referred to as IWR), 489.

[16]   Cited in Anderson, 120-121.

[17]   "Hans Blix Speaks His Mind on How US Doubted Him," *NYT* 6/16/2003.

[18]   Donald Rumsfeld, *Known and Unknown: A Memoir,* (New York : Penguin Books) 434-435.

[19]   U.S. British Draft Resolution on Iraq, 2/24/2003; "Words of Refusal: Three Nations Say No," *NYT,* 3/6/2003; Jeffrey Richelson (ed.), "Iraq and Weapons of Mass Destruction," National Security Archive, 2/11/2004, http://www.gwu.edu/~nsarchiv/NSAEBB/NSAEBB80/

[20]   Pew Research Center, Trends in Public Opinion About the War in Iraq, 2003-2007, http://pewresearch.org/pubs/431/trends-in-public-opinion-about-the-war-in-iraq-2003-2007

[21] Senate vote was 77-23,with 29 of 50 Democrats voting in favor. House vote was closer, 296-133, with 81 Democrats voting in favor. "Of Pre-emption and Appeasement, Box-Cutters and Liquid Fuel: Excerpts from the October 10, 2002, House Debate, *IWR*, 359-366; Authorization for Use of Military Force Against Iraq, (H.J.Res. 114), http://thomas.loc.gov/cgi-bin/query/D?c107:3:./temp/~c107IDVEF7.

[22] George W. Bush, Transcript 'Leave Iraq Within 48 Hours,' *CNN World*, March 17, 2003.

[23] Project for a New American Century, "An Open Letter to President Bush: Lead the World to Victory," *IWR*, 222-224; Robert Kagan and William Kristol, "What to do About Iraq," *IWR*, 243-250; Nicholas Lemann, "The Next World Order," *IWR*, 253-265. For the role of the "neo-cons," James Mann, *Rise of the Vulcans, The History of Bush's War Cabinet* (New York: Viking); Stefan Harper and Jonathan Clarke, *America Alone, The Neo-Conservatives and the Global Order,"* (New York: Cambridge University Press).

[24] Stinging critiques of the Bush War in Iraq are too numerous to list here. Among those which have formed the background for this paper: Ali A. Allawi, *The Occupation of Iraq* (New Haven, Yale University Press); Rajiv Chandrasekaran, *Imperial Life in Emerald City,* (New York, Vintage); Larry Diamond, *Squandered Victory* (New York: Henry Holt & Co.); David Phillips, *Losing Iraq* (New York: Westview Press); Thomas Ricks, *Fiasco* (New York: The Penguin Press); Anthony Shadid, *Night Draws Near* (New York: Henry Holt & Co.).

[25] "President Bush Takes Heat for WMD Jokes," *CNN Politcs,* 3/3/2004.

[26] See especially Diamond, *Squandered Victory, 53-178;* Chandrasekaran, 66-91; Shadid, 235-237.

[27] Shadid, 153-166.

[28] *Ibid.*, 186-235.

[29] National Intelligence Estimate: "Al Qaeda Damage Becoming More Scattered," *CNN Politics*, 9/26/2006.

[30] Anderson, 189.

[31] Juan Cole, "Sunni Baghdad Dark on Satellite: Kagan Proved Wrong Again," *Informed Comment, (IC)* 9/20/2008. http://www.juancole.com/2008/09/sunni-baghdad-dark-on-satellite-kagan.html.

[32] BBC, "World View of US Role Goes from Bad to Worse," 1/23/2007.

[33] Ray Close, "The Real Meaning of Fallujah," Guest Columnist in Juan Cole, *IC,* 4/30/2004.

[34] Dahr Jamail, *Democracy Now*, US Broadcast Exclusive- "Fallujah: the Hidden Massacre-on the US Use of Napalm-Like White Phosphorus Bombs," 11/08/2005.

[35] BBC, "US Used White Phosphorus in Iraq," 11/16/2005.

[36] "War Costs May Total $2.4 Trillion,*"* *USA Today*, 10/25/2007.

[37] "Barack Obama's Stirring 2012 Speech Against Iraq War," http://usliberals.about.com/od/extraordinaryspeeches/a/Obama2002War.htm.

[38] "In New Hampshire, Clinton Owns Up to Her Vote on Iraq War," *NYT,* 2//11/2008; "The Fine Print in Hillary's Promise to End the War, *Washington Post, (WP)*, 10/10/2007.

[39] Barack Obama, "My Plan for Iraq," *NYT,* 7/14/2008.

[40] Transcript of Obama/ McCain Debate, *CNN,* http://edition.cnn.com/ 2008/POLITICS/09/26/2008.

[41] Barack Obama, *The Audacity of Hope* (New York: Three Rivers Press). 308-309

[42] Oslo Peace Prize Committee, Press Release, 10/09/2009, http://www.nobelprize.org/ nobel_prizes/peace/laureates/2009/press.html

[43] Full Text of Obama's Nobel Peace Prize Speech," 12/12/2009, http://www.msnbc.msn.com/id/34360743/ns/politics-white_house/t/full-text-obamas-nobel-peace-prize-speech. /

[44] Cited in Bob Woodward, *Obama's Wars,* (New York: Simon & Schuster), 57.

[45] "Violence in Iraq Drops Sharply," *Reuters*, 10/22/2007.

[46] Administration officials, who sustained considerable criticism for "the surge," have strongly maintained that this decision was the reason why violence in Iraq dropped significantly in 2007-2008. Bush, *Decision Points,* 355-394; Dick Cheney, *In My Time* (New York: Threshhold Editions), 465-493. For diverse perspectives on this question, Dylan Matthew, "How Important Was the Surge?" Survey of 12 Iraqi Experts," *New American Prospect,* 7/25/2008.

[47] BBC, "Shoes Thrown at Bush on Iraq Trip," 12/15/ 2008, http://news.bbc.co.uk/ 2/hi/7782422.stm.

[48] "Civilian Killings Created Insurmountable Hurdle to Extended Troop Presence in Iraq," *WP,* 12/11/2012.

[49] White House Press Office, Remarks by President Ending the War in Iraq http://www.whitehouse.gov/the-press-office/2011/10/21/remarks-president-ending-war-iraq.

[50] Transcript, President Obama's Speech, Fort Bragg,, *NYT,* 12/14/2011.

[51] Amnesty International, "Amnesty International Annual Report-Iraq," 5/13//2011, http://www.amnestyusa.org/research/reports/annual-report-iraq-2011; Toby Dodge, "The Irresistible Rise of Nuri al-Maliki, March 12, 2012, *Open Democracy*, http://www.opendemocracy.net/toby-dodge/resistible-rise-of-nuri-al-maliki

[52] For early period Dov Zakheim, *A Vulcan's Tale (*Washington: Brookings Institution Press), 127-140, 156-183; Ahmed Rashid, *Descent Into Chaos,(*New York: Penguin) 171-195.

[53] Bergen, 192.

[54] Anderson, 211-212.

[55] Woodward, 88-89; David E. Sanger, *Confront and Conceal* (New York: Random House), 16-17.

[56] Rajiv Chandrasekaran, *Little America,(* New York: Knopf) 50-53.

[57] Woodward, 96-97.

[58] *Ibid,* 97.

[59] "Top US Commander in Afghanistan is Fired," *WP,* 5/12/2009.

[60] Sanger, 30-31.

[61] On Biden's views, Woodward, 166-169, 186; Chandrasekaran, *Little America*, 125-127.

[62] Woodward, 247, 292.

[63] Greg Miller, "US Military Campaign to Topple Resilient Taliban Hasn't Succeeded," *WP,* 10/26/2010; "Afghanistan: How Well is the U.S. Really Doing in Kandahar," *Time,* 11/09/2010.

[64] Ahmed Rashid, "NATO's Dangerous Wager With Karzai," *New York Review of Books,* *12/01/2010.*

[65] C.J. Chivers, "Putting Afghan Plan Into Action Proves Difficult," *NYT*, 3/08/2011; Carlotta Gall, "Winning Hearts While Flattening Vineyards is Rather Tricky," *NYT,* 3/11/2011.

[66] "An Afghan Comes Home to a Massacre," *NYT,* 3/12/2012.

[67] "Afghan Shootings Refocus Attention at Fort Lewis-McChord Base," *WP,* 3/13/2012; "Members of Stryker Combat Brigade in Afghanistan Accused of Killing Civilians for Sport," *WP*, 3/18/2010.

[68] Cited in Alex Kane, "5 Ways Obama is Just like George W. Bush,"Salon.com, 6/6/2013.

[69] Jo Becker and Scott Shane, "Secret 'Kill List' Proves A Test of Obama's Principles and Will," *NYT,* 5/20/2012.

[70] Cited by Spencer Ackerman, "The Obama Doctrine," *The American Prospect,* 3/19/2008.

[71] Role of militarism discussed in Carolyn Eisenberg "Imperial Crisis and Domestic Dissent," *Positions* (North Carolina: Duke University Press) and "The New Cold War," *Diplomatic History*, 29:3, 423-427. Andrew Bacevich, *The New American Militarism: How Americans Are Seduced by War*," (New York: Oxford) and *Washington Rules: America's Path to Permanent War*," (New York: Henry Holt & Co.) Chalmers Johnson, *Sorrows of Empire* (New York: Henry Holt& Co.).

[72] Ted Galen Carpenter, "The Iraq Debacle Continues," *The National Interest, 1/05/2013.*

[73] Patrick Cockburn, "The Death of the American Dream in Afghanistan," *The Independent*, 02/07/2012; Joshua Hersh, "Afghanistan: the Long and Winding Road," *Huffington Post*, 10/13/2012; Oleg Svet, "COIN's Failure in Afghanistan," *National Interest*, 08/31/2012.

[74] Robert Pape, "What Triggers the Suicide Bomber?" *LA Times,* 10/22/2010.

In: Change in the White House?   ISBN: 978-1-62948-920-9
Editor: Meena Bose   © 2014 Nova Science Publishers, Inc.

Chapter 8

BUSH, OBAMA, POLARIZATION AND NATIONAL SECURITY: SOME CONCLUDING THOUGHTS

Dov S. Zakheim

More than any conflict since the Vietnam War, which ended nearly four decades ago, the war in Iraq, and to a lesser extent the conflict in Afghanistan, have prompted a massive divide among Americans—that is, Americans in academia, the think tank world, and the media. Unlike Vietnam, which required the call-up of hundreds of thousands of draftees, and affected Americans of all walks of life, the later wars have been fought by volunteers. Only in those communities from which reservists have been drawn can the war be said to have affected a wider circle than the immediate one of the military and their families.

Certainly, with the passage of time, both the wars in Afghanistan and Iraq became increasingly unpopular. The former, termed Operation Iraqi Freedom, never won the depth of support that the war in Afghanistan, launched in the aftermath of the 9/11 tragedy, was able to mount. Yet as the Afghan War dragged on, with few tangible signs of lasting progress, with losses and serious injurieso slowly mounting, and with the American economic recession perceived to have been aggravated by wartime spending, Americans tired of that war as well.

Nevertheless, with the exception of a few major demonstrations, neither war has prompted the vitriolic public reaction that haunted the Vietnam operation from the mid-Sixties onwards. Few Americans have lambasted the military as they did during the Vietnam years; indeed, Madison Avenue, that reliable gauge of domestic popularity, has been including the military in its advertisements throughout the course of both wars. Nor have there been major or even minor campus revolts, and no shutdowns at all. There have been four major political conventions, two Republican and two Democratic, since the onset of both wars; none witnessed the turmoil that roiled Chicago in 1968.

The chapters in this volume therefore represent what is essentially a debate among elites. Long-time opponents of American involvement in military conflicts have found fault with both wars, and with both Presidents, Bush and Obama, who have conducted them. Right-leaning academics have generally been sympathetic to Bush, and his decision to go to war with Iraq, while critical of Obama's haste in withdrawing troops from Afghanistan. Their left-leaning counterparts have taken the opposite view. They criticize Bush for attacking Saddam on what proved to be the invalid pretext of seeking to eliminate weapons of mass destruction, and support what they view as Obama's measured efforts to withdraw from Afghanistan while preserving the tenuous political and economic progress that has been achieved since the 2002 defeat of the Taliban.

The debate over the conduct of both wars has not been limited to the wisdom of actually launching them. It has spawned criticism of what seems to be an ever-expanding role of presidential power—from the Bush Administration's attempt to implement the unitary theory of presidential power to the Obama Administration's ongoing targeting and killing of terrorists overseas, including, it is has been reported, Americans, without revealing the nature of those operations to the Congress, much less the American people.

The papers by Robert Spitzer and Carol Eisenberg exemplify the disappointment of many on the liberal/progressive side of the political spectrum with President Obama's policies policies, especially because he seemed to promise a sea-change from those of the Bush Administration, for which the Left had nothing but scorn. Still, both find far greater fault with President Bush.

Robert Spitzer points out that both Bush and Obama expanded their power at the expense of the Congress, and, in what he admits is a "broad brush" statement, asserts that "the Bush unitary theory was by definition categorically more aggressive and tendentious than anything contemplated or articulated by the Obama Administration, at least as of this writing." In fact, while the Obama Administration has not articulated any particular theory of presidential power or authority, its aggressive employment of drones on the battlefield while minimizing any disclosure of their use even to the Congress, could certainly qualify as an equally expansive pursuit of presidential fiat. This policy has been criticized, especially by those on the Left, for violating the right of habeas corpus to which all Americans are entitled (and, some would add, to which even foreign terrorists are entitled). Indeed, such criticism has been both far harsher, and more widespread among the public, than the objects of Spitzer's concern, for example, Obama's decision to intervene in the Libya conflict without fully conforming to the requirements of the War Powers Act, or his use, however more limited than Bush's, of signing statements to circumvent the intent of Congress.

Nevertheless, Spitzer is far more trenchant regarding Bush's decision to intervene in Iraq than he is with respect to anything Obama has done. While acknowledging that the "Congress provided the necessary green light , and Bush acted within that constitutional and legal framework," Spitzer nevertheless asserts that the Congress acted as it did because it was tricked into doing so: "In no instance in American history," he asserts rather tendentiously, "was the case for war—any war—built on as lengthy and prodigious a list of lies as the Iraq War." One wonders what Spitzer makes of the Gulf of Tonkin Resolution. Or for that matter, the 1898 declaration for war against Spain, which was prompted by an explosion on the warship *Maine* that was falsely attributed to that country.

More to the point perhaps, it should be noted that to this day, leading figures in the Bush Administration contend that they accepted the intelligence that was presented to them. That intelligence was not, as is often asserted, created from whole cloth. Saddam's generals sought to reassure him that the program was progressing; Saddam himself wanted the Iranians to believe he had such a program, in order to deter them. After all, he had already fought one bloody war with them in the 1980s and since then had both been defeated by the American-led coalition and was subject to the humiliation of a no-fly zone over his country. Spitzer's vitriol is, however, a good reflection of the emotions that the decision to go to war with Iraq have stoked over the past decade.

In a sense Spitzer is correct when he emphasizes that both presidents have, each in his own way, significantly expanded the powers of their office at the expense of the Congress, and, moreover, have prompted a "serious debate about the scope and limits of presidential power." Yet neither President Bush nor President Obama significantly modified their behavior in response to that debate. For example, President Bush showed no interest in closing the prison at Guantanamo, nor did he indicate any interest in prosecuting captured terrorists in civil courts. For his part, after initially seeking and failing both to close Guantanamo and to try terrorists on American soil, President Obama reverted to his predecessor's reliance on military tribunals to try captured terrorists.

Indeed, President Obama, freed from the burden of campaigning for re-election, has indicated that he will continue to broaden presidential prerogatives both in the civil and national security sectors. For example, since his re-election, the president has announced that he will sign an executive order for the Center for Disease Control to study gun violence, despite clear Congressional intent and legislation to the contrary. Similarly, he shows no inclination to ratchet back his reliance on drone attacks to prosecute what his predecessor called the "war on terror." In fact it appears that the number of those attacks has continued to rise. Moreover, by nominating, while the mastermind behind those attacks, White House assistant John Brennan, to head the Central Intelligence Agency, the president has indicated that he remains comfortable with his policy of relying on drone attacks to kill America's enemies, regardless of their citizenship

It is therefore questionable whether President Obama has been any more respectful of constitutional norms than his predecessor. While he may have issued fewer signing statements thus far in his presidency--and he has virtually four more years ahead of him--, and his ongoing prosecution of a war that is being kept secret from both the Congress and the American people, offers little prospect of any. diminution of what Spitzer would likely perceive as the abuse of presidential power. His argument that Obama's "constitutional presidency has been broadly consistent with his post-Watergate strongtrin-g presidency contemporaries, but ... he is no George W. Bush," does not meet the test of Washington reality.

Like Robert Spitzer, Carolyn Eisenberg is critical of both presidents, but reserves her harshest judgment for President Bush. Indeed, her indictment of Bush verges on the intemperate, rendering Spitzer's assessment mild by comparison. Eisenberg clearly is of the opinion that not only was the attack on Iraq unnecessary, so too was the war in Afghanistan. Reflecting a view that is widespread on the Left, she asserts that it has been "the usual practice of the United States and other countries to treat acts of terrorism, even when launched from inside another country, as a crime rather than a war." This in fact is not at all the case. The shooting of the Israeli ambassador to the UK triggered the Lebanon War of 1982; indeed, the assassination of Archduke Franz Ferdinand was the immediate cause of World War I.

Moreover, the notion that an act of terrorism should be "handled through investigation, arrest and criminal prosecution," as Eisenberg asserts, confuses a single act by an individual with a series of coordinated activities by a terrorist organization across international borders. Al Qaida and its affiliates, who assert they are at war with the United States, are hardly to be compared to Timothy McVeigh, even if at the same time they cannot be treated as enemy combatants as defined by the Geneva Conventions and. expect to be granted the same rights afforded to him.

In any event, the attack on Afghanistan's Taliban regime was due to its determination to harbor the Al Qaida terrorists. Eisenberg asserts that the Bush ultimatum to the Taliban was a sham, and that he always intended to go to war. Yet she does not explain why, in that case, the entire international community, including France, Germany, Canada and Russia, all of whom later opposed the attack on Iraq, sided with Bush and supported Operation Enduring Freedom, with all but the last contributing troops and/or materiel to the effort.

Eisenberg rightly criticizes the Bush Administration for turning to Iraq before it completed the job in Afghanistan. It certainly paid a high price for doing so: had it maintained its focus on the latter, neither al Qaida, nor the Taliban and its sister groups would likely have regrouped and launched what has been essentially a second Afghan War. Yet Eisenberg overreaches in her critique of the Iraq Operation.

Like many critics of the Iraq War, Eisenberg asserts that the 2002 National Security Strategy, which many believe laid the groundwork for that war, unveiled a novel approach to international threats " that went far beyond the notion of pre-emptive action , recognized by international law." Yet it is difficult to see how what the strategy termed "anticipatory action to defend ourselves"--which Eisenberg highlights in italics--is more radical than say, France's and Britain's declaration of war on Germany when the Nazis attacked Poland, a third country; or the 1991 Coalition attack on Iraq, which the United Nations mandated after Saddam's forces attacked Kuwait, a third country; or NATO's attack on Yugoslavia, which was also mandated by the UN; or, for that matter, America's declaration of war on Germany after it had been attacked not by that country but by Japan! Relative to each of those cases, the 2002 strategy seems almost passive.

Again, like many critics, Eisenberg asserts that the invasion of Iraq prompted "massive criticism" from around the world. This is simply incorrect. Far more countries contributed to the international coalition in Iraq than opposed the invasion. Those contributing troops included not only smaller states, but also South Korea, Japan, Italy, Spain and Poland. Many others contributed materiel. The objections of France, Germany and Canada do not constitute "massive" worldwide criticism.

Similarly, Eisenberg's assertions regarding domestic American opposition to the war, particularly prior to 2005, are simply misplaced. What she refers to as "an active and growing anti war movement" was hardly heard from prior to that date and never remotely approached either the magnitude or intensity of the opposition to the Vietnam War. That this was the case was due in no small part to the absence of the draft, which was a major motivator of the protests of the 'Sixties. This time the campuses remained quiet, even if professors were not.

Many of Eisenberg's specific comments about the conduct of the war have been articulated elsewhere, debated elsewhere, and, of course, refuted elsewhere by former Bush Administration officials. They need not be rehashed here. On the either hand, it is worth noting Eisenberg's unhappiness with the policies of Barack Obama, whose administration she, like many of her progressive colleagues, expected would mark a sharp departure from its predecessor.

In Eisenberg's view Obama did not fulfill the promise of his campaign rhetoric when he looked to Washington insiders to fill key national security positions. She notes that instead of bringing in new faces for his national security team, he drew its members from among those who worked for Bill Clinton. She complains that he did not replace his senior military advisors, something which presidents rarely if ever do when they take office. In particular, she cites his retention of Robert Gates as Secretary of Defense. She describes Gates as a former cold warrior who appeared moderate only relative to the extremists in the Bush Administration.

Nowhere does Eisenberg note that Gates signed a bipartisan report that was critical of the Bush team's handling of the Iraq War and that called for an early withdrawal from that country. Nor does she point out that Gates later opposed American involvement in the Libya Operation. Her unhappiness with Gates derives from a deeper distrust of US motives: like many on the Left, Eisenberg continues to bemoan the labeling of the Soviet Union as the "evil empire," even though subsequent events have vindicated Ronald Reagan's use of that graphic and memorable descriptor.

Nevertheless, whatever the accuracy, and, for that matter, validity, of Eisenberg's assertions, they reflect the deep disappointment of the Left with Barack Obama. This disappointment extends well beyond unease with what is perceived to be his high-handed approach to the Constitution, even if it does not match that of George W. Bush, and beyond his decision to surge forces in Afghanistan and to continue fighting the war throughout his entire first term and into his second. Instead, it is rooted in the belief, that, as Eisenberg puts it, American national security policy reflects "the powerful grip of military thinking and military institutions on American political life." And neither Eisenberg, nor those who share her view, have any idea how to loosen that grip anytime soon.

Richard Himelfarb provides a cautionary corrective to the long held views of the American Left that feature most prominently in Carolyn Eisenberg's paper. Himelfarb's essay nominally addresses the question of whether either Presidents Bush or Obama helped to bridge the yawning social, economic and cultural gap that bedevils contemporary American politics. In fact, however, it is essentially a sharp rebuttal of Gary Jacobson's book *A Divider, Not A Uniter*, and subsequent essays that take George W. Bush to task for exacerbating partisan divisions but and tend to overlook similar behavior by Barack Obama and his Administration.

Himelfarb notes that Jacobson, a respected liberal academic, takes Bush especially to task for employing specious arguments in support of his decision to launch the war in Iraq. In that regard, Jacobson's assertions are no different from the case that Spitzer and Eisenberg make in this volume. Himelfarb defends Bush, arguing that Bush's belief that Saddam possessed weapons of mass destruction was sincere, and that the Administration's "most frequently employed justification for war against Iraq was not the result of lying and deception."

Himelfarb goes on to make a larger point that goes well beyond the debate over Iraq, however. He argues that Obama has been no less partisan than Bush, nor any less deceptive. Moreover, he asserts that the Left, like the Right, is guilty of a variety of excesses, which Jacobson tends to gloss over.

Himelfarb makes a strong case. There certainly is enough blame to go around. For every partisan excess on Fox News, there is an equal and opposite provocation on MSNBC. Guantanamo has remained an open sore under Obama as it did under Bush. The Bush Administration's so-called "rendition program" appears to have survived the change of Administrations.

Himelfarb asserts that Bush's behavior in launching the Iraq War was no more or less devious that Obama's methods to pass health reform. His contention is highly debatable. It might be argued that Obama's efforts to pass health care legislation, no matter how high-handed, simply cannot be compared with the tactics the Bush Administration is alleged to have used to prompt a decision to go to war. On the other hand, the case can be made that whatever the sleight of hand that might have been employed to win Congressional support for Operation Iraqi Freedom, it has been more than matched by Obama's refusal to acknowledge even to the Congress that he is personally in charge of drone attacks that reputedly have targeted American citizens as well as foreign terrorists.

There is no quick resolution to the question of who has been guilty of more and greater misdeeds, Bush or Obama. On and on goes the slanging match between the respective supporters of the two presidents. Indeed, the debate shows no signs of ebbing in the aftermath of the bitterly contested 2012 presidential election and the tension over the debt ceiling, tax reform, sequestration, national security policy and the defense budget.

It is perhaps not surprising that many academics on both sides of the partisan divide have been no less vitriolic about those who do not share their views than have the politicians of each party and their most rabid supporters. No less surprising, giving the generally liberal orientation of most campuses, is the fact that other academics have reserved most of their bitterness for Bush, yet at the same time have been deeply disappointed with Obama, whose performance has fallen short of the "hope" that he offered and that they consequently expected. It is therefore hard to quarrel with Himelfarb's concluding observation that "the United States is a deeply divided country governed in the 21st century by a pair of principled presidents pursuing controversial, transformative policies.

John Graham and Veronica Stidvent point out that "the president cannot escape polarization because the president is typically perceived as the national leader of his party." They cite Jacobson's assertion that the president may be a strong polarizing influence; an observation to which Himmelfarb, for all his criticism of Jacobson's work, could agree, at least in its generic sense. Graham and Stidvent's focus is on the Congress, however, and specifically on how Bush and Obama dealt with that highly polarized institution.

The authors highlight three economic policy issues—the Bush tax cuts of 2001-2006, the Bush and Obama industry bailouts of the following three years, and Obama's stimulus package of 2009-10—that they feel will serve as indicators of "whether the White House was effective in persuading Congress to enact the president's proposal." They offer these issues as case studies of three strategies that a president might pursue: "cooperative bipartisanship," wherein the president engages both parties in order to reach a consensus; "partisanship," where there is no outreach to the other party; and "cross partisanship," whereby the president unifies his party and then tries to draw support from as many members of the other party as he can.

The authors note that Bush's approach on tax cuts was an example of the third strategy. He relied on a united Republican party in the Congress, and drew upon what became an increasingly diminishing, but still non-trivial, number of Democrats in support of the cuts. Bush was never able to make his cuts permanent, however, because he could not attract enough Democratic votes in the Senate to clear the 60 vote hurdle necessary to pass his proposed legislation.

Obama had initially sought to repeal the cuts, but could not muster enough support within his own party in order to do so. Instead he fell back upon the first of the three presidential strategies: he negotiated a series of deals with the Republicans that initially extended the tax cuts past 2012, as well as preserving several other tax breaks that the Republicans insisted upon, and then, after the 2012 elections, increasing taxes on the wealthiest Americans, but compromising with the Republicans by raising the threshold for higher rates from his preferred level of $250,000 to $400,000.

The authors point out that Obama, and indeed Bush, both employed a strategy of "cooperative bipartisanship" when they successfully sought to bail out the housing market and launched the initial phase of TARP legislation to bail out Wall Street. On the other hand, the Obama Administration fell back on a strategy of "cross-partisanship" when seeking passage of the far more controversial Dodd-Frank business legislation, the Obama stimulus package of 2009, and the "cash for clunkers" legislation.

Graham and Stidevent assert that "the fundamental lesson of the case studies is that it is feasible—though certainly not easy—for the White House to overcome partisan polarization in the Congress and enact priority legislation." In fact, these cases may be the exception. The 2012 election actually increased polarization in the Senate. Whereas more Democrats were elected to that body, several moderate Republicans departed, notably Olympia Snowe, who retired, and Richard Lugar, who was defeated in the Indiana primary race (the seat was won by a Democrat).

President Obama has been unable to obtain legislation on many of his key priorities, the most notable of which are his proposals to increase taxes and cut defense in order to avoid sequestration. Moreover, as the authors themselves acknowledge, the lessons they wish to draw "may be less applicable to foreign and military affairs." Their rationale for this situation is, however, somewhat misplaced. It is not because of "the stronger constitutional role of the president on these issues and the historical tendency for these issues to have less partisan content." On the contrary, while the president's constitutional role has indeed expanded, as several of the authors in this volume have noted, the partisan divide over both defense strategy and defense spending, as reflected in the deadlock over sequestration, has grown wider. Democrats feel that defense needs to contribute its "fair share" toward deficit reduction. Republicans argue that defense made that contribution in the 2011 National Defense Authorization Act which reduced spending by $487 billion over ten years.

Indeed, if there is bipartisanship on the question of defense spending, it tends to push in the opposite direction favored by the White House. On the one hand, there certainly are some Republicans, mostly associated with the Tea Party, who would favor defense cuts. In that sense, the White House might be able to pursue a strategy of cross-partisanship. On the other hand, however, many Democrats with military bases or defense industry in their districts have been reluctant to cut defense spending to the extent the White House would prefer. While a compromise will ultimately certainly be reached to avert the full multi-year force of sequestration, it is unlikely to call for the level of defense cuts that the Administration would prefer. In that sense, Graham and Stidman offer some excellent advice to the current resident of the White House: "presidents should give laser-like attention to the political interests of Senators from the opposing party who are potential cross-over votes." President Obama has done this on occasion; he needs to do it more often if he is to have the legislation he prefers enacted into law.

Two questions, one of policy and the other of process, transcend the partisan debates that have embroiled both Presidents Bush and Obama as well as the Congress. Stanley Renshon addresses the policy question, while John Burke looks at process. The policy question can be framed as: "does President Obama's approach to national security reflect a coherent '"doctrine'"? Many analysts, including Renshon, believe that it does. There is much to be said for this argument. Unlike many other promises issuing from candidate Obama, his belief that international security is subordinate to domestic concerns colored his presidency during his first term and promises to be a dominant theme in his second.

Renshon argues that what he terms the "real" Obama doctrine consists of three elements: redemptive transformation, which incorporates his view that nation-building begins at home; managing what he believes to be America's diminished primacy, for example, his initial rejection of American exceptionalism; and "hidden hand" leadership, for example, Washington's minimalist approach to the Libya operation. While, as Renshon notes, the president appeared to veer away from his critique of American exceptionalism during his first term, there are already several indications that in his second term he is likely to hew even more closely to the other elements of policy that Renshon elevates to a full-blown doctrine.

One example of the president's management of what he believes to be a decline in American primacy is his approach to nuclear weapons. It has become increasingly clear that president's offhand remark to Russian president Medvedev that he would significantly reduce America's nuclear arsenal will come to pass. Having already obtained a formal arms reduction treaty, President Obama appears ready to sidestep any need for future agreements by simply employing the budget to reduce America's nuclear arsenal. He will simply underfund nuclear modernization. In the current budgetary climate, with mandatory defense cuts already in place and more likely to be mandated, the Congress would be hard-pressed to restore most of the funds that the Administration would deny the strategic nuclear program. In a sense, Obama would thus not only be managing America's decline, he would actually hasten it.

Another example is the Administration's decision to delay a carrier deployment to the Indian Ocean/Arabian Gulf, ostensibly because of the likelihood that the dreaded sequester wouldill become a reality. Reducing the Indian Ocean force to one carrier precludes the Navy's ability to mount round-the-clock operations. In so doing, the Administration has reinforced the impression privately held by many Middle Eastern observers and policy makers that America is shifting its focus from the Middle East to East Asia. They can only conclude that a declining America no longer can protect its interests in both regions as it has done for the past four decades. (In fact it appears that in mid-February 2013 the United States had only one carrier deployed overseas.)

The second Obama term also promises more of what Renshon refuses to term "leading from behind," if it indeed will lead at all. It appears that contrary to what Renshon asserts, Secretary of State Hillary Cinton urged the president to become even more actively engaged in the crushing of the Ghaddafi regime. Instead, he followed a middle path between Hillary Clinton's preferences and the caution urged by Secretary of Defense Robert Gates.

The president was even more cautious when it came to arming the Syrian rebels. In fact, America not only did not lead from behind, it did not lead at all. In this case the White House did not pursue a path midway between those advised by his Secretaries of State and Defense, he actually is reported to have overridden both, in electing not to arm the opposition even as tens of thousands of civilians were being slaughtered by Bashar Assad's forces.

Washington has provided some support to the French forced battling the Islamic extremists in Mali. Yet it has done so with the utmost reluctance, indicating yet again that President Obama is not fully committed to leading from behind or from anywhere. The Administration had clearly preferred that African forces take the lead in combating the Islamists, and that Washington's role was to train these forces. There was no mistaking the Administration's annoyance at Paris for seizing the initiative and dispatching troops to the beleaguered west African state. Moreover, Washington's initial demand that France pay for the refueling of its aircraft and the airlift of its troops was nothing less than mean-spirited.

The Bush Administration did nothing of the kind when it lifted coalition forces to the Afghan and Iraqi theaters.

Whether the aforementioned actions constitute a full-blown doctrine may be debatable. Not every president has promulgated a doctrine, even if he pursued a consistent set of policies. Moreover, President Obama is hardly unique in setting policy direction. Presidents Nixon and Carter, both authors of eponymous doctrines, certainly did so. So too did Ronald Reagan, contrary to what many believe. So too did George H.W. Bush, who brought to the office more foreign and security policy experience than any president since Nixon.

Even if there is no clear Obama Doctrine, his policies certainly constitute a pattern that reflects the characteristics Renshon outlines. Moreover, there is no indication that he will veer away from those policies during his second term. Indeed, both his inaugural address and his 2013 State of the Union address underscore that pattern. And it is a disturbing pattern indeed.

With respect to process, John Burke examines what many have termed "the Scowcroft Model" of national security decision making, which has been the model for all administrations since Brent Scowcroft served as national security advisor to Gerald Ford and then held the same job, arguably with far greater influence, under George H.W. Bush. Burke describes the Scowcroft model's

> most notable features are meetings of the principals chaired by the NSC advisor in the absence of the president…informing its deliberations are deputies' meetings chaired by the deputy NSC advisor and composed of department, agency and NSC staff representatives…[whose] work in turn is assisted by a variety of working groups, again drawn from NSC staff and departmental personnel. [In addition] the NSC advisor [acts] as an honest broker, attentive to full and fair policy analysis and deliberation and concerned with the quality of advice reaching the president and the effectiveness of procedures producing it….as well as giving due attention to and management concern for the organization and processes that bear upon foreign and national security policy making.

Burke claims that neither Condoleeza Rice nor retired General Jim Jones were truly able to act as "honest brokers," though for different reasons. In Rice's case, Burke notes that she had to deal with three highly experienced and "bureaucratically skilled" players: Vice President Cheney, Secretary of Defense Rumsfeld and Secretary of State Powell. Moreover, once it became increasingly likely that there would be a war with Iraq, Burke feels that Rice seemed to lose control of a process she had managed reasonably well until then. Her cites claims that the process became "dysfunctional."

In fact, Rice deserves far more credit than she has received from the many "tell-all" volumes that have appeared in print, and that Burke cites. It was not merely the case that Rice had to contend with veteran bureaucratic players—she was the only National Security Advisor that ever had to deal simultaneously with three top officials who had all previously held senior White House posts. Rumsfeld and Cheney had both been White House Chiefs of Staff. Powell had held Rice's job before she did. In addition, Rumsfeld and Cheney were close friends; the two men would speak on the phone several times each day. (They now own homes near each other on Maryland's Eastern Shore). Finally, Rumsfeld and Powell clearly did not see eye to eye, while the Secretary of State and the Vice President did not get along terribly well.

Brent Scowcroft never had to deal with such circumstances: in his first stint as NSA, he knew better than to clash with his former boss at the White House, Henry Kissinger. In his second stint, he had the good fortune of working with three collegially minded men—Jim Baker, a very different Dick Cheney at Defense, and the president himself, with whom he was both personally close and later co-authored a memoir.

For Rice to have survived four years in her job, when so many of her predecessors never managed to do so, is nothing short of miraculous. It was indeed, as Burke indicates, her closeness to the president—they visibly spoke to each other on a unique "frequency"—that enabled her to cope with the special stresses of her job.

The problem for Rice, therefore, was not one of her faulty management, or even a faulty process. It was the problem of personality. Every presidential candidate has a coterie of close advisors that he brings with him into major policy positions once elected to office. Usually, these advisors fill high sub-cabinet level positions, but they tend to be protégés of other senior individuals who assume cabinet rank.

In some cases, that of George H.W. Bush being the prime example, the president chooses personnel that are likely to work well together, which is not the same thing as agreeing on every issue. In other cases, however, the president will choose people he may not know well, and therefore will have no idea of their ability to be team players. Nixon's choice of William Rogers as Secretary of State together with Henry Kissinger as National Security Advisor, is an example of the latter case., Kissinger outfoxed Rogers, eventually pushing him out and replacing him. Carter's choice of Zbigniew Brzezinski, his senior national security advisor during the 1976 campaign, for the post of NSA, had a tense relationship with Cyrus Vance, the establishment lawyer whom Carter named Secretary of State. Vance resigned over the Desert One fiasco, the failed attempt to rescue the American hostages in Iran. Reagan's close friend and associate Caspar Weinberger, who became Secretary of Defense, clashed with General Alexander Haig, whom Reagan knew less well when he named him Secretary of State; Haig resigned in 1983.

Powell and Rumsfeld had both advised Bush during the 2000 presidential campaign. Rumsfeld had actually briefed Bush on missile defense during a meeting of the "Vulcans" (Bush's top foreign policy team) at the Governor's mansion in Austin. But Bush appears not to have focused on whether Powell would get along well with the Rumsfeld-Cheney axis, about which he knew because it was Cheney who suggested Rumsfeld for Defense Secretary when Senator Dan Coates was dropped from consideration for that position. Nor does Bush appear to have considered whether very senior white males like Rumsfeld and Cheney would take seriously a woman who had been a relatively junior staffer when they previously held office. In the event, they did not.

Personality issues also undermined General Jones' relatively brief tenure as national security advisor. Jones had not sought the post of National Security Advisor, but as a lifelong dedicated Marine, he could not say no when it was offered to him by his commander-in-chief. Obama had chosen Jones in large part to give his Administration some credibility with the tightly knit national security community, both domestic and international. It was not, however, a matter of Jones having to cope with clashing egos at State and Defense, however, because Hillary Clinton and Bob Gates both proved to be excellent team players. Instead, Jones had to cope with the fact that both his deputy, Tom Donilon, and his National Security Council Chief of Staff, Dennis McDonough, were close associates, and had better access to the president than he did. Both had worked for Obama in the 2008 presidential campaign. In addition, Donilon's brother Mike had been appointed counselor to Vice President Joe Biden, while Donilon's wife, Cathy Russell, became Jill Biden's chief of staff.

It should come as no wonder, then, that Jones was quickly frustrated in his new job, or that he was unable to prevent the constant back-channel communications to the president that undermined his authority. With the passage of time, as Obama gained more confidence as Commander-in-Chief, and as he came to rely increasingly not only on Donilon and McDonough but also on Clinton and Gates, Jones became dispensable. His resignation was a foregone conclusion months before it took place. That Donilon succeeded him also came as no surprise to Washington's national security community.

Burke rightly asks whether Donilon has served as an "honest broker." He cites critics who argue that the NSC remains dysfunctional and devoid of solid management. Yet it is arguable that Donilon has done what a president who is prepared personally to authorize drone attacks would want him to do. President Obama has certainly been afforded different points of view, for example, regarding whether when and how to intervene in Libya and Syria. Donilon does not appear to have suppressed these viewpoints; nevertheless, he clearly sees his job as an implementer of the president's decisions. And that apparently is what the president wants.

As Burke rightly notes, at the end of the day, neither the Scowcroft model, and, it might be said, no model, "does not necessarily provide(s) substance and content in its own right…vision, ideas, strategy and tactics matter—they are the substance of policy choice." That is not what processes are about. In fact, one of the government bureaucracy's primary shortcomings, as it has continued to grow incessantly over the past decades, has been the predilection of officials to avoid substantive decisions by burying themselves in process. And process, even a robust one that has stood the test of time like Brent Scowcroft's, can only go so far. Ultimately, it is the president who must choose the personalities that will formulate and recommend policy options, and it is the president who must choose from among those options. The "buck" still stops at his desk.

Presidents Bush and Obama had very different methods of deciding policy. They had different approaches to choosing their most senior advisors. Most important of all, they held very different world views.

The contrast between the policies of both men, particularly with respect to national security writ large, which includes economic security, reflects the deep and ongoing divisions within American society about the best means for maintaining stability and security in a rapidly evolving international environment. Obama, and Bush before him, have offered very different visions of America's role in the world, the importance of the military to that role, and the priority that should be assigned to national security budgets relative to domestic programs. The essays in this volume address these visions from a variety of viewpoints. Taken together, however, they reflect the depth of public debate over these issues, one that is likely to go unresolved for an extended period of time, regardless of the policies pursued by the second Obama Administration, or for that matter, those of the Administration that will take office in 2017.

INDEX

#

2001 recession, 59
21st century, 52, 77, 136
9/11, 5, 6, 7, 10, 11, 19, 29, 32, 40, 41, 47, 48, 51, 52, 59, 85, 103, 105, 111, 131

A

abolition, 80
Abraham, 40, 80
abuse, 133
access, 16, 112, 114, 140
accommodation, 79
accounting, 88
advertisements, 131
affirmative action, 51
Afghanistan, vii, ix, 6, 7, 8, 40, 81, 82, 84, 88, 89, 94, 97, 100, 101, 105, 111, 112, 113, 115, 118, 119, 121, 122, 123, 124, 125, 126, 129, 130, 131, 133, 134, 135
Africa, 19, 126
African-American, 78
age, 78, 125
agencies, 6, 17, 18, 24, 35, 47, 51, 62, 91, 95
aggression, 114
agility, 62
Air Force, 123
Al Qaeda, 25, 48, 112, 113, 114, 118, 119, 120, 121, 122, 123, 128
Alexander Hamilton, 30
alternative energy, 46
American Bar Association, 33
American Presidency, vii, ix, 3, 30, 31, 57
anger, 43, 44, 112, 117, 125
anthrax, 48
anxiety, 43

apoplexy, 16
appointees, 25, 122
appointments, 6, 96, 119
appropriations, 4, 23, 25
Appropriations Act, 24, 34
architects, 93
armed forces, 19, 20, 120, 121
arms sales, 93
arrest, 112, 133
Asia, 80
assassination, 126, 133
assault, 117
assertiveness, 77
assessment, vii, 17, 38, 42, 43, 47, 48, 133
assets, 7, 84
asymmetry, 9
atmosphere, 32, 100
attitudes, 12, 59
Attorney General, 17, 22
audits, 16
authoritarianism, 12, 44
authority(s), 4, 5, 12, 15, 16, 23, 24, 25, 28, 29, 32, 34, 44, 49, 63, 65, 101, 103, 116, 125, 132, 141
automotive sector, 63, 67
aversion, 113

B

bail, 64, 137
balance sheet, 64
bankers, 65
bankruptcy, 65, 66
banks, 63, 64, 65
base, 15, 16, 37, 38, 46, 116, 118, 120, 123, 124, 125
benefits, 6, 49, 50, 62, 68, 94, 112, 119
bias, 9, 39, 45
Bible, 44
bilateral relationship, 84

144 Index

biological weapons, 114
Blacks, 44
blame, 5, 9, 29, 38, 43, 45, 99, 114, 135
bleeding, 66
blogs, 86
bondholders, 65
Bosnia, 20
bounds, 101
brainstorming, 69
Britain, 47, 84, 112, 134
brutality, 41, 48
Budget Committee, 61
budget cuts, 84
budget deficit, 8
Bulgaria, 115
bullying, 119
bureaucracy, 3, 28, 141
burn, 117
Bush administration, vii, 4, 5, 6, 9, 11, 16, 17, 18, 19, 21, 27, 28, 31, 39, 40, 41, 46, 47, 48, 50, 64, 100, 116, 119, 120, 126
businesses, 68, 117

C

Cabinet, viii, 86, 99, 128
Camp David, 105
campaigns, 50
cancer, 112
candidates, 61
capital gains, 60, 69
Capitol Hill, 48, 86, 101
caricature, 51
case law, 24, 26
case studies, 8, 57, 58, 68, 136, 137
cash, 8, 65, 66, 67, 113, 137
casting, 57, 118
CBS, 55, 88
center-left coalition, 12
challenges, vii, 4, 23, 24, 26, 103, 104, 124
chaos, 116
chemical(s), 19, 114, 117, 124
Chicago, 10, 30, 33, 54, 70, 78, 118, 131
Chief of Staff, 119, 140
child mortality, 112
children, 12, 44, 112, 124, 125, 126
China, 47
Christians, 37, 38, 41, 42, 44, 45, 50
CIA, 47, 89, 93, 94, 100, 101, 106, 113, 114, 119, 122, 123
city(s), 62, 75, 114, 120, 121, 127, 128
citizens, 16, 78, 81, 136
citizenship, 133

civil liberties, 5
civil rights, 78
clarity, 81, 95
classes, 38
cleft palate, 112
clients, 62
climate, 45, 96, 119, 138
clone, 29
cluster bomb, 117
clusters, 114
CNN, 70, 127, 128, 129
coal, 68
Cold War, 77, 82, 84, 104, 119, 126, 130, 135
collaboration, 63
collateral, 81
collateral damage, 81
College Station, 31
colleges, 67
Colombia, 23
commander-in-chief, 20, 21, 140
commerce, 105
commercial, 62
commercial bank, 62
communism, 111
community(s), 16, 44, 62, 78, 84, 96, 115, 123, 131, 134, 140, 141
compensation, 64, 67
competitors, 79, 118
complications, 123
composition, 120
conception, 18, 23, 84
conductor, 106
conference, vii, 60, 68, 86, 120
conflict, 25, 58, 77, 100, 115, 117, 120, 131, 132
congress, 3, 5, 16, 18, 19, 20, 21, 22, 23, 24, 25, 26, 27, 29, 30, 32, 33, 34, 35, 39, 45, 48, 50, 52, 57, 58, 59, 61, 63, 64, 65, 66, 68, 69, 70, 84, 112, 115, 132, 133, 136, 137, 138
Congressional Budget Office, 43
consensus, 8, 13, 47, 58, 65, 69, 77, 95, 136
Consolidated Appropriations Act, 25
conspiracy, 43
Constitution, 5, 15, 17, 18, 22, 23, 24, 25, 26, 27, 30, 31, 32, 33, 35, 44, 51, 135
constitutional authority, 4, 15, 24, 25, 29
constitutional challenges, 23
constitutional crisis, 5
constitutional issues, 24
constitutional limitations, 4, 24
construction, 26, 88
consulting, 62
consumers, 64, 65, 67
controversial, 15, 28, 48, 52, 64, 136, 137

convention, 104
conversations, 99
conviction, 81
cooperation, 57, 67, 81, 103, 124
coordination, 20, 106
corruption, 121
cost, 6, 21, 29, 32, 46, 49, 112, 117
counsel, 94, 105
courtship, 43
creditors, 66
crimes, 121
criminal acts, 125
criminality, 116
criticism, 16, 24, 25, 26, 28, 47, 48, 95, 97, 115, 129, 132, 134, 136
Cuba, 16
culture, 79, 85, 126
Czech Republic, 87

displacement, 117
disposition, 28, 111
dissatisfaction, 43, 120
dissenting opinion, 98
distortions, 44
DNA, 97
DOC, 32
domestic investment, 82
domestic issues, 59
domestic policy, 7, 57, 58, 78, 81, 83, 85, 95, 102
domestic violence, 125
dominant strategy, 9
Down syndrome, 52
downsizing, 8, 85
draft, 117, 134
dramatic departures, 6
drawing, 118, 120
dumping, 117

D

danger, 24, 76, 111, 116, 125
deaths, 118, 121
decision-making process, 94
defects, 112
deficit, 49, 50, 61, 137
democracy, 5, 7, 19, 29, 48, 79
Democrat, 11, 137
Democratic Party, 11, 12, 68, 77, 96
democratization, 21
demographic characteristics, 12
demonstrations, 131
denial, 124
Department of Defense, 106
Department of Justice, 32
deployments, 16, 124
depth, 120, 131, 141
despair, 125
destruction, 6, 19, 114, 116
detainees, 4, 16, 24, 28
detention, 16, 25
deterrence, 114
deviation, 83
dignity, 89
diplomacy, 34, 84
directives, 104, 105
directors, 76
disability, 112
disappointment, 132, 135
disaster, 5, 8, 32, 47, 97, 100
disclosure, 16, 25, 62, 132
discrimination, 51
disorder, 112

E

East Asia, 138
economic crisis, 44
economic growth, 59
economic policy, 57, 58, 69, 136
economic progress, 132
Edgar Allen Poe, 33
editors, vii
education, 10, 44, 45, 46, 78
Egypt, 19, 85
elders, 44, 51
election, 15, 39, 43, 49, 50, 51, 58, 61, 62, 63, 69, 96, 117, 122, 124, 133, 136, 137
electricity, 116
emergency, 23, 66
employment, 78, 132
empowerment, 77
enemies, 52, 79, 81, 111, 116, 126, 133
enemy combatants, 5, 16, 17, 117, 134
energy, 44, 68, 82, 93, 96, 104
energy efficiency, 68
energy security, 82
enforcement, 84
environment, 8, 9, 67, 84, 141
equality, 7
Europe, 66, 80
evidence, 5, 8, 10, 11, 19, 24, 40, 41, 47, 48, 51, 52, 76, 92, 98, 114, 116
evil, 41, 119, 126, 135
evolution, 10
executive branch, 4, 17, 18, 23, 24, 25, 33, 126
executive orders, 5, 7, 16
executive power, 4, 15, 17, 18, 22, 23, 27, 28, 29, 66

146 Index

exercise, vii, 12, 17, 26, 27, 39, 50, 77, 83, 84, 85
expenditures, 85, 118
extremists, 135, 138

F

fairness, 7, 45, 95
faith, 82, 86, 125
false belief, 10, 11, 12
families, 61, 63, 67, 123, 124, 125, 131
Fannie Mae, 62, 63
fantasy, 123
far right, 44, 62
farmers, 121
fear(s), 77, 114, 124
federal government, 52, 63, 78
Federal Reserve, 59
Federal Reserve Board, 59
Federalist Papers, 17, 30
ferret, 124
financial, 6, 8, 12, 62, 63, 64, 65, 66, 67
financial crisis, 8
financial institutions, 62, 63, 64
financial regulation, 8
financial sector, 64
financial system, 8, 63
fires, 117
FISA, 15
flexibility, 122
food, 67, 116
force, 5, 6, 7, 19, 43, 47, 51, 77, 78, 82, 83, 85, 94,
    115, 117, 118, 119, 120, 125, 126, 137, 138
Ford, 22, 27, 28, 33, 65, 92, 139
foreclosure, 63
foreign affairs, 6, 7, 34, 95, 96, 102
foreign banks, 64
foreign policy, vii, ix, 29, 75, 76, 77, 78, 79, 81, 82,
    84, 85, 89, 91, 92, 96, 97, 98, 99, 100, 101, 103,
    104, 118, 126, 140
formula, 50
France, 7, 47, 83, 84, 89, 101, 134, 138
fraud, 65
Fraud Enforcement and Recovery Act, 24
Freddie Mac, 62, 63
freedom, 3, 48, 82, 89, 113
funding, 25, 49, 58
funds, 62, 64, 65, 66, 68, 93, 138

G

GDP, 59, 60
general election, 6, 118

General Motors, 64
Geneva Convention, 134
George Mitchell, 97
Germany, ix, 47, 134
global climate change, 12
glue, 103
God, 11, 41, 45
governance, 38
government intervention, 46
governments, 115, 122
governor, 43
Grand National Assembly, 87
grants, 67
gravity, 63
Great Britain, 83
Great Depression, 8, 63, 67, 69, 79
Great Recession, 57, 58, 62, 66, 67, 69
Greeks, 89
grotesque, 21, 112
growth, 59, 60
Guantanamo, 16, 80, 133, 135
guardian, 88
guidance, 3, 103
guidelines, 102
guilt, 78
guilty, 38, 51, 125, 135, 136

H

Haiti, 97
handwriting, 108
healing, 37
health, 8, 13, 42, 43, 44, 46, 48, 49, 50, 52, 67, 78,
    118, 135
health care, 8, 13, 43, 44, 46, 48, 50, 78, 118, 135
health care costs, 118
health insurance, 50
highway system, 82
history, 6, 19, 22, 39, 46, 48, 65, 67, 80, 82, 95, 111,
    119, 121, 132
homeland security, 104
homeowners, 63
homes, 63, 117, 121, 124, 139
host, vii, 43, 55
hostility(s), 12, 18, 20, 21, 43, 111, 116
hot spots, 4
House, vii, viii, 5, 8, 9, 12, 13, 26, 27, 32, 44, 49, 50,
    59, 61, 62, 64, 65, 66, 67, 68, 69, 70, 71, 104,
    105, 128, 129, 137, 139
House of Representatives, 8, 32, 64
housing, 62, 63, 64, 65, 67, 69, 137
housing boom, 62
human, 6, 12, 24, 111, 112, 117, 125, 126

Index 147

human right(s), 117
humanitarian disaster, 5, 32
hunting, 113, 118, 126
hybrid, 75
hypothesis, 57, 68

I

ideals, 7, 77, 78, 79, 80, 85, 118, 119
identity, 79, 85
ideology, 12, 28, 45
idiosyncratic, 125
imagination, 16
immigration, 12, 45
immunity, 6, 121
income, 39, 43, 59, 61, 62, 63, 67, 78
income tax, 59, 61
incumbents, 44
independence, 31, 44, 51
individuals, 48, 140
Indonesia, 44
industry(s), 8, 57, 58, 66, 82, 136, 137
information sharing, 25
infrastructure, 68, 82
initiation, 20
INS, 24
inspections, 99
inspectors, 47, 114, 115
institutions, 3, 7, 64, 77, 111, 126, 135
insurance policy, 122
insurgency, 6, 40, 116, 122, 124
intellect, 111
intelligence, 16, 40, 47, 51, 84, 101, 113, 115, 132
Intelligence Reform and Terrorism Prevention Act, 7
interagency coordination, 93, 105
interest groups, 48
interest rates, 59
international institutions, 7, 77
international law, 6, 17, 77, 114, 117, 118, 134
international relations, 77
internationalism, 7, 77, 85, 86
interrogations, 16
intervention, 20, 21, 83, 84, 89, 107
investment(s), 62, 64, 82
investors, 62
Iowa, 78
Iran, 4, 84, 89, 92, 93, 100, 105, 140
Iraq War, 6, 10, 11, 13, 18, 19, 21, 29, 31, 52, 53, 117, 118, 121, 127, 128, 132, 134, 135
irony, 29, 121
isolation, 92, 102
Israel, 47, 48

issues, vii, viii, ix, 9, 13, 24, 58, 78, 79, 86, 94, 95, 96, 98, 99, 100, 103, 105, 123, 136, 137, 140, 141
Italy, 134

J

Japan, 134
Jews, 44
jihad, 30
jobless, 59, 69
judicial power, 4, 24
justification, 19, 47, 48, 135

K

Keynes, 32
kill, 5, 6, 108, 112, 126, 133
kinship, 37, 38
Korea, 40, 47
Kosovo, 40, 87
Kuwait, 115, 134

L

labeling, 12, 135
laws, 16, 17, 25, 26, 46
lawyers, 17, 28
lead, 7, 8, 11, 48, 66, 76, 77, 83, 89, 92, 93, 95, 97, 138
leadership, vii, 7, 57, 58, 61, 62, 66, 67, 69, 75, 81, 83, 84, 85, 89, 97, 104, 119, 138
leaks, 102
Lebanon, 133
legality, 22
legislation, 4, 8, 9, 13, 16, 22, 24, 26, 27, 43, 46, 48, 49, 50, 57, 58, 59, 64, 65, 68, 69, 91, 133, 135, 136, 137
legs, 112
lending, 63, 65, 66
lens, 92
leukemia, 112
liberty, 17
light, 8, 19, 42, 69, 101, 132
liquidity, 64
loans, 64, 65, 66
Louisiana, 49
loyalty, 126
lying, 39, 47, 135

148 Index

M

machinery, 94
magnitude, 7, 21, 134
majority, 7, 9, 10, 11, 12, 13, 37, 38, 41, 42, 44, 49,
    59, 65, 115
man, 23, 80, 99, 115, 119, 121, 122
management, 91, 92, 93, 95, 102, 138, 139, 140, 141
mantle, 26
Marine Corps, 96
mark up, 108
market share, 65
marketing, 11, 39
Maryland, 139
mass, 7, 66
materials, 108
matter, 23, 25, 27, 51, 76, 93, 95, 99, 104, 126, 132,
    134, 135, 140, 141
media, 51, 82, 93, 96, 97, 98, 100, 104, 131
median, 11
Medicaid, 46, 49, 67
medical, 84, 112, 118
medical assistance, 84
Medicare, 45, 46, 49, 50
Medicare Modernization Act, 45
medicine, 63
membership, 92, 93
messages, 27, 39
messengers, 39
Mexico, 114
Miami, 88
Middle East, vii, 4, 19, 48, 52, 83, 116, 117, 126,
    138
military, 6, 7, 8, 16, 19, 20, 21, 22, 25, 29, 32, 41,
    48, 51, 59, 77, 81, 82, 83, 84, 85, 89, 96, 97, 101,
    102, 106, 111, 112, 114, 115, 116, 117, 118, 119,
    120, 121, 122, 123, 124, 125, 126, 131, 133, 134,
    135, 137, 141
military tribunals, 16, 133
militia, 113, 116
miniature, 16
Minneapolis, 62
minorities, 8
mission, 20, 116, 120, 123, 125
Missouri, 67
models, 104
moderates, 11, 61, 62
modernization, 138
mold, 12, 98, 116
momentum, 126
monopoly, 37, 51
Montana, 68
Morocco, 89

motivation, 124
MR, 79
murder, 116, 125
music, 113, 127

N

nation building, 82
National Defense Authorization Act, 25, 137
National Economic Council, 93, 105
national emergency, 20
National Intelligence Estimate, 128
national interests, 85
National Public Radio, 32
national security, ix, 4, 5, 15, 40, 84, 91, 93, 95, 96,
    97, 98, 99, 101, 102, 104, 105, 115, 119, 120,
    124, 126, 133, 134, 135, 136, 137, 139, 140, 141
National Security Council, 91, 92, 93, 95, 98, 106,
    119, 122, 140
nation-building, 88, 113, 138
Native Americans, 80
NATO, 7, 20, 21, 84, 89, 96, 101, 113, 122, 123,
    124, 126, 130, 134
natural disaster(s), 82
negative consequences, 99
neglect, 113
negotiation, 59
New Deal, 43
Nicaragua, 93
No Child Left Behind, 45
nominee, 52, 76
North Korea, 47, 95
NSA, 4, 140
nuclear program, 114, 138
nuclear weapons, 19, 40, 47, 95, 138

O

Obama Administration, 30, 34, 35, 36, 81, 120, 132,
    137, 141
obedience, 44
objective reality, 45
Office of Management and Budget, 33, 105
officials, 3, 17, 28, 94, 101, 105, 114, 116, 118, 125,
    129, 134, 139, 141
oil, 82, 118
oil revenues, 118
OMB, 34
omission, 100
Operation Enduring Freedom, 113, 134
Operation Iraqi Freedom, 131, 136
operations, 85, 94, 97, 112, 116, 132, 138

Index
149

opportunities, 3, 8, 77
organize, 3, 86, 91
outreach, 120, 136
overlap, 18
oversight, 17, 63, 92, 116

P

Pakistan, 97, 101, 113, 114, 119, 123, 124, 126
parents, 111
Parliament, 80, 87
participants, 3, 95, 98, 103
Pashtun, 113, 121
Patriot Act, 7
payroll, 62, 68, 120
peace, 5, 47, 114, 115, 129
Pentagon, 55, 94, 100, 106, 112, 117, 122, 123
permission, 64
perpetrators, 6, 112, 115
Persian Gulf War, 19
personal control, 98
personal history, 10
personal life, 78
personal relationship, 4, 94, 100
personality, 76, 140
persuasion, 11
phosphorus, 112, 117
physicians, 50, 112
platform, 15, 18
playing, 46, 83, 99, 113
poison, 48
Poland, 134
polarization, 8, 9, 10, 11, 12, 38, 57, 58, 67, 68, 69, 136, 137
police, 96, 112
policy, vii, 3, 4, 6, 11, 21, 22, 25, 29, 39, 42, 45, 46, 58, 63, 69, 76, 77, 78, 79, 80, 81, 85, 91, 92, 93, 94, 95, 96, 97, 98, 99, 100, 101, 102, 103, 104, 105, 106, 111, 124, 132, 133, 135, 136, 137, 138, 139, 140, 141
policy choice, 104, 141
policy initiative, 58, 79
policy makers, 63, 138
policy making, vii, 139
policy options, 91, 102, 141
policymakers, 112
political leaders, vii, 51
political party, vii, 28
political power, 116
politics, vii, ix, 5, 21, 29, 30, 32, 33, 34, 37, 38, 39, 42, 43, 45, 52, 57, 97, 119, 129, 135
popular support, 11
population, 19, 43, 116, 124

populism, 44
poverty, 69
precedent(s), 3, 20, 21, 23, 51
prejudice, 44, 51
preparation, 113
presidency, vii, viii, ix, 3, 4, 6, 8, 13, 15, 16, 17, 19, 22, 23, 24, 26, 28, 29, 30, 37, 38, 39, 42, 43, 44, 45, 46, 50, 52, 60, 76, 79, 83, 91, 92, 94, 96, 98, 101, 103, 104, 105, 108, 133, 138
President Clinton, 47, 49
President Obama, vii, 31, 32, 35, 36, 51, 55, 66, 67, 75, 76, 77, 78, 80, 81, 83, 85, 86, 87, 89, 96, 98, 111, 120, 122, 123, 125, 126, 127, 129, 132, 133, 137, 138, 139, 141
presidential authority, 23
presidential campaign, vii, 42, 76, 78, 82, 140
presidential performance, 38
presidential politics, 104
primacy, 7, 8, 81, 82, 83, 84, 85, 138
principles, 16, 44, 111, 119
prisoners, 4, 16, 24, 117, 121
profiteering, 126
program administration, 64
project, 116
proliferation, 63
protection, 24, 75
psychology, 12, 77
public affairs, 96
public concern, 118
public investment, 46
public opinion, 4, 10, 37, 38, 39, 43
public schools, 68
public support, vii, 40, 51
purity, 9

Q

qualifications, 119
query, 128
questioning, 22, 50

R

race, 10, 59, 100, 137
racism, 44, 45
radicalism, 12, 43
rash, 118
rating agencies, 62
reactions, 10, 12, 19
reading, 8, 11
real estate, 62
realism, 7, 103

150 Index

reality, 7, 8, 10, 41, 93, 123, 133, 138
reasoning, 10, 13
recall, 10, 12, 61
recession, 43, 59, 63, 69, 118, 131
recognition, 78, 85, 119
recommendations, 91, 92, 99, 122
reconciliation, 49, 59
reconciliation procedure, 59
reconstruction, 94
recovery, 11, 57, 58, 59, 64, 67, 69
reelection, 5, 8, 9, 44
reform(s), 8, 32, 43, 44, 45, 46, 48, 49, 50, 52, 70, 92, 135
refugees, 117
regulatory agencies, 17
rejection, 43, 138
relatives, 116
relief, 59, 62, 64, 67, 68, 75
religion, 12, 124
remorse, 78
rendition, 135
renewable energy, 68
reporters, 39, 51
Republican Party, 46
requirements, 5, 62, 63, 132
resentment, 12, 44, 51, 120
reserves, 133
resistance, 61, 62, 66, 115
resolution, 21, 32, 47, 99, 115, 136
resources, 5, 6, 7, 116, 124
response, 4, 11, 40, 84, 85, 97, 101, 112, 117, 133
restrictions, 23, 25
retirement, 61
revenue, 61
rhetoric, 7, 12, 13, 37, 39, 48, 51, 78, 82, 103, 116, 126, 134
rights, 134
risk(s), 5, 8, 20, 58, 62, 65, 81, 84, 87, 114, 123
routes, 113
routines, 3
rule of law, 121
rules, 5, 17, 48, 49, 59, 119
Russia, 25, 47, 134

S

Saddam Hussein, 4, 6, 7, 18, 19, 31, 40, 41, 47, 48, 51, 94, 114, 115, 116, 117
safety, 24, 62, 124
sanctions, 84, 89
savings, 88
scholarship, vii, 37, 38, 39, 45, 51
school, 15, 67, 117

science, 12, 38, 51, 52, 77, 105
scope, 4, 15, 20, 46, 76, 85, 118, 133
Secretary of Defense, ix, 47, 94, 97, 106, 119, 123, 135, 138, 139, 140
Secretary of the Treasury, 79
security(s), 48, 59, 62, 65, 82, 91, 93, 97, 99, 103, 105, 113, 115, 116, 117, 118, 122, 123, 124, 125, 126, 134, 138, 139, 140, 141
security forces, 117, 118, 123, 124, 126
segregation, 80
self-confidence, 76
self-presentation, 10
seller, 118
Senate, 6, 8, 9, 20, 21, 24, 25, 34, 44, 49, 58, 59, 60, 61, 62, 64, 65, 66, 67, 68, 69, 70, 71, 86, 96, 108, 118, 123, 128, 136, 137
Senate Foreign Relations Committee, 108, 123
senior military commanders, 6
September 11, 40, 94, 104, 118
services, 122
settlements, 100
severe stress, 63
sham, 134
shape, 10
shores, 112
showing, 117, 126
signs, 61, 122, 124, 131, 136
slavery, 80
smallpox, 48
social attitudes, 12
Social Security, 46, 49
socialism, 11, 43
society, 124, 141
solution, 123
Somalia, 126
South Korea, 80, 134
Soviet Union, 135
Spain, 87, 115, 132, 134
specialists, 116
speech, 17, 42, 80, 81, 118, 119, 129
spelling, 104
spending, 9, 24, 45, 46, 62, 64, 67, 68, 78, 84, 88, 131, 137
spin, 42, 100
Spring, 13, 30, 32, 53, 87, 88, 89
stability, 5, 101, 120, 124, 141
staff members, 96
state(s), 9, 16, 17, 25, 49, 61, 67, 68, 69, 88, 89, 91, 96, 98, 104, 105, 112, 119, 123, 134, 138
State of the Union address, 8, 139
stimulus, 8, 11, 42, 43, 46, 57, 58, 61, 62, 67, 68, 78, 136, 137
stock, 59, 63, 64

Index

151

stock markets, 64
stock value, 63
strategic planning, 98
stress, 112
strictures(s), 17, 28, 29, 34, 92, 93, 98
style, 10, 25, 43, 93, 102
succession, 111
suicide, 116
Sun, 86
Sunnis, 117, 120
supplier(s), 47, 65, 66
Supreme Court, 17, 24, 27
surveillance, 15, 16, 17, 126
survivors, 112
sweat, 100
sympathy, 112
Syria, 19, 83, 84, 85, 87, 89, 141

T

tactics, 9, 13, 17, 38, 46, 48, 50, 52, 95, 104, 114, 136, 141
Taliban, 112, 113, 114, 121, 123, 124, 126, 127, 129, 132, 134
target, 6, 7, 9, 124
Task Force, 33
tax breaks, 136
tax credits, 68
tax cuts, 8, 39, 45, 49, 57, 58, 59, 60, 61, 62, 68, 136
tax increase, 61
tax rates, 61
tax reform, 136
taxes, 13, 43, 50, 60, 61, 62, 117, 136, 137
teams, 101, 104, 113, 114
techniques, 16
technology, 68, 69, 105, 118, 126
telephone, 17
temperament, 126
tenants, 77, 81, 85
tension(s), 100, 101, 136
tenure, 43, 79, 94, 96, 97, 98, 101, 103, 140
territorial, 104
territory, 113
terrorism, ix, 6, 7, 8, 48, 105, 111, 112, 114, 118, 125, 133
terrorist attack, 5, 40, 59
terrorist groups, 47, 51
terrorist organization, 133
terrorists, 5, 6, 7, 18, 19, 47, 48, 113, 114, 118, 121, 124, 126, 132, 133, 134, 136
threats, 7, 8, 59, 77, 119, 134
time frame, 32, 59
time warp, 31

tones, 103
torture, 17, 28, 80, 121
Toyota, 65
trade, 105
training, 112, 118, 124
traits, 44
transactions, 62
transcripts, 108
transformation, 7, 46, 79, 81, 85, 138
transgression, 77
transition period, 119
transparency, 49
trauma, 11, 19
Treasury, 63, 64, 65, 66, 95, 105
Treasury Secretary, 95
treaties, 17, 77
treatment, 4, 24, 80
Trinidad, 87
Troubled Asset Relief program (TARP), 8
Turkey, 87

U

U.N. Security Council, 20, 32
U.S. economy, 59, 63, 69
UK, 133
unemployment insurance, 68
unhappiness, 123, 134, 135
unilateralism, 6, 85
United Nations (UN), 84, 99, 104, 113, 114, 115, 116, 134
United States (USA), vii, ix, 7, 19, 20, 24, 26, 31, 32, 42, 43, 45, 48, 51, 52, 57, 70, 71, 75, 77, 79, 80, 81, 82, 83, 84, 87, 89, 111, 112, 114, 115, 117, 118, 119, 120, 121, 123, 124, 125, 126, 127, 128, 133, 136, 138
uranium, 112
urban, 116
USSR, 119

V

vehicles, 80, 126
venture capital, 59
veto, 15, 16, 22, 24, 25, 26, 27, 28, 29, 36
Vice President, 15, 16, 23, 30, 94, 95, 96, 100, 105, 122, 139, 141
victims, 9
Vietnam, 40, 131, 134
Viking, 107, 128
violence, 48, 116, 120, 129, 133

152 Index

vision(s), 17, 42, 52, 76, 78, 96, 98, 100, 103, 112, 118, 141
vote, 9, 32, 45, 49, 57, 58, 59, 60, 61, 62, 64, 65, 66, 67, 115, 118, 128, 136
voters, 10, 44, 65, 119, 122
voting, 9, 59, 69, 128
voting record, 69

W

war, ix, 6, 11, 15, 16, 18, 19, 20, 21, 29, 30, 32, 33, 37, 38, 40, 41, 42, 45, 47, 48, 50, 51, 52, 67, 80, 81, 82, 87, 88, 94, 99, 106, 111, 112, 114, 115, 116, 117, 118, 121, 124, 125, 126, 127, 129, 131, 132, 133, 134, 135, 136, 139
War on Terror, 55
War Powers Act, 5, 19, 20, 30, 132
warlords, 113
Washington, 30, 31, 35, 39, 53, 55, 63, 71, 80, 83, 84, 85, 87, 88, 89, 93, 105, 106, 107, 108, 112, 113, 119, 121, 122, 123, 124, 125, 128, 129, 130, 133, 134, 138, 141
water, 116, 117, 125
weapons, 5, 10, 18, 19, 40, 47, 48, 80, 114, 115, 116, 117, 132, 135

weapons of mass destruction, 5, 10, 19, 114, 115, 116, 132, 135
web, 21
well-being, 124
West Wing, 86
White House, vii, 4, 13, 24, 25, 26, 28, 35, 36, 42, 48, 50, 52, 57, 58, 59, 61, 62, 63, 65, 66, 68, 69, 73, 83, 86, 87, 88, 96, 97, 100, 101, 104, 107, 109, 118, 119, 121, 122, 123, 126, 127, 129, 133, 136, 137, 138, 139, 140
withdrawal, 5, 6, 81, 84, 101, 118, 135
WMD, 10, 40, 41, 47, 48, 51, 128
working groups, 92, 93, 139
world order, 82
World Trade Center, 112
World War I, 92, 118, 133
worldview, 75, 76
worldwide, 85, 134
worry, 5, 9, 76

Y

Yale University, 70, 128
yarn, 29
Yemen, 126
Yugoslavia, 20, 134